Getting the most out of your
Table Saw

Rockwell Handbooks

GETTING THE MOST OUT OF YOUR DRILL PRESS
GETTING THE MOST OUT OF YOUR TABLE SAW
GETTING THE MOST OUT OF YOUR BAND SAW

Getting the most out of your
Table Saw

a Rockwell Publication

A complete handbook describing the table saw in the home workshop with more than three hundred photographic illustrations and line drawings.

Rockwell International

Power Tool Division
400 North Lexington Avenue
Pittsburgh, Pennsylvania 15208

Foreword

"Getting The Most Out Of Your Table Saw" is published as a service to power tool users. Because different makes, models, and sizes of machines vary in their performance and features, the editors have tried to make the information in this handbook as general as possible.

The table saw is one of the most basic and useful tools to be found in the home workshop. It can be used for almost all simple cutting operations with a minimum of effort and a maximum of efficiency. However, the table saw can also be utilized in a wide field of complex and intricate operations.

The table saw is a safe tool. But, as with any power tool, certain safety precautions must be followed. These procedures are included throughout the book and detailed in Chapter 2. For clarity, guards and other safety devices have been removed from illustrations depicting procedures described by the text. To avoid injury the operator should insure that guards and other safety devices are in place and properly operating before using the saw. You should also be attentive to future improvements and new development techniques for guards and other devices which will enchance the safe operation of the saw.

This book was designed to accommodate both the beginner, wanting to learn the basic operations of the table saw, and the skilled artisan, needing information about a single area of cutting.

Originally published in 1937, this handbook has been reprinted many times, and has evolved into both a compendium and a final word about table saws. This most recent edition includes all applicable information from previous editions, as well as the latest in woodworking techniques. Material for this book was based on information gathered from sources throughout the power tool industry. It is the greatest hope and desire of the editors that you will "get the most out of your table saw," after reading this book.

Copyright © 1937, 1949, 1953, Rockwell Manufacturing Company
Copyright © 1978 Rockwell International Corporation
Published by Rockwell International

Brief quotations may be used in critical articles and reviews. For any other reproduction of this book, including electronic, mechanical, photocopying, recording or other means, written permission must be obtained from the publisher.

Text prepared and book designed by
Robert Scharff & Associates

Library of Congress Catalog Card Number: 78-56311

Manufactured in the United States of America

Contents

FORWARD	iv
1. GETTING TO KNOW THE TABLE SAW	1
2. BEFORE OPERATING THE TABLE SAW	11
3. BASIC OPERATION OF THE TABLE SAW	23
4. BASIC USE OF THE DADO HEAD	39
5. SPECIAL SAW AND DADO OPERATIONS	45
6. SPECIAL JIGS AND HOW TO USE THEM	61
7. POPULAR WOOD JOINTS	69
8. USING THE MOLDING CUTTERHEAD	95
9. OTHER USES OF THE TABLE SAW	107
10. SHARPENING SAW BLADES	111
INCH/MILLIMETER CONVERSIONS	118
INDEX	119

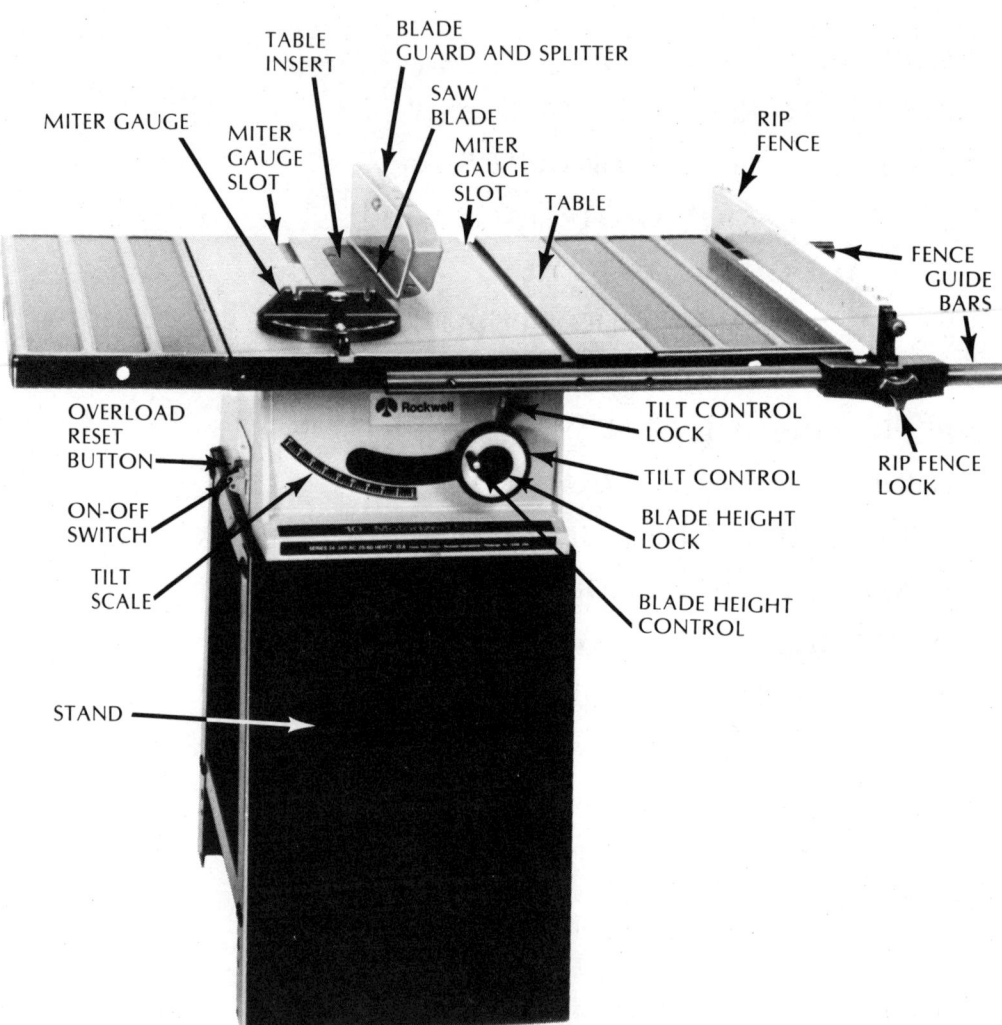

Fig. 1-1: Basic parts of a 10-inch table saw.

Chapter 1

GETTING TO KNOW THE TABLE SAW *

The table saw, also called the bench, variety, or stationary circular saw, is one of the oldest known stationary power tools used in woodworking. It is estimated that better than 80 percent of all woodworking involves sawing, so the value of a clean cutting precision tool for this purpose is apparent. Anyone who has used a handsaw and then accomplished similar tasks using a power tool, knows the value of the table saw. There is an increase in production and a decrease in expended energy. These two advantages by no means cover its total usefulness. There is also a gain in accuracy because the machine is organized to minimize the possibility of human error.

The table saw is the basic machine in any woodworking shop for performing the fundamental operations of *straight line sawing*. It is not a difficult tool to operate. Plain ripping and crosscutting come naturally to most operators, and other jobs requiring more know-how are easily learned. In fact, there are only six basic saw cuts in all woodworking: rip, bevel rip, crosscut, bevel crosscut, miter, and bevel miter. All other cuts, no matter how intricate, are combinations of these basic cuts.

SIZES AND CONSTRUCTION

The size of a table saw is known by the largest diameter saw blade it will accommodate. Popular sizes for home or school workshops range from 9 to 12 inches. Table saws for industrial use are available up to 24 inches in diameter, but the 14- and 16-inch sizes are not commonly used. (Note: All dimensions in this book are given in English measurements. A chart for metric conversion is given on page 118.)

Saw capacity is determined approximately by blade size. For example, a 10-inch saw will cut through wood up to 3 1/4 inches thick; a 12-inch saw will cut to 4 1/8 inch thickness with the blade at 90 degrees.

The operation of the modern table saw (Fig. 1-1) is simple. The saw blade is mounted on a threaded shaft called an arbor that is turned by a motor; the blade projects through a table on which the work is rested. The arbor must be tilted to cut bevels, chamfers, and certain types of miters. There is a handle to raise and lower the blade, to tilt the blade, a device to lock the blade at any degree of tilt or height, and a scale to show the degree of tilt.

While direct-drive motor arrangements are employed, the arbor of most modern table saws is usually coupled to the motor by means of a belt and pulleys. The belt and-pulley drive has certain advantages over direct-drive motor arrangements. For instance, the maximum thickness of wood that can be sawed is greater, because it is not necessary to keep the arbor down to leave room under the table for a motor—only enough for an arbor pulley. It is easier to change from one motor to another in case of motor failure or in case the saw is transferred from one shop to another having a different current supply. The belt drive machine does not coast as long as the direct-drive machine after it is turned off. This adds to the safety of the belt-drive machine.

Two methods of accurately guiding the workpiece past the blade are available with table saws: a rip fence and a miter gauge.

*NOTE: *In order to clearly illustrate certain procedures described in this chapter, the blade guard and other safety devices have been removed. For safe operation of the table saw, guards and other safety devices must always be utilized.*

 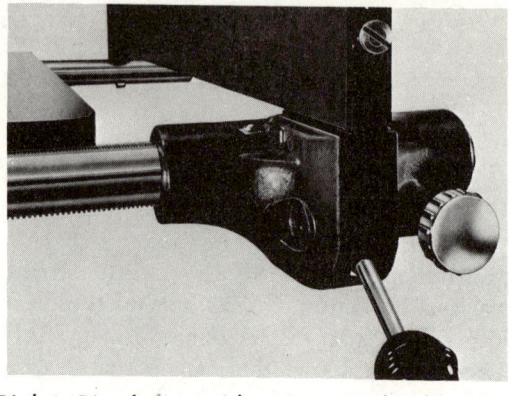

Fig. 1-2: (Left) Standard rip fence controls. (Right) Rip fence with micro-set knob.

The metal *rip fence* (Fig. 1-2) is guided by means of bars fastened to the ends of the table. On most saws the front bar is calibrated to show the distance the fence is set from the saw blade. It is used for all ripping operations. Clamp handles or knobs fasten it securely in place. On some rip fences there is a micro-set knob for fine adjustments as well. In all cases, it is important that the fence does not pinch the workpiece between it and the blade.

Fig. 1-3: Miter gauge in place on the table.

The *miter gauge* (Fig. 1-3) is used for all crosscutting operations. It slides in slots in the table top. There is one slot to the left and one to the right of the saw blade. Some saws permit the use of the miter gauge in either slot. Many miter gauges are equipped with positive stops at 45 and 90 degrees.

The bench-type table saw (Fig. 1-4A) and the cabinet-or floor-type (Fig. 1-4B) are both popular with the bench type costing a little less. Most often the bench-type saw is mounted on its own stand which is better than taking up room on the workbench. The stand can be purchased or made in your own shop.

Protective Devices. Three protective devices are standard on most table saws: the blade guard, anti-kickback fingers, and a splitter or spreader (Fig. 1-5). The blade guard serves primarily to keep fingers away from the side of the moving blade, but it also helps to deflect flying chips which can otherwise be a threat to the eyes. Because protection has always been an important consideration to manufacturers, many different kinds of guards have been developed. The most popular today are the plastic, see-through guards. For added safety, some manufacturers tint the plastic guard with an "alert" orange color.

Many illustrations in this book (and others of its kind) show the saw in use with the blade guard removed. This is done only in the interest of the clarity of the illustration and should not be construed as a normal working procedure.

The splitter or spreader is a piece of metal directly behind the saw blade which helps keep the kerf (saw cut) open. This

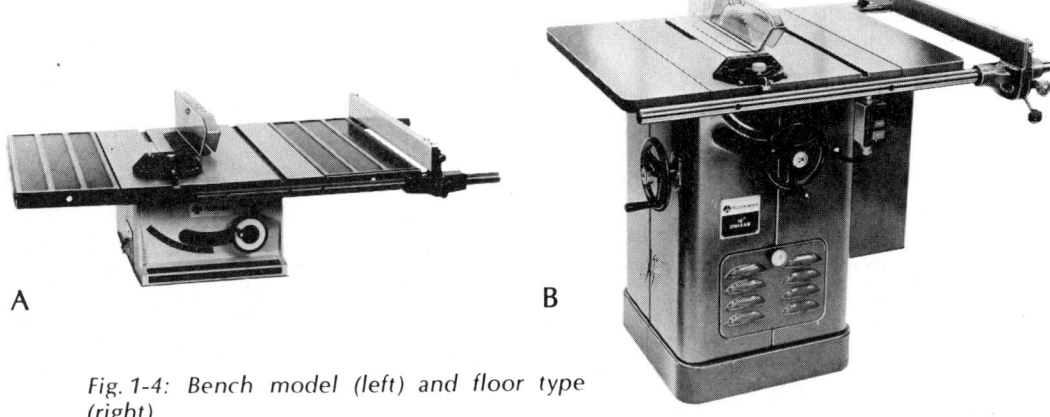

Fig. 1-4: Bench model (left) and floor type (right).

Fig. 1-5: Blade guard, anti-kickback fingers, and splitter in action.

helps prevent the wood from binding on the blade and causing kickback. Thus it is especially important to use the splitter for all ripping operations. Most splitters are equipped with metal fingers or pawls that provide added anti-kickback protection.

To increase the safety of the saw, some manufacturers offer belt and pulley guards as accessories for their saws (Fig. 1-6).

Power and Speed. The speed of a table saw for woodworking is not very critical. A wide range of speeds will be found satisfactory and manufacturers' recommendations should be followed. At a constant motor speed, the arbor speed can be from 3450 to 3800 rpm for a 12-inch blade and 3800 to 4000 rpm for a 9- or 10-inch blade. When an ac-dc universal motor is used, the speed will not remain constant but will, of course, be less under a load. When this kind of motor is used, the no-load speed will be up to 50 percent faster than a constant speed motor. A 9-inch saw requires 3/4 to 1 hp. A 10-inch saw takes 1 to 3 hp, while a 12-inch saw needs 5 to 7 1/2 hp to maintain the fast feed and high rate of production usually expected of a machine of this size. The motor, regardless of size, should be protected by a thermal overload with a manual reset button.

When it comes to actually cutting the wood, it will be found that the wiring in the shop is as important as the size of horsepower rating of the motor. In other words,

Fig. 1-6: Motor pulley and belt guard.

the motor cannot and will not put out any more power than goes into it from the power line. A line that is intended for lights only will not properly carry a power tool motor. Wire that is heavy enough for a short distance will be too light for a greater distance. The line that is adequate for one tool, may have to be replaced when two, three, or more tools plus some lights are to be run on one line. Have an electrician check the line before you go to any expense getting larger and more powerful motors. It may be necessary to have a suitable circuit installed.

What to Look for When Buying a Table Saw. Table saws are sold in many different models, each with its own characteristics and features. However, certain general quality and operating features will apply to every model, and it is well for all prospective tool users to study their anticipated purchase for the following items. Here are some points to check when buying a table saw:

1. The controls should all be conveniently placed within easy reach and they should perform their function in a satisfactory manner. Check especially the on-off switch for the motor to be sure it is within reach and that an emergency stop can be made without groping or fumbling.

2. Look for a table that is smooth, for ease in feeding the work, accuracy and a good appearance.

3. Take a 6-inch scale and measure the width of the blade slot in the table insert. It should be as narrow as possible. Then tilt the blade to a full 45 degrees, and the blade still should not strike the insert. If the insert has a wide slot or if it has to be removed to tilt the blade, then a hazardous condition exists in which the work could splinter or narrow pieces could fall into the opening and be thrown back into your face.

4. It is desirable for the rip capacity of a table saw to be no less than 24 inches, since this enables you to rip to the center of a 48 inch panel, which is a common size. Ripping capacity depends on how far the rip fence can be extended on the rip fence guide bars.

5. Check the table of the saw with the blade raised 1 inch above the table surface. It is desirable to have 12 inches or more of the table in front of the blade. This will enable you to support on the table any board up to 1 inch thick and 12 inches wide, while you are crosscutting it.

6. The blade should protrude above the table at least far enough to cut a 2 X 4 on a 45-degree bevel with the 2 X 4 laid flat (Fig. 1-7). This means a minimum of 1 5/8-inches capacity with the blade tilted 45 degrees. The depth of cut with the blade at 90 degrees should be at least 2 inches.

Fig. 1-7: Sawing a 45 degree bevel on a 2 x 4.

7. The guard should be designed for safety, minimum interference, and maximum visibility. Be sure that the guard includes a splitter and kickback fingers, which adds to the safety, minimizes drag on the motor, and prevents kickbacks.

8. Look under the table to see if it is adequately ribbed for strength and for the purpose of maintaining original accuracy.

9. The rip fence should automatically align itself with the miter gauge grooves of the table, and this alignment should be easily adjustable. To be truly accurate the fence should lock both front and rear and extend the full length of the table.

10. Inquire as to whether the arbor bearings can easily be replaced.

SAW BLADES

While there are many different kinds of table saw blades, all have one thing in common: They must cut a kerf slightly wider than their body to avoid binding and overheating. This necessary clearance is accomplished in one of three ways:

1. By setting or bending teeth to one side or the other alternately to create added width at tips. Such blades are called *flatground* blades (Fig. 1-8A) and their kerfs are about 1/8 inch (large teeth) to 3/32 inch (small teeth). The teeth must be kept sharp and properly set or the blade will wander from the cut line and bind. Flat-ground or set-tooth blades are easy to resharpen.

2. By grinding or tapering the blade sides to leave the tooth tips wider. If the blade is thin-rimmed (Fig. 1-8B), the blade gets its clearance because the material between the teeth and the hub has been ground out leaving the ends of the teeth the original thickness of the blade. On the other hand, the hollow-ground or taper-rim blade (Fig. 1-8C) receives its clearance from the fact that the material from the tip of the teeth to hub is ground in a taper. The hollow-ground blade permits full-depth cuts and makes a kerf of about 3/32 inch. The thin rimmed blade is limited to the depth of the taper (usually about 1-1/2 inches), but the kerf is usually narrower. Both the hollow-ground and thin rimmed blades cut smoother than the equivalent flat-ground types. They are both easy to recondition.

3. By brazing on tungsten carbide tooth tips that are slightly wider than the blade. The carbide-tipped swage blade (Fig. 1-8D) may be flat-ground (straight across) or beveled in alternate directions. The kerf is about 1/8 inch. While such blades wear longer than other types, they are more expensive in original cost, and if dulled or damaged, the blades must be factory reconditioned.

In addition to the blade type, the sizes and shapes of the blade teeth and gullets determine the kind of work a blade will do. There are several types of common blades (Fig. 1-9).

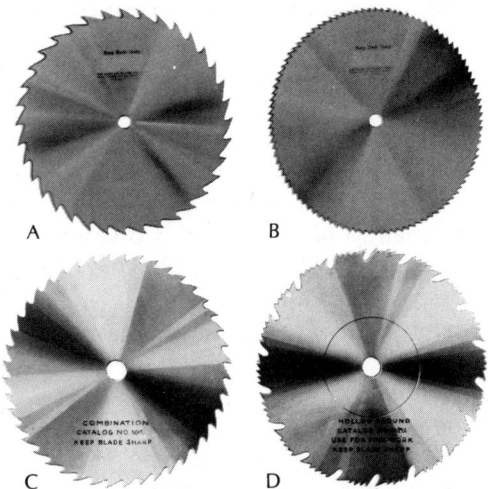

Fig. 1-9: Typical tooth pattern of (A) Rip; (B) crosscut; (C) standard combination; and (D) novelty-tooth blades.

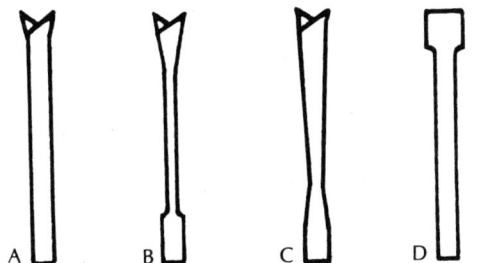

Fig. 1-8: (A) Flatground; (B) thin-rimmed; (C) hollow-ground; and (D) carbide-tipped blade.

Crosscut Blade. The crosscut blade is a flatground blade designed for cutting across wood grain. Its fine crosscut teeth are set alternately and are filed with a bevel on both the face and back. The teeth are small in size and are filed to a sharp point so that they will sever the wood fibers as they move across the grain. The gullets are small because only a fine sawdust is produced when crosscutting. The crosscut blade may also be used for cutting plywood, veneer, and various other composition materials.

Rip Blade. The rip blade is a flat-ground blade designed for cutting with the wood grain of all varieties of wood. The teeth are set alternately and are filed straight across to form a chisel-like cutting edge. Since, during ripping operations, the chisel-like teeth gouge lengths of wood fibers, they must be larger (fewer in number). The gullets are deeper than a typical crosscut blade.

Combination Blade. Table saws usually come equipped with a *standard combination blade* which will crosscut, miter, and rip comparatively equally well. The teeth of this all-purpose blade, sometimes called a *chisel-tooth flat-ground combination blade*, resemble those of a rip blade and are set for fast cutting. The cut, however, is not very smooth, but it is a good blade for all-around cutting especially for construction work.

Another popular combination blade is the so-called *novelty-tooth flat-ground combination blade*, which is divided into segments and provides either two or four cutter teeth and raker teeth in each segment, with a deep gullet between. The two-cutter type will rip a little easier than the four-cutter, but the cut is not so smooth, and it has a tendency to splinter more than the four-cutter type. However, both novelty-tooth types give a smoother cut than the standard combination blade.

In addition to the standard and the novelty-tooth types, there are several other combination blades (Fig. 1-10) which may be used in woodworking. The most important of these are described here.

Hard-tip combination blade. The hard-tip combination blade (Fig. 1-10A) offers fast, accurate cutting of hardwoods and plastic. Use of a lubricant, together with its skip-tooth design, makes it excellent for cutting lightweight aluminum extrusions and other soft, nonferrous metals. The flame-hardened, quenched teeth stay sharp longer, but are harder to resharpen and do not cut as smoothly as the other combination blades.

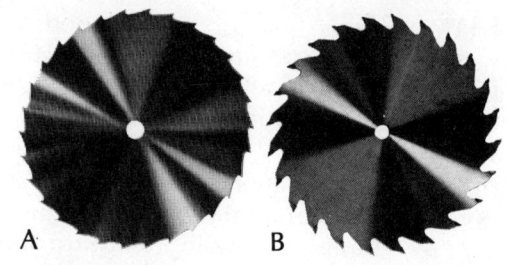

Fig. 1-10: (A) Hard-tip and (B) carbide-tipped combination blades.

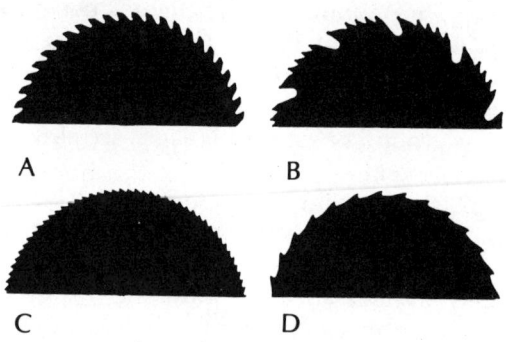

Fig. 1-11: Other popular blades: (A) Alternate bevel-ground, carbide-tipped; (B) hollow-ground planer; (C) plywood; and (D) nonferrous metal blade.

Carbide-tipped combination blade. The carbide-tipped combination blade (Figs. 1-10B and 1-11A) rips and crosscuts like any other blade, however, it remains sharp for long periods of continuous operation and outlasts ordinary blades many times over. It is ideal for cutting asbestos board, hardboard, plastic, and similar materials.

Planer saw blade. The planer saw blade generally has four cutting teeth and one raker, and the teeth have no set. The blade is tapered or hollow-ground (Fig. 1-11B), so that it is several gauges thinner near the hub than at the rim. Sometimes called a *miter blade*, it is generally used by cabinetmakers when cutting stock to finish dimensions, because it cuts very smoothly both with and across the grain.

Plywood blade. The plywood blade (Fig. 1-11C) is a fine tooth cutting blade with either a thin-rim taper or a hollow-ground.

It does an excellent job on plywood. It makes cuts with smooth finishes—ideal for glue joints.

Nonferrous-metal blade. The nonferrous-metal blade (Fig. 1-11D) is taperground for smooth, free sawing of most metals except iron and steel. Because sparks are produced your eyes must be protected. For best results with this blade, lubricate the teeth with tallow (candle wax) and feed the work slowly. The metal-slitting blade (Fig. 1-12A) is useful for neat and accurate cutting of light sheet metal, but should not be used on thicker metals or other materials.

Abrasive or Cutoff Wheels. Abrasive wheels for use on the table saw arbor can be obtained in a number of different grades, thicknesses, and diameters. For average shop use, an 8-inch diameter, 3/32-inch-thick, resin-bonded wheel (Fig. 1-12B) is the most satisfactory. Almost any material can be cut with abrasive wheels. Aluminum-oxide wheels are used for cutting steel and nonferrous metals, while silicon carbide wheels work best for plastics, hard rubber, and similar materials. Cutting operations are performed dry and at the regular saw speed of about 8,000 surface feet per minute (sfm). Wheels are mounted on the saw arbor. Heavy paper washers or blotters are often placed on the arbor. As with any abrasive process, proper ventilation is important.

USEFUL TABLE SAW ACCESSORIES

There are many useful commercial accessories available that will make your table saw even more versatile. Use only recommended accessories. Consult your owner's manual for the recommended accessories for your model saw. The use of improper accessories may cause hazards.

Some of the more popular and useful table saw accessories are described here.

Dado Heads. While there are several dado heads on the market, the two most popular are still the conventional dado set

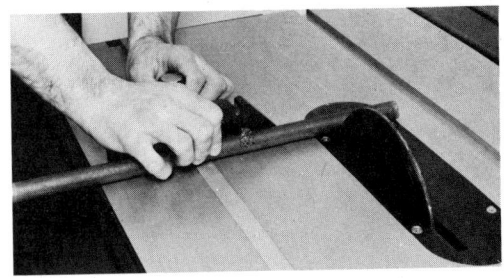

Fig. 1-12: (A) Metal-slitting blade.

Fig. 1-12: (B) Abrasive or cutoff wheel.

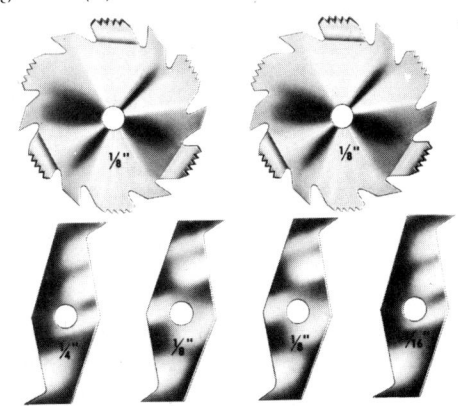

Fig. 1-13: (Above) Standard dado head, (Right) inside and outside cutters.

and the adjustable wobble blade. The conventional or standard dado set (Fig. 1-13) consists of two outside saws, each about 1/8-inch thick, whose teeth are not given any set, and inside saws, or "chippers" as they are called—one 1/4-inch thick, two 1/8-inch (some heads include two additional 1/8-inch chippers instead of the 1/4-inch one), and one 1/16-inch thick (thickness at the hub). The cutting portions of the inside cutters or chippers are widened to overlap the adjacent cutter or saw. When assembling a cutter head, arrange the two outside cutters so that the larger raker teeth on one are opposite the small cutting teeth on the other. This produces a smoother cutting and easier running head. Be also sure the swaged teeth of the inside cutters are placed in the gullets of the outside cutters, not against the teeth, so the head cuts clean and the chips have exit clearance. Stagger the inside cutters so their teeth do not come together. For example, if three cutters are used, they should be set approximately 120 degrees apart. The design of the cutting teeth of the dado-head set permits cutting with the grain, across the grain, or at an angle.

The second type is a single blade with self-contained adjustable-wobbler units (Fig. 1-14) that can be set to cause the blade rim to wobble from side-to-side a predetermined amount as the blade revolves. These blades cut kerfs from a 3/16 inch (or 1/4 inch) minimum up to 13/16 inch and can be adjusted by rotation of a dial without removing the dado head from the saw arbor. While the dial is calibrated in 1/16-inch increments, the adjustment is continuous rather than stepped so that variations of less than 1/16 inch can be made. With most wobbler units, the arbor nut locks both the adjustment and the blade on the arbor. These adjustable dado heads are usually available with eight carbide-tipped teeth (Fig. 1-14A) and with 24 combination teeth for high speed

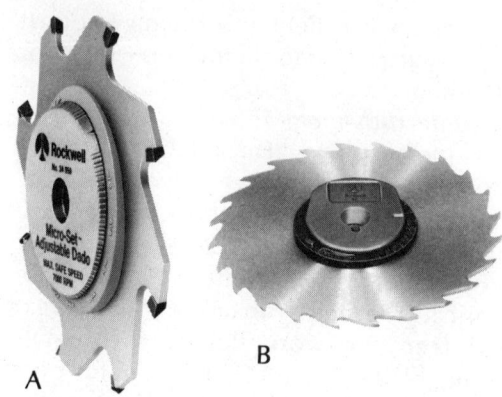

Fig. 1-14: Two types of adjustable dado heads.

Fig. 1-15: Clamp attachment.

cutting (Fig. 1-14B).

Clamp Attachment. The clamp attachment (Fig. 1-15) is very useful in crosscutting or mitering operations. It allows you to clamp work tightly and securely to your miter gauge, thus eliminating completely any tendency for the work to creep toward or away from the saw blade. It makes cross-cutting and mitering safer since the hands need not come near the blade. It is also very useful when cross-cutting longer material as the clamps will hold the work on the miter gauge, which frees the left hand to support the longer work.

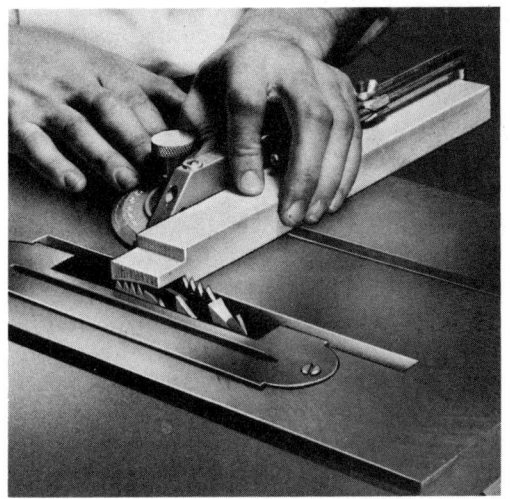

Fig. 1-16: Stop rod.

Fig. 1-17: Tenoning jig.

Stop Rod. Fitted to the miter gauge, a stop rod attachment holds short workpieces to prevent their creeping, and positions them for cutting at a predetermined length. The stop rod (Fig. 1-16) is set in the miter gauge on the side away from the saw blade.

Tenoning Jig. The tenoning jig (Fig. 1-17) is a useful accessory for making tenons and grooves on the table saw. It slides in the left miter gauge slot at an adjustable distance from the saw blade, and holds stock up to 2 3/4-inches thick, any width within the capacity of the saw. Tenons can be cut to full capacity. A clamp holds the workpiece firmly and in the correct position.

Table Extension. The table extension (Fig. 1-18) accessory is used to increase the

Fig. 1-18: Table extension.

circular saw table size and is very useful in cutting large panel stock. This table may be left on the saw at all times.

Sanding Disk. The sanding disk accessory will turn your table saw into a disk sander. When using a sanding disk in place of the saw blade, a special table insert is sometimes required.

Molding Cutterhead. Straight molding or shaping can be done on the table saw. The saw blade is replaced with a molding cutterhead (Fig. 1-19), which includes sets of formed knives or cutter shapes.

An assortment of knives or cutter shapes are available to fit molding heads. These shapes offer almost unlimited possibilities for making molding shapes on the table saw. But, remember that in many cases a special auxiliary wood facing for the rip fence is required. It should be made with a cutout in the center that gives clearance to the cutterhead when the knives are at their highest cutting point. Remove the standard table insert from the saw table, and replace it with a throat insert having an opening sufficiently large to accommodate the molding head and cutters.

Safety Goggles. Safety goggles or safety glasses should be worn when operating any power tool and this includes the table saw.

Shop Vacuum. While not an attachment to your saw, a shop vacuum (Fig. 1-20) is an accessory that helps keep your machine free of sawdust and other debris. This versatile device can also be used for other clean-up jobs around the shop and home.

While these are the most useful manufactured table-saw accessories and work helpers, there are other devices, less extensive in scope but extremely handy for particular jobs. Most can be easily made right in the shop. Many such devices are described in this book.

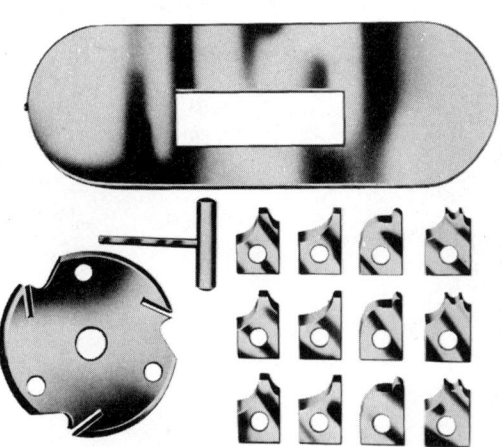

Fig. 1-19: Molding cutterhead, table insert, wrench and assorted molding cutters.

Fig. 1-20: Shop vacuum.

Chapter 2

BEFORE OPERATING THE TABLE SAW

It is important to know your table saw before operating it. The information in this chapter is of a general nature, applicable to most table saws. For specific data on your table saw, carefully check the owner's manual that came with it. By using the owner's manual along with this book, you will be able to get the most out of your table saw.

INSTALLATION

The table saw should be installed in a spot that leaves enough room to handle the size of the anticipated work materials. Generally the cabinet type of saw should be placed in the center of the shop, with plenty of space on both sides, and to the front and back. Room on all sides is required for ripping or crosscutting long boards or large panels. The bench type of machine can be put on a workbench, but this is usually not satisfactory. The table of the saw will be uncomfortably high, and interference will occur with the wall or with other things on the bench. So the bench type table saw is more readily usable when mounted on a steel or wooden stand of its own. It, too, should be placed in the center of the shop to allow room on all sides. Many table saw stands have accessory casters available which allow movement of the machine to the center of the shop when being used (Fig. 2-1).

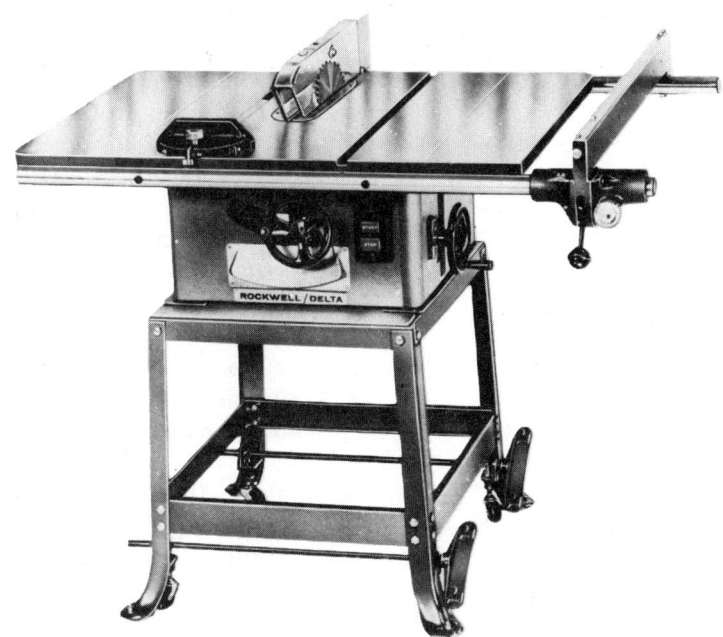

Fig. 2-1: Retractable casters or rollers permit the saw to be moved about the shop.

Fig. 2-2: Table saw-jointer combination.

Sometimes a common stand is used for both the table saw and the jointer (Fig. 2-2). This combination works out well, as work flows back and forth between the saw and the jointer. For example, to produce a board of certain width, the edge is jointed, and the board is sawed to about 1/16 inch oversize. The board is then jointed on the sawed edge to bring it to size. Smoothing with the jointer usually follows sawing. The surface of the table of the saw should be the correct height so that a board on the saw will just clear the top edge of the fence of the jointer.

The correct height of the table will be less than waist-high in all cases, and will vary from one shop to another because a tall person is comfortable with a higher mounting of the saw than a short person. A height of 34 inches from the floor to the table top is a good reference point. There are several arrangements that can be made in which a shop vacuum can be used to pick up the sawdust. Of course, cabinet type table saws are usually provided with a self-contained sawdust box fitted with a clean-out door. Be sure to provide an ample light source, natural or artificial, to enable easy reading of dials and controls.

The table saw should be unpacked and assembled according to the manufacturer's instructions. In order to obtain the maximum efficiency from your table saw's motor, the wire from the source of power to the machine should be of the proper size. Check with an electrician to be sure. Also, be sure that the electric line is fused with a 15-ampere fuse. If an ordinary type of fuse blows during the initial fraction of a second when the machine is turned on, do not put in a new one of higher rating. Instead, replace it with a fuse of the same rating, but of the "slow-blow" or delay type which contains a special fusible link that withstands a momentary overload without giving way.

Before plugging the cord into the wall or floor outlet, look at the name plate on your machine to see that its voltage supply needs are the same as that used in the house. If you ordered a table saw for use on a 240-volt line, be sure the name plate is marked 240 volts. Unless the voltage is delivered to within plus or minus ten percent of the motor name-plate rating, operation may not be satisfactory. If the motor runs hot or is short of power, call your local power company to check your voltage.

The table saw, as any other power tool, should always be grounded while in use. This precaution will protect the operator against possible electric shock should a short circuit or ground develop while the tool is being connected to the power outlet or during operation of the tool. Most table saws offer assured grounding protection for your safety. In accordance with a ruling of the National Electric Code, it is equipped with a three-wire cord, one wire being a ground wire. For your complete safety while operating this saw, remember that the three-conductor attachment plug naturally requires a three-prong outlet (Fig. 2-3A). Just insert the three-pronged plug, and the machine is instantly grounded if the receptacle is properly installed.

To permit use of this tool with a two-prong receptacle, an adapter (Fig. 2-3B) is

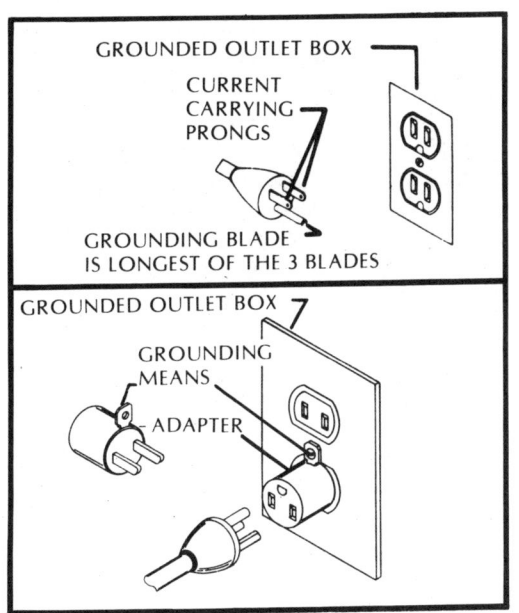

Fig. 2-3: (A) Grounded outlet and (B) grounding adapter.

once, but cannot be restarted without inserting the switch toggle.

Fig. 2-4: A method of locking the power switch in the OFF position.

Fig. 2-5: A special switch that locks in the OFF position.

available. (Such adapters are *not* applicable in Canada.) When using the adapter, the extending green wire should be connected to the outlet-plate retaining screw, provided that the outlet itself is grounded, or to any other known permanent ground, such as a water or an electric-conduct pipe. *Caution: If an extension cord is used, be sure it is a three-wire cord and large enough to prevent excessive voltage loss.*

If there are young children in the family, it is wise to make your table saw "kidproof." The best way to accomplish this is to lock the power in the "OFF" position using a padlock (Fig. 2-4). Some saws are equipped with a special switch such as shown in Fig. 2-5 that lock the saw when it is in the "OFF" position. This can be done by grasping the switch toggle and pulling it out of the switch. With the switch toggle removed the switch will not operate. However, should the switch toggle be removed while the saw is running, the saw can be turned "OFF"

SAW ADJUSTMENTS

Most table saws are thoroughly tested, inspected, and accurately aligned before leaving the factory. However, moving parts will wear, and the abrasive action of dust and dirt adds to this wear. Rough handling during transportation can also throw the machine out of alignment (Fig. 2-6).

A

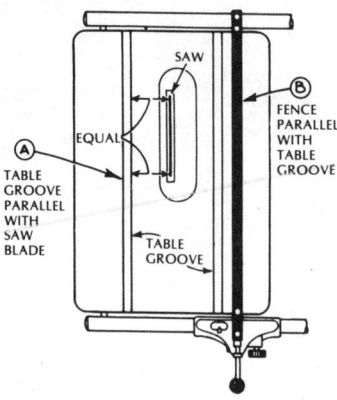

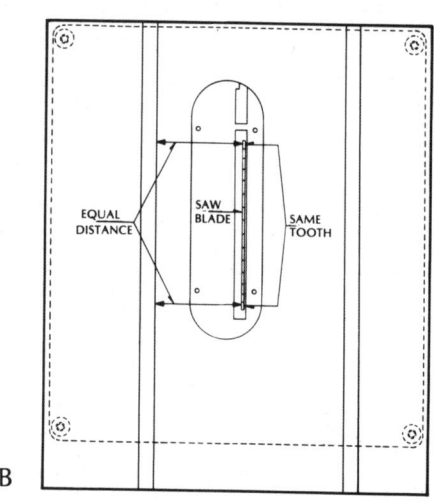

B

Fig. 2-6: A correctly aligned table saw.

Eventually, adjustment and realignment are necessary to maintain accuracy in any machine—regardless of the care with which the tool is manufactured. Usually, the instruction manual which comes with the machine describes how to make these adjustments.

Blade-Table Alignment. Since the rip fence and miter gauge both rely on the table for their alignment, it is of critical importance that the table itself be correctly squared with the saw blade (Fig. 2-6). However, before making any adjustments, be sure to disconnect the plug from the power source.

To check the blade-table alignment, crank the blade up to maximum elevation, and mark one of the teeth with a crayon (Fig. 2-7A). Turn the blade until the marked tooth is even with the surface of the table, and carefully measure the distance, at a right angle to the blade, from the marked tooth to the edge of the miter gauge slot. Then rotate the blade until the marked

Fig. 2-7: Checking blade-table alignment.

tooth is even with the surface of the table at the other end of the blade slot, and measure again (Fig. 2-7B). The two measurements should be identical; otherwise, the blade is out of alignment and will have to be adjusted.

Another way to check this alignment is to set the miter gauge at exactly 90 degrees, using a combination square and a flat-ground saw blade, as shown in Fig. 2-8. Place the miter gauge in its slot and, again with the combination square, make sure that the face of the gauge is at 90 degrees to the blade. (Hold the square against the flat of the blade, and not against a raked-out

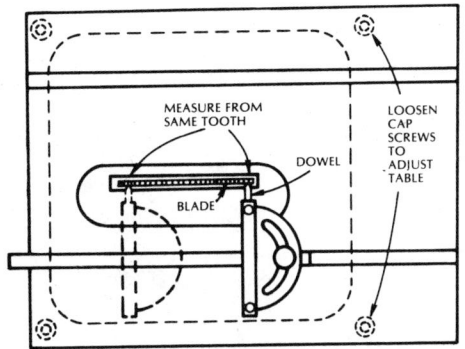

Fig. 2-8: Another method of checking blade-table alignment.

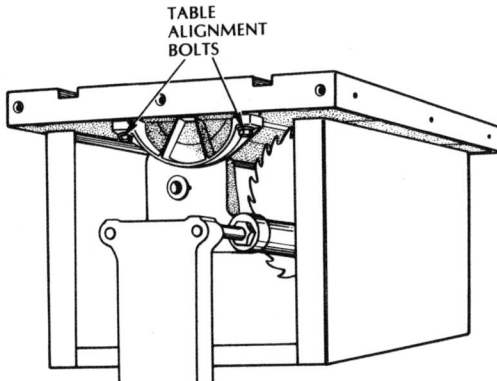

Fig. 2-9: Many saws have four bolts (two in the front, two in the back) that must be loosened to re-align the table.

bly to the table. Because of the variations in this adjustment, be sure to follow directions in the owner's manual.

To check the vertical blade alignment, crank the tilt control as far as it will go with the blade in the straight-up position. Then check with the combination square to see if the blade is at exactly 90 degrees, vertical to the table surface (Fig. 2-10). If not, sawdust in the tilt-mechanism track (Fig. 2-11) may be preventing the tilt from riding all the way against the stop. You may also have to correct the stop itself, which is usually done by adjusting a bolt. When this has been done and the blade is positioned at 90 degrees, check the tilt indicator. This should read exactly 0 degrees when the blade is in the vertical position. To adjust the pointer, simply loosen the screw that

Fig. 2-10: Checking vertical position of the blade.

Fig. 2-11: Be sure that sawdust in the tilt-mechanism track does not interfer with blade's alignment.

Fig. 2-12: Re-setting tilt-scale pointer.

tooth.) If you find that the blade is out of alignment, the necessary adjustment can be made easily by slightly loosening the screws or bolts which hold the table to the trunnions or to the saw base (Fig. 2-9). After slackening the screws or bolts slightly, the table or trunnions are bumped over with a rubber or rawhide mallet, and a recheck is made until the table shows square with the blade and the saw is positioned properly in the table insert slot. The table should again be checked for accuracy after the fasteners have been tightened. On some saws, the table adjustment is made by turning a single screw which rides against the table trunnion. On a few saws, adjustment is made by loosening the bolts that hold the arbor assem-

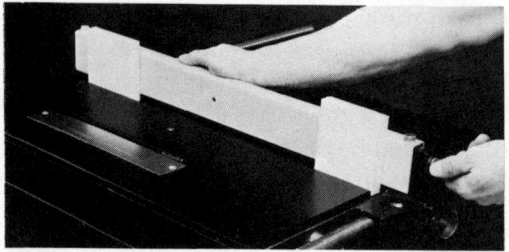

Fig. 2-13: To check ripping accuracy, lock fence against blocks in miter gauge slot.

Fig. 2-14: Measuring the miter-gauge slots.

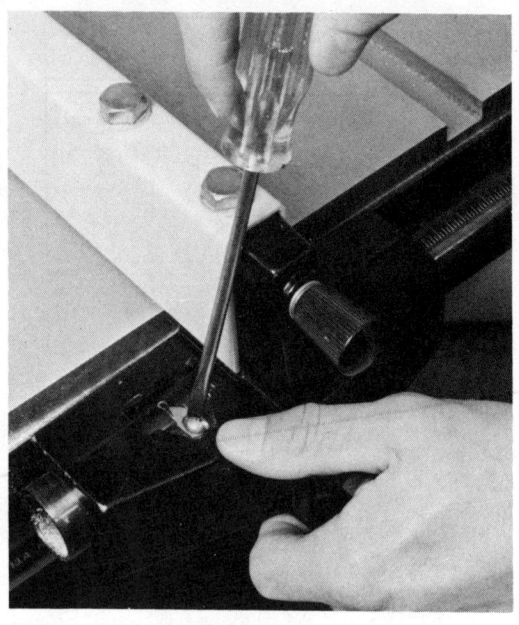

Fig. 2-15: Re-setting the rip-fence pointer.

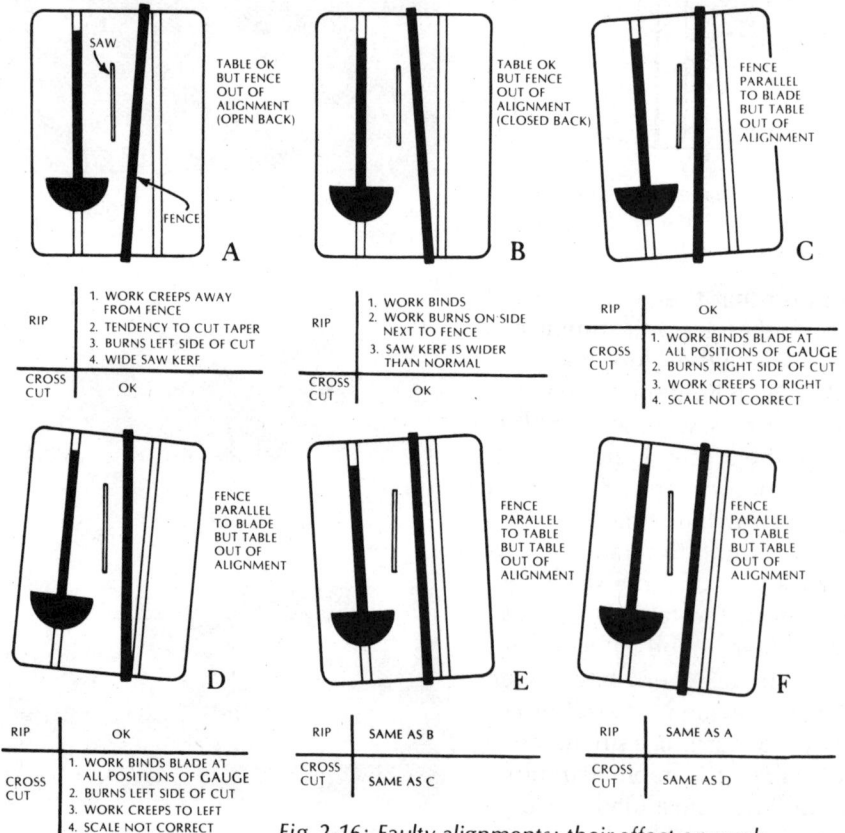

Fig. 2-16: Faulty alignments; their affect on work.

holds it to the arbor and set it correctly. (Fig. 2-12). In a few instances, this may require bending the pointer.

The Rip Fence. Set the rip fence so that, when the front clamp is tightened onto the guide bar, the fence will be parallel to the miter-gauge slot (Fig. 2-13). Adjust if necessary, following the manufacturer's instructions. When the fence is parallel to one of the miter-gauge slots in the table, it is automatically parallel to the other miter-gauge groove (Fig. 2-14). Grooves are milled simultaneously during manufacture and will definitely be parallel to each other. The fence can be used either to the right or to the left of the blade, but the position to the right of the blade is used most of the time.

The pointer on the rip fence indicating the ripping width is set by moving the fence over until it lightly touches the blade, and then setting the pointer to zero on the graduated front bar (Fig. 2-15). A recheck on this setting should be made by ripping a board to a certain width according to the saw scale and then checking the width with an ordinary rule. For example, rip a board with the pointer of the fence on some convenient setting—say 3 inches. Measure the board and set the pointer to the width of the cut board. If the board is 3-1/16 inches wide, set the pointer to 3-1/16 inches. It will then read correctly at any position, until the blade is changed. The kerf varies from blade to blade and the pointer should be set each time the blade is changed. The same holds true if the blade is sharpened and set. Remember that the cut is plus or minus the kerf.

Fig. 2-16 shows all of the possible variations of faulty table alignment. A and B are fence faults only. It will be noted in these cases, that the crosscut is okay. When the table is out of alignment, the crosscut always binds. Hence, if a ripping cut binds or pulls away from the fence, a check should be made on a crosscut. If a crosscut binds, the table needs adjustment. If the

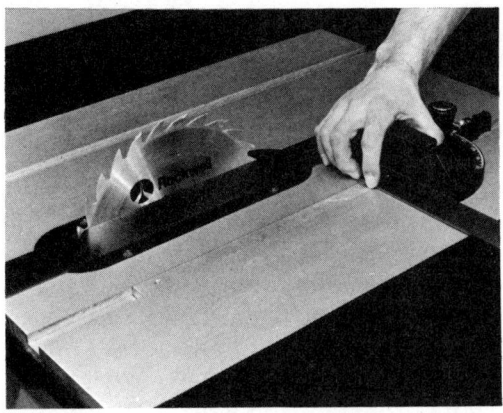

Fig. 2-17: Checking the miter gauge.

crosscut is okay, the fault is at the fence. Smooth, accurate operation of any table saw depends to a considerable extent on proper table adjustment, and this should be checked at regular intervals.

The Miter Gauge. The miter gauge is likewise checked for squareness. To check, place a square against the face of the miter gauge set at 90 degrees and along one of the miter gauge slots, as shown in Fig. 2-17. Another method of checking is to lock the gauge at the 90-degree position, and then make a trial cut on a fairly wide board. Check the board with the square, and if it is accurate, set the pointer on the miter gauge to the 90-degree mark. If the gauge has a stop link, set the link to maintain the setting. Make a similar check of the 45-degree positions, being careful in making the test cut to avoid any creeping of the work. If the scale does not give a proper reading, loosen the retaining screw and adjust the pointer accordingly. The table alignment should always be made before adjusting the miter gauge.

The miter gauge should glide smoothly and easily in its slot. If it does not, sprinkle a bit of silicone compound or powdered graphite in the slot, and slide the gauge back and forth until it moves freely; then clean and wax both the slide bar and the slot. Also check for burrs on the gauge or slot and remove them with a fine file.

The Tilt Angle Scale. Check to be sure that the tilt angle scale reads 0 degrees when the blade is set at 90 degrees (vertical) to the table. Also check at 45 degrees. Adjust the scale if necessary.

REPLACING A SAW BLADE

Before replacing a blade, **make sure the saw is disconnected from the power source.** Then remove the table insert. Place a block of soft wood against the front of the saw blade to keep it from turning. Then with a properly sized wrench, loosen the blade nut (Fig. 2-18) by turning it in a clockwise direction when looking at the end of the arbor shaft. (A few saws have an arrangement for using two wrenches for removing the arbor nut.) Once the nut is taken off, remove the flange and the blade.

Install the new saw blade on the arbor, making sure the teeth of the blade are pointing down at the front of the table.

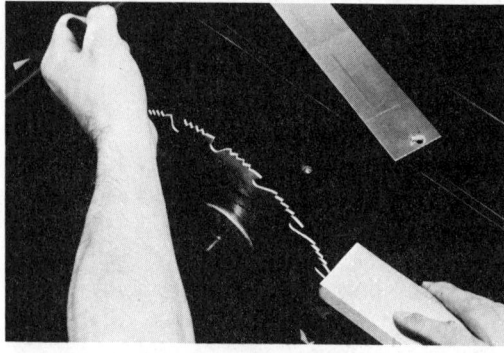

Fig. 2-18: Changing the saw blade.

Then replace the arbor flange and the blade nut. Tighten the nut securely and replace the insert plate. Rotate the blade by hand to make sure it is running free and clear.

OTHER MAINTENANCE TIPS

Although the table saw requires little maintenance, the following checks should be made on occasion to make sure problems do not arise:

1. Check all nuts, bolts, and screws for tightness. Check the arbor bearings by cranking the blade all the way up, and then trying to wiggle it. If you can feel play, replace the arbor bearings. Check the elevation and tilt gears and sliding surfaces to make certain these are functioning properly.

2. Check the belts to make certain they are in good condition. Keep them just snug enough to operate smoothly without slipping.

3. Make sure the pulleys are aligned and tight on the shafts. If necessary to align them, use a narrow board with a double bevel on one edge as a guide.

4. Make sure all safety devices operate easily, especially the blade guard.

5. Regular oil or grease is *not* recommended for lubrication of any of the mov-

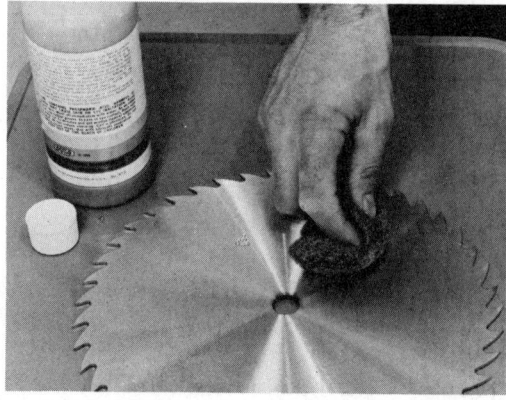

Fig. 2-19: Cleaning a saw blade with solvent.

Fig. 2-20: Applying wax to saw table.

ing parts of the saw, because it would only serve to catch the sawdust and clog the raising and tilting mechanisms, and so on. Use one of the available silicone products or powdered graphite for lubrication of the moving parts.

6. Keep all working parts free from sawdust and other substances that might have an abrasive effect on the parts. Also clean out the sawdust from underneath the table at regular intervals.

7. Blade teeth tend to become clogged with sawdust and resin. This causes draggings during the cut. Clean frequently (Fig. 2-19), using a resin solvent when necessary, and apply a light coating of oil to prevent rust.

8. Never use solvents to clean plastic parts. Solvents could possibly dissolve or otherwise damage the material. Only a soft damp cloth should be used to clean plastic.

9. Make sure the insert plate is in good condition and flush with the table surface. Replace it if necessary. See the manufacturer's instruction manual for adjusting procedure.

10. Keep all machine surfaces, such as the table top, free of rust or corrosion. Coat the surface of the table and all of the bright parts of the saw with wax. Automobile paste wax (Fig. 2-20) is very good for this purpose. Buff the wax to a glossy finish. This will fill the pores of the castings and prevent rust. It will make the table top extra smooth, causing the work to slide freely without sticking and jerking. It will make the machine safer and more pleasant to use.

TROUBLESHOOTING GUIDE

In spite of how well a table saw is maintained, problems do come along. The following troubleshooting guide will help solve the more common problems

Trouble: *Saw will not start*
Probable Cause
1. Saw not plugged in.
2. Fuse blown or circuit breaker tripped.
3. Cord damaged.
4. Overload relay not set.

Remedy
1. Plug in saw.
2. Replace fuse or reset circuit breaker.
3. Have cord replaced.
4. Push overload reset button.

Trouble: *Overload kicks out frequently.*
Probable Cause
1. Extension cord too light or too long.
2. Feeding stock too fast.
3. Blade in poor condition (dull, warped, gummed).
4. Blade binding due to misaligned rip fence.
5. Blade binding due to warped wood.
6. Low supply voltage.

Remedy
1. Replace with adequate size cord.
2. Feed stock more slowly.
3. Clean or replace blade.
4. Check and adjust rip fence.
5. Select another piece of wood.
6. Contact your electric company.

Trouble: *Material binds on splitter*
Probable Cause
1. Splitter not aligned correctly with blade.

Remedy
1. Check and align splitter with blade.

Trouble: *Material pinches blade when ripping.*
Probable Cause
1. Rip fence not aligned with blade.
2. Warped wood.

Remedy
1. Check and adjust rip fence.
2. Select another piece of wood.

TROUBLESHOOTING GUIDE (Cont.)

Trouble: *Material kicked back from blade*

Probable Cause
1. Rip fence out of alignment.
2. Splitter not aligned with blade.
3. Feeding stock without rip fence.
4. Splitter not in place.
5. Dull pitch-coated blade.
6. Letting go of material before it is past saw blade.
7. Anti-kickback fingers dull.

Remedy
1. Align rip fence with miter gauge slot.
2. Align splitter with blade.
3. Install and use rip fence.
4. Install and use splitter (with guard).
5. Replace or clean blade.
6. Push material all the way past saw blade before releasing work.
7. Sharpen kickback fingers.

Trouble: *Does not make accurate 45- and 90-degree rip cuts.*

Probable Cause
1. Tilt angle pointer not accurate.

Remedy
1. Check blade with square and adjust to zero.

Trouble: *Does not make accurate 45- and 90-degree crosscuts*

Probable Cause
1. Miter gauge out of adjustment.

Remedy
1. Adjust miter gauge.

Trouble: *Saw makes unsatisfactory cuts*

Probable Cause
1. Dull blade.
2. Blade mounted backwards.
3. Gum or pitch on blade.
4. Incorrect blade for work being done.
5. Gum or pitch on table causing erratic feed.
6. Blade not properly sharpened.

Remedy
1. Replace blade.
2. Turn blade around.
3. Remove blade and clean with turpentine and coarse steel wool.
4. Change the blade.
5. Clean table with turpentine and steel wool.
6. Replace blade and then rewax.

Trouble: *Blade does not come up to speed*

Probable Cause
1. Extension cord too light or too long.
2. Low supply voltage.
3. Motor wired for different voltage.

Remedy
1. Replace with adequate size cord.
2. Contact your electric company.
3. Make sure motor and supply are the same voltage.

Trouble: *Machine vibrates excessively*

Probable Cause
1. Saw not mounted securely on stand or work bench.
2. Stand or bench on uneven floor.
3. Damaged saw blade.
4. Bent motor or arbor pulley.
5. Uneven belt.

Remedy
1. Tighten all mounting hardware.
2. Reposition on flat level surface; fasten to floor if necessary.
3. Replace blade.
4. Check pulleys. Replace if necessary.
5. Check belt. Replace if necessary.

Trouble: *Rip fence binds on guide rails*

Probable Cause
1. End clamp blocks of rip fence not adjusted correctly.

Remedy
1. Loosen screws and move front and rear clamp blocks on rip fence.

SAFETY AND THE TABLE SAW

Safety and craftsmanlike work are both dependent on a thorough knowledge of your tool and the proper methods of using it. As mentioned earlier, the table saw is easy to use, but like all power tools there is a certain amount of hazard. Using the table saw with the respect and caution demanded as far as safety precautions are concerned will considerably lessen the possibility of personal injury. However, if normal safety precautions are overlooked or completely ignored, the operator may be injured.

For guiding the beginner, the following safety precautions are important.

1. Know your table saw. Read the owner's manual very carefully. Learn the saw's applications and limitations, as well as the specific potential hazards.

2. Tighten all clamps and levers before starting the machine, and make no adjustments while the saw is running. In fact, it is a good idea to disconnect the tool before making adjustments and when changing accessories such as blades and cutters. This will avoid accidental starting.

3. Maintain the table saw in top condition. Keep it clean for best and safest performance. Never use a dull saw blade or one that does not have sufficient set. It may cause kickback.

4. Dress properly. Jewelry, neckties, loose clothing, or gloves can get caught in the cutting tool or workpiece. Nonslip footwear is recommended.

5. Use safety glasses or goggles. Also wear a face shield or dust mask if the cutting operation is dusty. If using the saw for extended periods of operation, wear earplugs or earmuffs.

6. Leave no tools or pieces of wood on the saw table when it is in operation, and keep the floor around the machine clean and in good condition. Keep the work area well lighted.

7. Always use the blade guard, splitter, and anti-kickback fingers on all *through-sawing* operations. Through-sawing operations are those where the blade cuts completely through the workpiece as in ripping or crosscutting.

8. Always hold the work firmly against the table, miter gauge, or fence.

9. Always use a push stick for ripping narrow stock and always push the material between the saw blade and the fence completely past the blade.

10. Never perform any operation "freehand" which means using only your hands to support or guide the workpiece. Always use either the fence or the miter gauge to position and guide the work.

11. Never stand or have any part of your body in line with the path of the saw blade.

12. Never reach behind or over tne moving cutting tool with either hand for any reason.

13. Move the rip fence out of the way before crosscutting.

14. When cutting moldings, never let the stock get between the fence and the molding cutterhead. See the owner's manual for details to molding applications.

15. Feed work into a blade or cutter against the direction or rotation of the blade or cutter only. Do not force the saw. It will do the job better and be safer at the rate for which it was designed.

16. Never use the fence as a cutoff gauge when crosscutting.

17. Never attempt to free a stalled saw blade without first disconnecting the saw from the power source.

18. Provide adequate support to the rear and sides of the saw table for wide or long workpieces.

19. Avoid awkward operations and hand positions where a sudden slip could cause your hand to move into the cutting tool.

20. Do not take your eyes off the work you are doing, and do not talk to anyone while using the table saw. All children and visitors should be kept a safe distance from the work area.

21. Never leave the table saw running

unattended. Turn the power to *off* and do not leave the tool until it comes to a complete stop.

22. Do not operate a table saw while under the influence of drugs, alcohol, or any medication. Continual alertness is most important when operating any tool.

Avoiding Kickback. If, for any reason, the saw blade should bind in the workpiece, it can kick the stock back toward the operator with great force and speed. Also, if any piece of scrap (or other object) is left on the table and slides into the revolving blade, it can be thrown with considerable force. Actually, kickback is one of the greatest hazards in running a table saw and must be avoided. Some of the common causes of kickback are as follows:

1. Using a dull saw or a saw with insufficient set.

2. Cutting "freehand" or ripping badly warped wood.

3. Failure to use the splitter guard and anti-kickback fingers.

4. Crosscutting against the ripping fence without using a clearance block.

5. Pieces of stock dropped on an unguarded saw blade.

6. Letting go of material before it is past the saw blade.

7. Ripping stock with loose or large, unsound knots.

Chapter 3

BASIC OPERATION OF THE TABLE SAW *

In Chapter 1, it was stated that there are only six basic saw cuts in woodworking—rip, bevel rip, crosscut, bevel crosscut, miter, and bevel miter. All other cuts, no matter how intricate, are combinations of these basic cuts (Fig. 3-1). It is essential, therefore, to master the basic cuts in order to use any power saw to its fullest capabilities.

Still another interesting fact is that perhaps 90 percent of all operations on the table saw are ripping and crosscutting. It should be noted again that a table saw should *not* be used in these through-sawing operations without the saw guard in place. In the many photographs shown in this book, the guard has been removed for the sake of clarity. **Use all guards and safety devices recommended by the manufacturer.**

It is important to remember that the table saw teeth above the table's surface rotate in the direction of the operator, and enter the top surface of the workpiece first (Fig. 3-2A). Therefore, place the wood with the finished side upward. This applies to plain plywood (Fig. 3-2B), veneers, and any

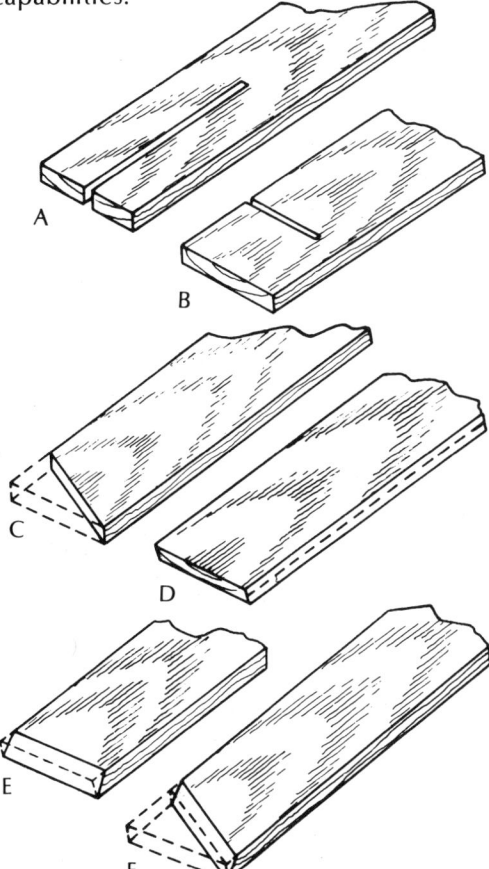

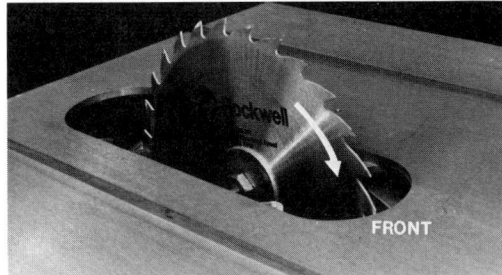

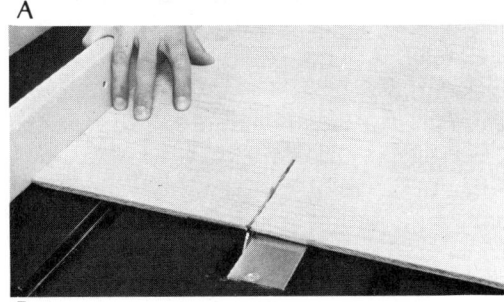

Fig. 3-1: The six basic cuts: (A) Rip; (B) crosscut; (C) miter; (D) bevel rip; (E) bevel crosscut; and (F) bevel miter.

Fig. 3-2: (A) How a table saw blade cuts. (B) Keep the good side up when cutting plywood.

*NOTE: *In order to clearly illustrate certain procedures described in this chapter, the blade guard and other safety devices have been removed. For safe operation of the table saw, guards and other safety devices must always be utilized.*

... of plywood with laminates attached. ...en both sides of the wood are finished, ...se a fine-tooth blade with minimum set, or use a hollow-ground saw blade with the teeth widely spaced. Also keep in mind that the kerf is the slot normally formed by the saw blade (Fig. 3-3). Its width will differ depending on the style, the gauge, and the amount of set on the teeth of the saw blade. The kerf should always be on the waste side of the cut line.

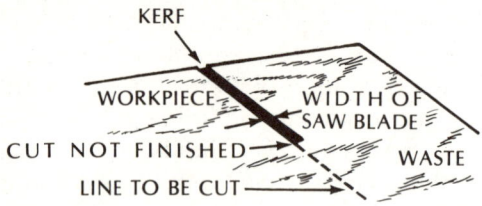

Fig. 3-3: *The saw blade's kerf.*

RIPPING

Ripping is the operation of making a *lengthwise* cut through a board. One edge of the work rides against the guide fence while the flat side of the board rests on the table. Therefore, before attempting to rip a board, make certain that one edge is straight so it can ride against the fence and that one surface is flat and smooth so it can lay flat on the saw table. A board with a crooked or curved edge can cause the saw blade to stick (bind) and kick the piece back toward the operator. It could also buckle (bend or twist) on the saw blade. The danger in a buckle or a kickback is that if your hands are near the saw blade at the time, one or both hands may be jerked loose and thrown into the blade. The approved sawing method is aimed at preventing kickbacks or buckles. As an extra precaution, the hands are kept in the clear "just in case." Kickbacks and buckles will not occur if the saw blade is sharp and has good set, and if the work has reasonably true surfaces to guide it along the fence and support it without rocking. Also, the guard has anti-kickback fingers and a splitter to prevent the saw kerf from closing behind and binding on the blade.

Do not rip material with loose or large, unsound knots. If a knot becomes loose just after it is cut in two, it can fly out with a great deal of force. Knock out loose knots with a hammer before starting the sawing operation. If possible, in all ripping operations, employ the splitter to keep the kerf open behind the blade.

Ripping Wide Stock. Stock is considered wide when it measures at least 4 inches between the fence and the blade. Adjust the height of the ripsaw or combination blade approximately 1/8 to 1/4 inch above the thickness of the stock (Fig. 3-4). While there seems to be some disagreement as to how the blade should be set, the 1/8 to 1/4 inch setting is by far the safest way to position the blade. It gives a very smooth cut. True, with maximum blade projection there is the least friction on the rim of the blade and less chance of burning the workpiece. The blade also cuts faster. But using the blade this way may cause excessive chipping of the wood and greater exposure to the whirling blade. Most experts recommend that the blade projection should be no more than 1/4 inch above the stock.

Fig. 3-4: *Recommended blade projection.*

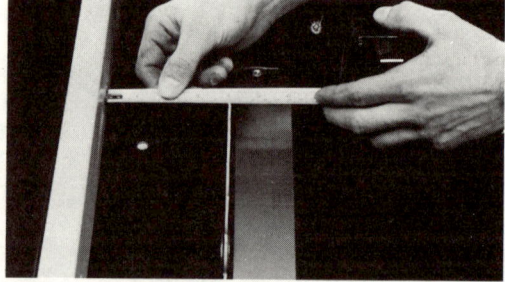

Fig. 3-5: *Rip fence is set by measuring from it to the blade.*

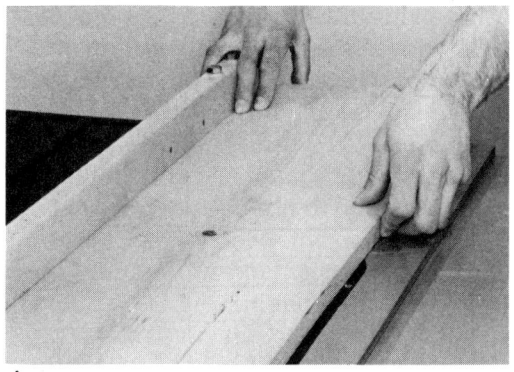

Fig. 3-6: (A) Keep the fingers over the fence. (B) The completion of the cut.

To adjust the rip fence for the proper width of the cut, hold a rule at right angles to it, or hold a large square against it and measure the desired width to the blade (Fig. 3-5). Another simple method is to place the marked workpiece against the rip fence and then move the fence until the cutting line is directly in line with the saw blade. When the blade has set teeth, be sure to check against one that points toward the fence. Also remember the thickness of the kerf; rip on the waste side of the marked line. (Note: While the rip fence can be located on either the right or left side of the saw blade, the following instructions are based on a right side location. If, for any reason you prefer to locate the fence to the left, correct these instructions accordingly.)

Start the motor, and when the blade comes to full speed, advance the workpiece, holding it down and against the fence. Never stand in the line of the saw cut when ripping. Hold the work with both hands. Use the left hand to hold the work in position against the fence and the right hand, with the fingers hooked over the fence, to feed the work forward (Fig. 3-6A). Keep the left hand in its original position, snugging the workpiece to the fence throughout the pass, but do not continue with the left hand beyond the front edge of the blade. Feed with the right hand until the work is past the saw blade. Once the work is beyond the saw blade and the anti-kickback fingers, the hand is removed from the work. When this is done, the work will either stay on the table and tilt up slightly to be caught by the rear end of the guard or will slide off the table to the floor (Fig. 3-6B). Alternately, the feed can continue to the end of the table, after which the work is lifted and brought back along the outside edge of the fence. The waste stock remains on the table and is not touched with the hands until the saw is stopped, unless it is a large piece allowing safe removal.

Ripping Narrow Stock. If the ripped work is less than 3 inches wide, a push stick should be used to complete the feed. That is, when the stock is over the front of the table, pick up the push stick in the right hand. Continue to apply pressure with the push stick (Fig. 3-7) to complete the cut and

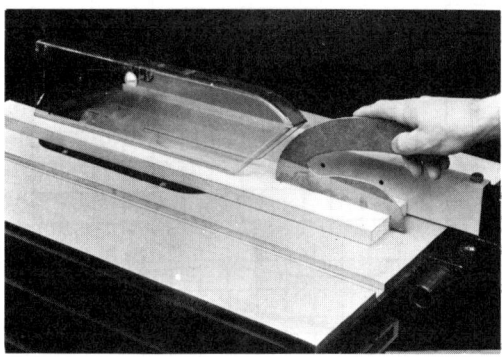

Fig. 3-7: Using a push stick for cutting narrow stock.

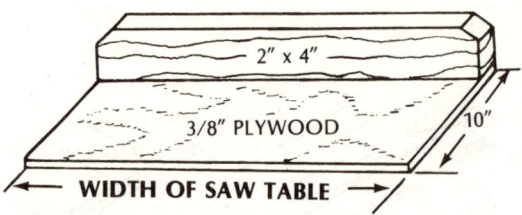

Fig. 3-13: An auxiliary wood table fence.

Fig. 3-14: The auxiliary table in use.

Fig. 3-15: Using a drill press for support.

PARTS CHART FOR CROSSCUT SUPPORT

PIECE	THICK	WIDTH	LENGTH
A	3/4	2 7/8	22 1/2
B	3/4	3/4	2 7/8
C	5/8	1 7/8 DIA.	—
D	1/2 DIA.	—	2 1/4
E	3/4	3 5/8	27
F	3/4	1 3/4	30
G	3/4	3 5/8	29
H	1 5/8	3 5/8	20
I	3/4	3 3/4	20

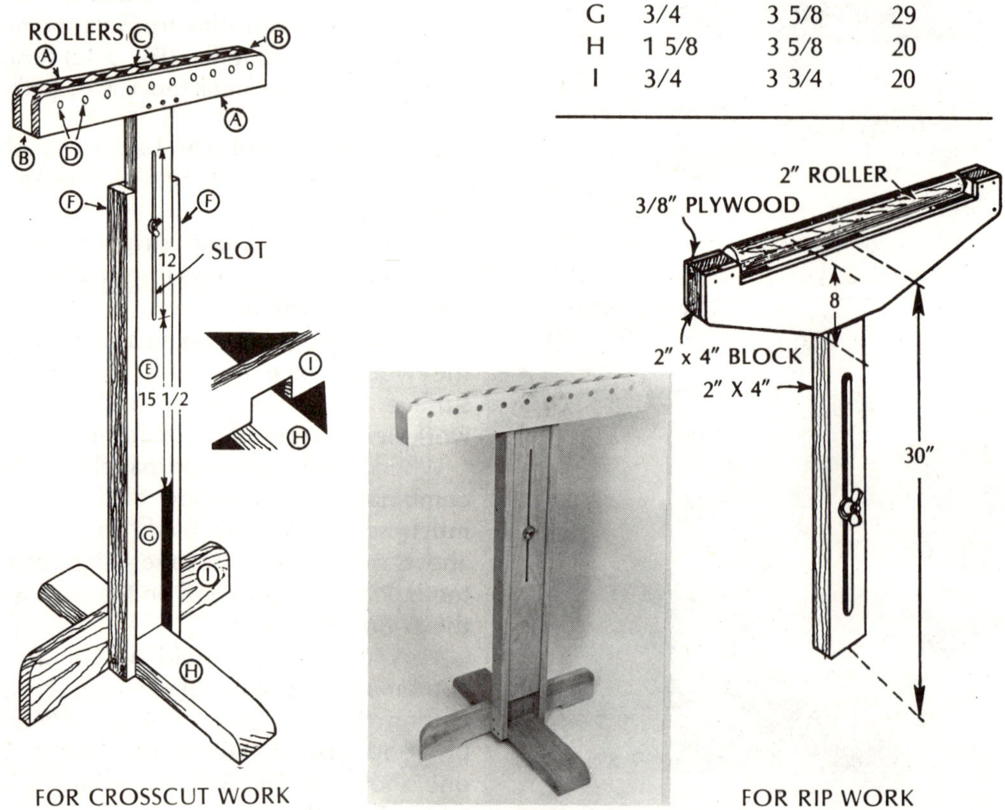

FOR CROSSCUT WORK

FOR RIP WORK

Fig. 3-16: Drawing shows roller support for both rip and crosscut work.

plywood table fence. Then place the thin stock on the table against the fence; hold and feed it with a thick piece. The auxiliary table can be reused for various other cutting operations (Fig. 3-14).

Ripping Long Stock. The major problem when ripping long stock is that the board may sag down behind the saw. To prevent this from occurring, some kind of outfeed is needed to support the stock. While another power tool (Fig. 3-15) or bench at the proper height will do, a homemade roller support (Fig. 3-16) is recommended as an outfeed table.

Another method of ripping long stock (Fig. 3-17) is to saw slightly more than half the length. Turn off the saw, draw the material back out of the saw, turn it over end to end, start the saw again, and complete the cut from the other end. Figure 3-18 shows a setup that is good for ripping long thin stock. Use a push stick or block to complete the cut.

Resawing. Resawing is the operation of ripping a thick board to make a thin board. If the work does not exceed the capacity of the saw, the cut can be treated as a regular ripping operation. But, before attempting this operation, it is necessary to make a jig called a "fingerboard" or "featherboard." A featherboard is a board cut off at an angle of 60 degrees. At that cut end, a series of parallel cuts is made part way through the board (Fig. 3-19).

The featherboard is clamped to the saw table on the infeed side, in such a way that it bears against the workpiece to be resawed and has its long edge opposite the front of the saw. It holds the stock firmly against the ripping fence, and its "fingers" prevent it from being thrown back. If it were clamped farther away from the operator, it would bear against the saw cut and pinch the blade.

If the board thickness is within the maximum capacity of the blade, it can be resawed in one pass. If it is thicker, but not more than twice as thick, it can be resawed

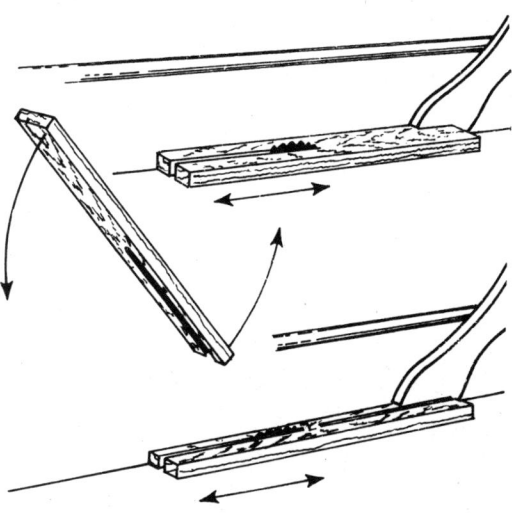

Fig. 3-17: One method of ripping long work.

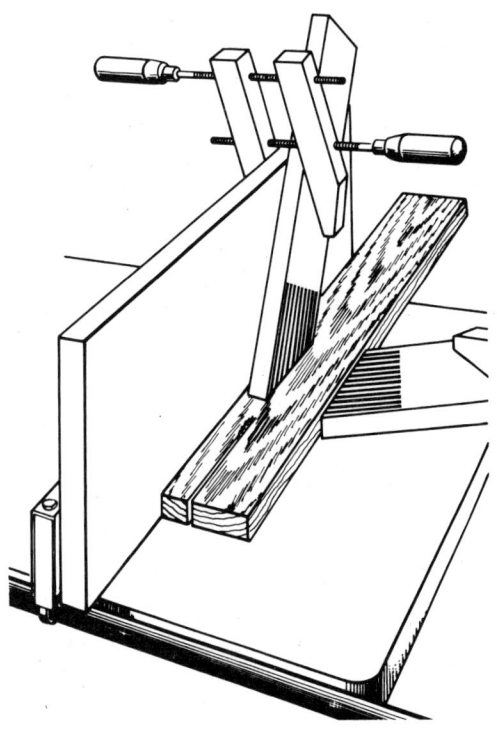

Fig. 3-18: Another setup for ripping long, thin stock.

29

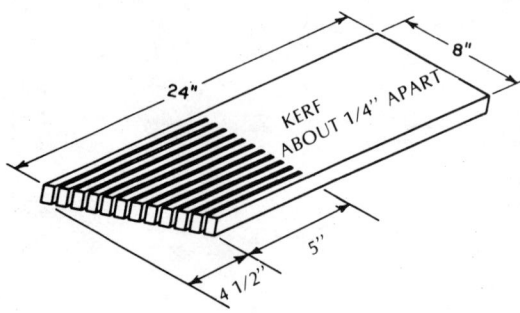

Fig. 3-19: Typical featherboard.

Fig. 3-20: Typical resawing setup.

A

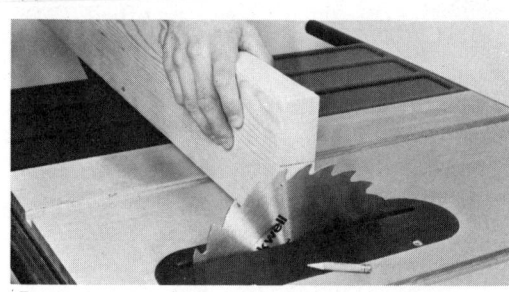

B

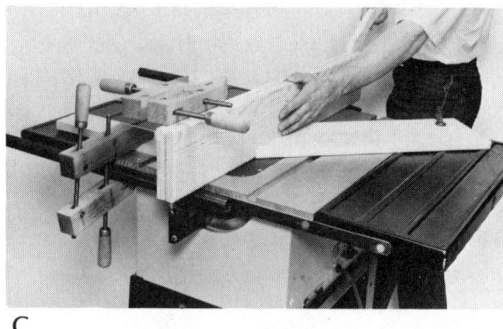

C

Fig. 3-21: Another simple and safe resawing setup.

in two passes, one with each edge down (Fig. 3-20). If it is more than twice as thick, two passes may come close enough to severing it, making it possible to finish the job by handsawing or on a band saw. That is, the cuts made on the table saw help in either case to make the rest of the cut straight and to reduce the handsawing operation. It is not easy to resaw a thick plank entirely on a band saw, because the blade has a tendency to weave in and out. The cuts made on the table saw help it to keep a straight line.

When two passes are required, it is necessary to remove the saw-blade guard; extra care must be exercised to keep your hands away from the blade. It is also a good safety procedure to attach an auxiliary wood fence arrangement to the metal one (Fig. 3-21A). Then use two featherboards one to apply pressure from the top and the other to hold the work against the auxiliary fence. Set the blade height (Fig. 3-21B) so that the first cut will be slightly more than half the width of the stock. (When resawing hardwood, it is best to make a shallow cut first then raise the blade so it extends above the work surface about 1/4" more

A

B

Fig. 3-22: (A) Straight crosscutting; (B) miter crosscutting.

than half the stock width.) To feed the material hold it at the top and sides (Fig. 3-21C). *Never* hold it at the end to push. When you make the second cut, if there is any tendency for the first-cut kerf to squeeze closed, use wedges to hold it open.

CROSSCUTTING

Crosscutting is sawing through (across the grain) a piece of stock or cutting across the narrowest dimension while using the miter gauge to guide it. All rectangular workpieces that are to be cut from one edge to the other (narrow dimension) must be crosscut. If the cut is at 90 degrees to the board edge against the miter-gauge face, it is a *straight crosscut* (Fig. 3-22A). A *miter crosscut* is a cut for which this angle is other than 90 degrees (Fig. 3-22B).

When making a straight crosscut, set and lock the miter gauge at the 0 degree position. Draw a line on the stock at the cutoff point, making the line long enough to use for sighting. A mark scribed on the table insert in line with the saw blade (Fig. 3-23) is most helpful in positioning the work against the miter-gauge face. Shift the work to the side as necessary to align your cutoff mark with the saw blade. If the scrap piece is at the left, the cutoff mark should be aligned with the right side of the blade so that the kerf will be in the scrap and vice versa. The miter gauge itself may be used in either table slot. If you are using the left-hand slot, hold the miter-gauge handle with the right hand, and use the left hand

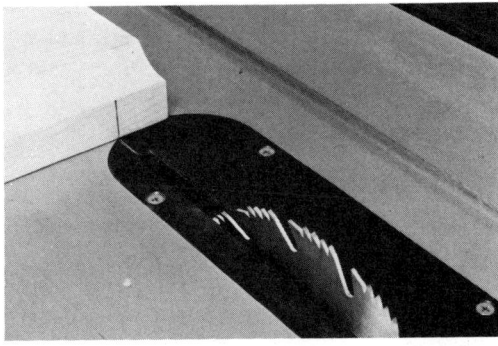

Fig. 3-23: A scribed mark on the table insert in line with the blade is useful for setting crosscut work.

Fig. 3-24: Method of guiding a miter gauge.

to hold the material (Fig. 3-24). Reverse these hand positions if the miter gauge is in the right-hand slot on the table. Remember to keep both hands on the same side of the saw blade; never place them on opposite sides since it can cause the blade to bind and result in a kickback.

With the stock positioned correctly and blade set about an 1/8 to 1/4 inch above the stock, start the cut slowly and hold the work firmly against the miter gauge and the table. One of the rules for operating a table saw, regardless of the cut, is that you never hang onto or touch a free (scrap) piece of work. Hold the supported piece, not the free piece that is cut off. The feed in crosscutting continues until the work is cut in two, then the miter gauge and work are pulled back to the starting point. Before pulling the work back, it is a good practice to give the work a little sideways shift to move the work slightly away from the saw blade. Never pick up any short length of free work from the table while the saw is running. A safe operator never touches a cutoff piece until the blade stops. Never use the fence as a cutoff gauge when crosscutting.

To prevent a long board from wobbling, the miter gauge can be fitted with an auxiliary face board that should be at least one inch higher than the maximum depth of the cut, and should extend 12 inches or more on either side of the blade. This auxiliary face board can be fastened to the front of the miter gauge by putting wood screws through the holes provided in the miter-gauge body and into the face board. Other methods of holding the fence to the miter gauge body are shown in Fig. 3-25. A scale (rule) can be fitted into the face board (Fig. 3-26) and a piece of coarse abrasive cloth can be glued to it to help prevent creeping. An additional safeguard against both wobbling and creeping is the miter-gauge hold-down clamp (Fig. 3-27).

When stock width is such that the

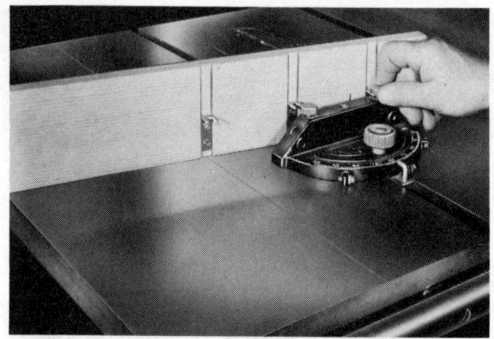
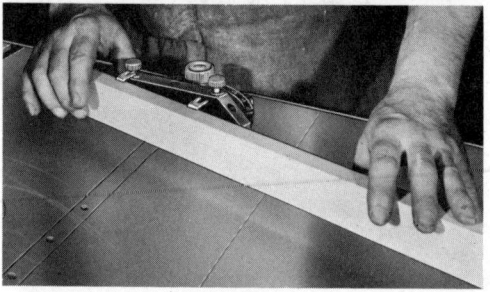
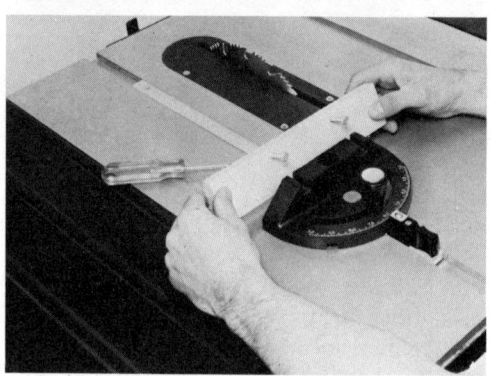

Fig. 3-25: Methods of fastening auxiliary woodfacing to miter gauge.

starting position locates the miter-gauge head off the table, it is a good idea to use the miter gauge backwards (Fig. 3-28). This means that one hand will be pulling the miter gauge against the forward edge of the workpiece while the other hand is pushing against the opposite edge. When doing this, however, be sure to support the work throughout the entire operation.

On a long piece of work, the overhanging ends will tend to drop down a little at the end of the cut unless properly supported. Of course, a roller support (Fig.

3-16) is one of the best ways to handle long work when crosscutting. The support is used parallel to the saw, the work riding on hardwood rollers which turn on dowel pins (Fig. 3-29). To cut extra long boards, or panels, the crosscut gauge shown in Fig. 3-30 is ideal.

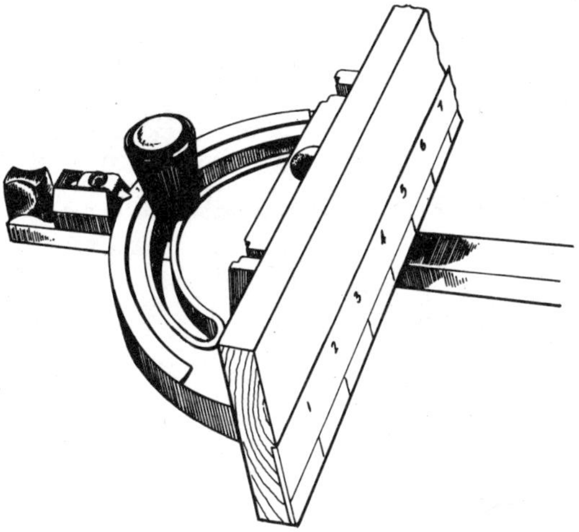

Fig. 3-26: An auxiliary face board with a built-in ruler.

Fig. 3-29: Using a roller support when crosscutting.

Crosscutting Stock to Length. If a number of short pieces are to be cut to the same length, the best method is to use a rip fence to which a clearance block or straddle block is clamped as a stop (Fig. 3-31A). The stop block can also be clamped to the table as in Fig. 3-31B. Hold the stock against the miter gauge while cutting, but be sure to use the clearance block; otherwise, a kickback is certain to result. Also use the guard over the saw and the splitter guard so that cut-off pieces will not be picked up by the back teeth and thrown forward.

Use a stop rod to cut longer pieces to length (see page 9) with the miter gauge, and move the rip fence out of the way. Square one end first on all of the pieces. Put the stop rod on the miter gauge. Measure the distance from the end of the stop rod to one tooth set to the left. Then place the squared end against the stop rod and make the cut (Fig. 3-32).

If the workpieces are longer than the stop rod will reach, an auxiliary face board will have to be made and screwed to the miter gauge. Remove the rip fence from

Fig. 3-27: Using a clamp attachment while crosscutting.

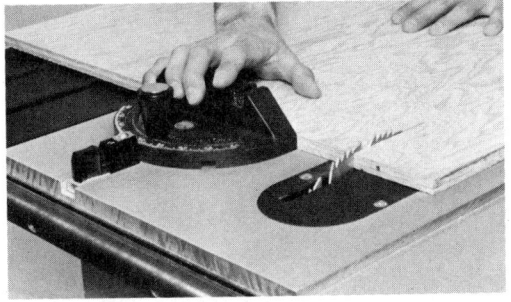

Fig. 3-28: Reversing the miter gauge in its slot.

the machine, and be sure to make the auxiliary face board long enough on both sides so that it will not tip the miter gauge. Nail, screw, or clamp a stop to the auxiliary face board at the correct length (Fig. 3-33). A simple adjustment stop block for the fence is illustrated in Fig. 3-34.

When cutting material to length in a production setup, two miter gauges can be used to good advantage. The one on the

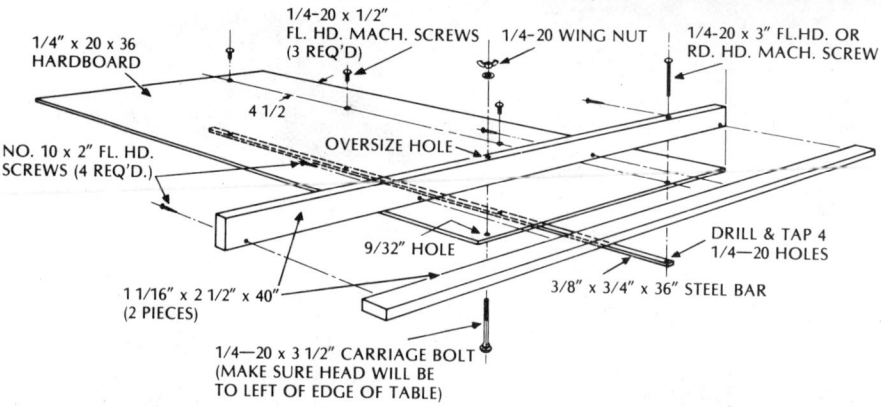

Fig. 3-30: Panel crosscut gauge.

A.

B

Fig. 3-31: Two ways of using a stop block.

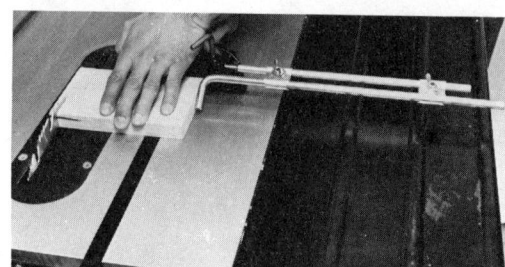

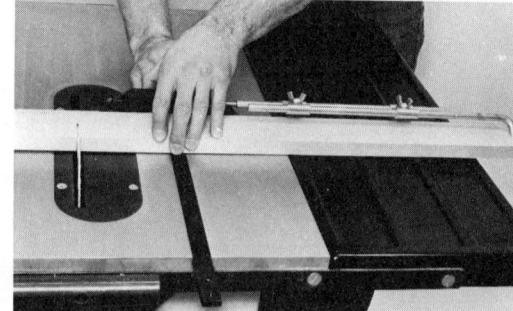

Fig. 3-32: Stop rods are most valuable when crosscutting to length.

Fig. 3-33: A block of wood clamped to the auxiliary facing.

MITERING

Mitering is crosscutting with the miter gauge set at an angle other than zero. To set the angle, put the gauge at the desired angle and lock it. You may also draw the desired cutoff angle on the workpiece. Then set the miter-gauge angle until this cutoff line aligns with the saw blade and locks in place. In either case, the cut is made in the same manner as the straight crosscut. The saw cut should be on the scrap or waste side.

right side is used to cut the left-end square; the one on the left has a stop block fastened to a wooden auxiliary face board, for cutting the second end to exact length.

The gauge can be set in either a closed or open position (Fig. 3-35). However, if the board is wide, or if the saw table is not large enough in front of the blade, the closed position is preferred. The reason is that when the open position is used, part or all of the miter gauge may be off the table and the work will rock.

Two miter guages can be used in making miter cuts. This is useful when a job calls for frequent readjustment of a single miter gauge in order to make mating cuts. This will occur when the stock is so shaped that it cannot be flipped over, such as cutting moldings that are not flat on both sides.

Fig. 3-34: A simple stop block.

All miter cuts tend to creep (Fig. 3-36) slightly during the course of cutting. That is, when the miter gauge is used in the

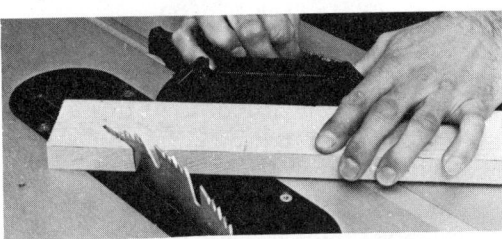

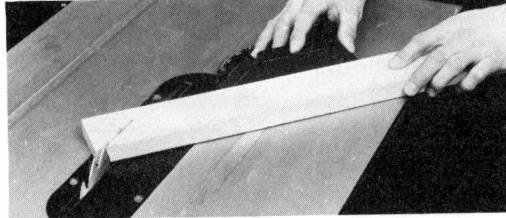

Fig. 3-35: A miter can be cut in either open or closed position.

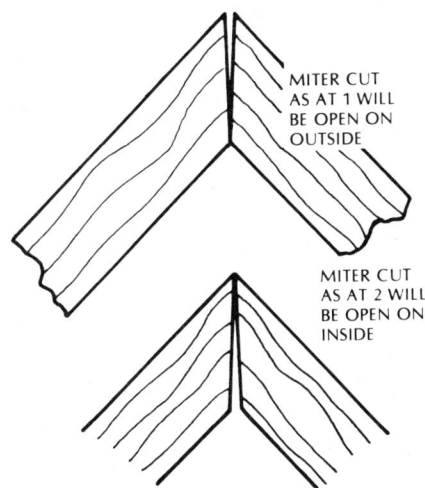

Fig. 3-36: Results of creeping.

35

closed position, the work will creep away from the blade. Because of the vibration of the moving parts, it is virtually impossible to prevent creeping unless special precautions are taken. One of the best solutions is the already discussed miter gauge clamp attachment. It can be left on the miter gauge most of the time, even when not being used, and then it will always be handy when needed.

Another noncreep device is an auxiliary wood face board with disappearing anchor points (Fig. 3-37). This can be used alone, or in connection with the clamp attachment. The points of the screws are filed sharp, and in most cases the slight marking of the work is not objectionable. When the points are not wanted, the screws are simply turned out enough to hide the points.

Several types of jigs can be used for accurate mitering. These are described in detail in Chapter 6.

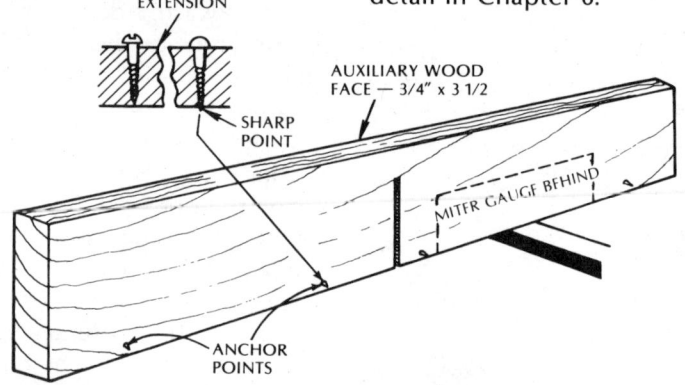

Fig. 3-37: An auxiliary miter gauge facing with disappearing anchor points.

Fig. 3-38: Sighting the cuttoff line.

BEVEL-ANGLE SAWING

There are three basic bevel cuts—the bevel-rip, bevel-crosscut, and bevel-miter or compound miter. Modern table saw blades tilt either to the right or to the left but never both ways. Since the majority of operators are right-handed, a right tilting machine is usually preferred. This puts the work on the left side of the blade.

The tilt scale indicates the angle of tilt from the blade's vertical position.

Bevel Ripping. Mark the angle of the cutoff line on the top and both ends of the workpiece and set the blade at this angle. Then mark a pencil line on the table in front of the blade remembering that the kerf should be on the waste piece. Locate the fence to align the bottom of the cutoff mark with this pencil mark. You can double-check the position before cutting by sighting from the back along the top cutoff line of the work to the blade.

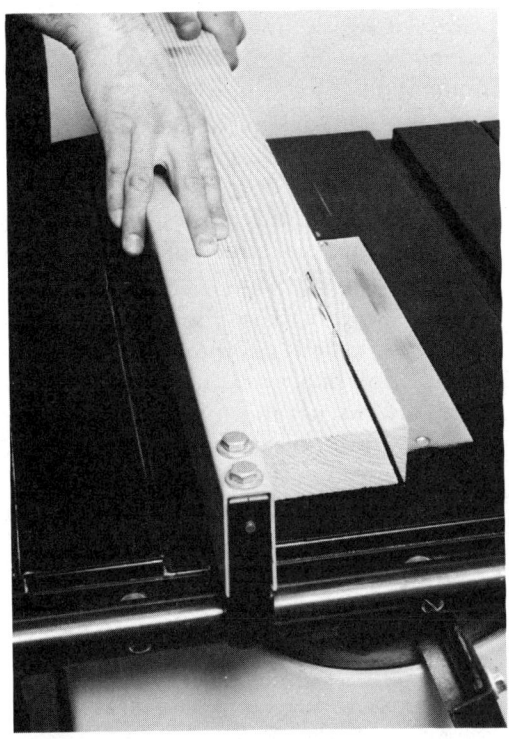

Fig. 3-39: Bevel ripping.

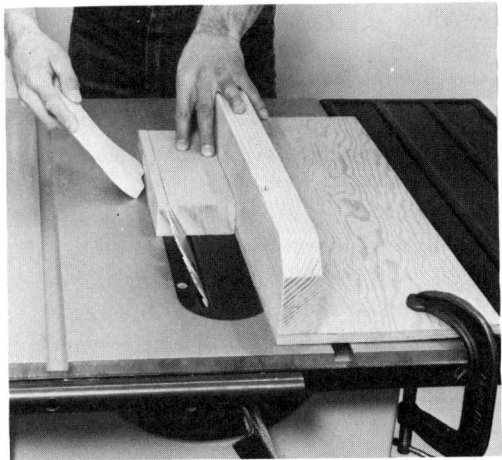

Fig. 3-40: Using an auxiliary table fence to bevel rip.

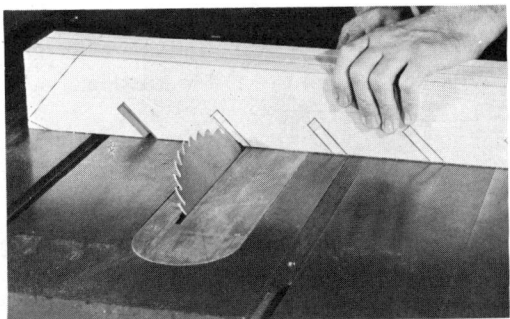

Fig. 3-41: Examples of bevel crosscutting.

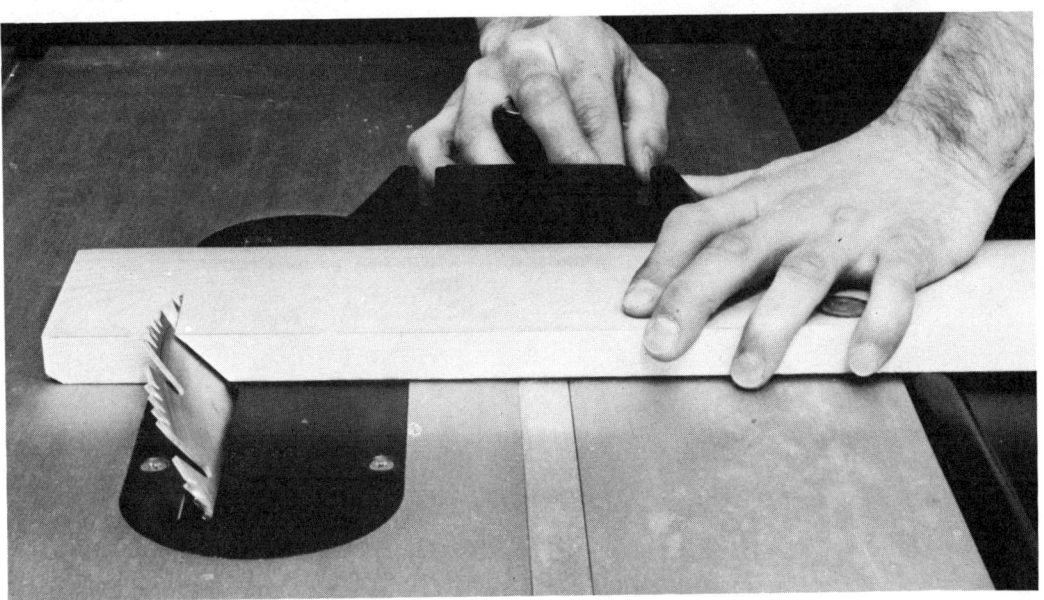

When the exact degree of the marked angle on the stock is not known, the blade can be adjusted to the desired angle by sighting along the marked lines (Fig. 3-38). This is done, of course, before the rip fence is positioned and located in place. Once the blade is set at the desired angle and adjusted to the correct height (about 1/8 or 1/4 inch above the work), and the workpiece and fence are located properly, the cut is completed in the same way you would a straight rip (Fig. 3-39).

Many times, when the blade tilts to the right, it is best to locate the fence on the left of the blade. This is especially true when bevel ripping narrow stock. If the fence on your saw cannot be positioned to the left of the blade, an auxiliary wood table fence (Fig. 3-13) should be clamped to the table parallel to the blade (Fig. 3-40).

Bevel Crosscutting. When bevel crosscutting, the miter gauge should be located in the table slot, tilting the blade away from the gauge. The blade is set at the desired angle and the work properly aligned in the way described for bevel ripping. Then hold the stock firmly against the gauge and make the cut as you would any crosscut (Fig. 3-41).

Bevel Miter. The bevel-miter cut, sometimes called a compound-angle is a combination of a miter cut and a bevel. To make this cut, set the miter gauge to the proper angle, and set up the workpiece as already described for bevel crosscutting. The cut itself is made in the same manner (Fig. 3-42). The combination of the blade set at an angle and the miter gauge set at an angle results in a compound angle (See page 52).

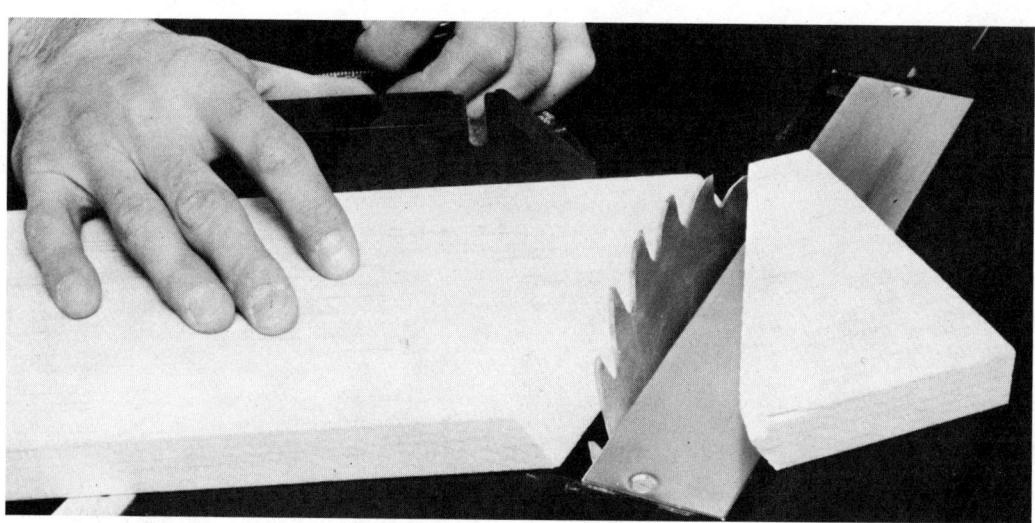

Fig. 3-42: Bevel miter.

Chapter 4

BASIC USE OF THE DADO HEAD *

The main use of a dado head is to cut grooves, dadoes, and rabbets. A groove is a slot cut with the grain of the wood, while a dado is a slot cut at right angles to the edge grain. A rabbet is similar to a groove or dado but along the end or edge of a board. (Fig. 4-1). All three of these cuts can also be made with a regular saw blade.

To make a groove, dado, or rabbet, set the saw blade at less than the stock thickness and make repeat passes to widen the normal kerf to the desired width of the slot. While the saw blade, repeat-pass method is good for an occasional groove, dado, or rabbet, the purchase of a dado head is a wise choice if such cuts are needed often. This accessory can perform tasks other than cutting grooves, dadoes, and rabbets.

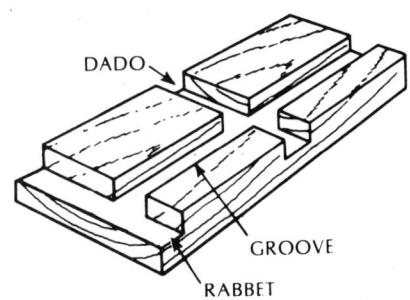

Fig. 4-1: A groove, dado, and rabbet. Details on cutting rabbets with a dado head are given in Chapter 5.

BASIC DADO OPERATIONS

A description of the various types of dado heads was given in Chapter 1. For dado-head mounting and width-spacing (or adjustable-dado setting) instructions, refer to the instructions furnished with the accessory. When using the standard type dado head, make sure that the cutters are heavily swaged and arranged so that this heavy portion falls in the gullets of the outside saws, as shown in Fig. 4-2A. The saw and cutter overlap as shown in Fig. 4-2B, (a) being the outside saw, (b) the inside cutter, and (c) a paper washer or washers which can be used as needed to control the exact width of the groove. A 1/4 inch groove or dado is cut by using the two outside saws arranged as shown in Fig. 4-2C. The teeth of the saws should be positioned so that the raker on one saw is beside the cutting teeth on the other saw.

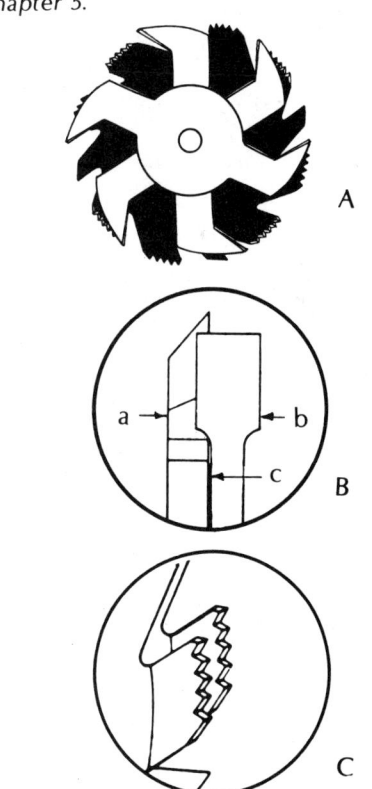

Fig. 4-2: Standard dado head adjustments.

*NOTE: *In order to clearly illustrate certain procedures described in this chapter, the blade guard and other safety devices have been removed. For safe operation of the table saw, guards and other safety devices must always be utilized.*

Once assembled and/or set, the dado head—either the adjustable or the standard type—is fitted and secured to the arbor in the same manner as a regular saw blade (Fig. 4-3). The guard, splitter, and anti-kickback-finger assembly cannot be used when using the dado head and must be removed from the saw. Also, the standard table insert must be replaced with a dado insert which has a slot wide enough to accommodate a full-width dado head.

A dado head should not be used for through sawing—only for cutting partway through (or into) a piece of stock. Furthermore, when using a dado head in the bevel position, make certain that it does not strike and destroy the table insert. Some manufacturers even recommend that a dado head should not be used in a bevel cutting position. (Check the owner's manual for your saw.)

Because grooving and dadoing are done on the underside of the work and because of the varying widths of the cuts, the work must be aligned with a dado head differently than with a saw blade. One way of positioning the dado head for grooving is to use a ruler (Fig. 4-4). However, remember, that when measuring to a dado head, measure to the tooth closest to the fence; rotate the arbor by hand to find this closest tooth. Also, when measuring to an adjustable dado, rotate the blade (by hand) to establish the nearest approach of blade teeth to the fence (they wobble nearer and further), and then measure accordingly.

Rather than using the ruler method, you can mark "groove lines" on the top of the workpiece and sight along these lines to the extreme tooth sides of the dado head (or adjustable dado). Whether you sight or use a ruler, it is a good idea to test your setting on a piece of scrap.

The easiest way to position the stock in the miter gauge is to draw dado lines on the workpiece top and leading edge, and then do the aligning by eye. For more accuracy, make a cut in a piece of scrap

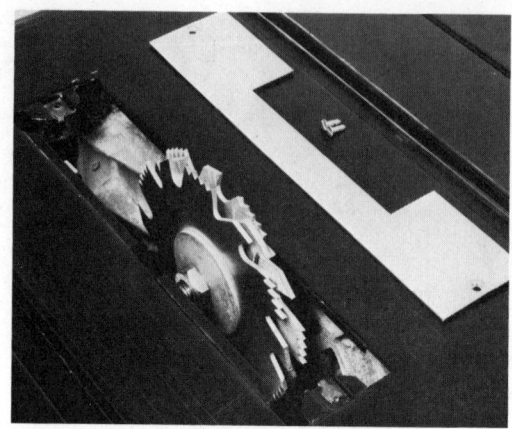

Fig. 4-3: Standard dado head in position.

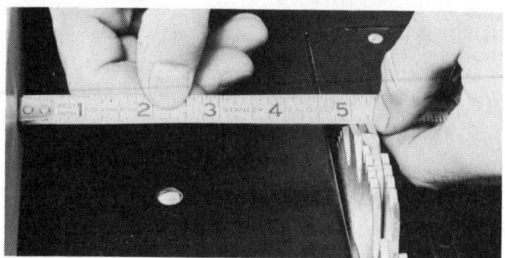

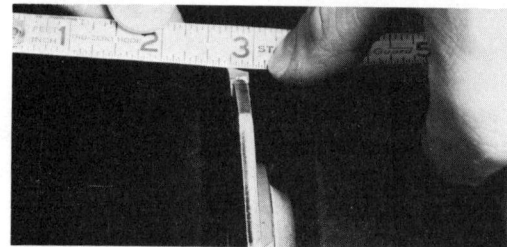

Fig. 4-4: Measuring groove lines for (Above) standard dado head and (Below) adjustable type.

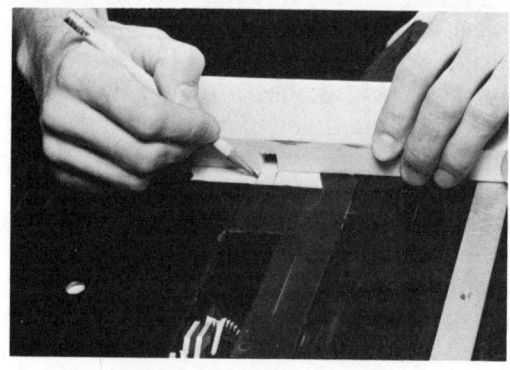

Fig. 4-5: Measuring a dado cut.

wood clamped in the miter gauge. Bring the miter gauge back to the front edge of the table, turn the saw off, and mark the cut edges on the table surface. If the marks are not too visible, use masking tape on the table (Fig. 4-5).

Cutting Grooves. Grooving, or ploughing as it is sometimes called, is done in the same manner as straight ripping (Fig. 4-6). That is, the fence is used as a guide in grooving. Raise the dado head to the depth of the groove and move the fence to the correct position. It is a good idea to clamp a featherboard to the fence directly above

Fig. 4-6: Cutting a groove.

the work, to hold the workpiece firmly against the table. Since the dado head takes a big "bite" out of the stock, every precaution must be taken to prevent kickback. In fact, the depth-of-cut should be limited as follows:

Softwood (in inches)		Hardwood (in inches)	
Wide	Deep	Wide	Deep
1/8	1 1/4	1/8	5/8
1/4	1	1/4	1/2
3/8	7/8	3/8	7/16
1/2	3/4	1/2	3/8
5/8	5/8	5/8	5/16
3/4	1/2	3/4	1/4
13/16	3/8	13/16	3/16

Make each pass without altering the workpiece setup, continuing to increase the dado elevation, as indicated in the table, until the desired depth is reached. Slowly feed the workpiece into the head, applying side pressure to hold the stock against the rip fence to keep it in line. When raising the dado head to the depth-of-cut, remember that the maximum depth is produced by the tooth tips as they pass by the vertical centerline of the cutter. This depth can be measured by a ruler (Fig. 4-7).

If a groove, larger than the dado head can provide, is needed, it must be made in two or more passes, all at the same elevation setting. It is preferable to make the two outside cuts first, aligning each carefully with its respective side of the groove (Fig. 4-8). The center cuts can then be made without particular attention to alignment. Simply have each cut overlap

Fig. 4-7: Measuring the dado depth-of-cut.

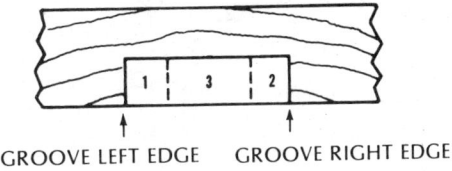

GROOVE LEFT EDGE   GROOVE RIGHT EDGE

Fig. 4-8: Steps in cutting an extra wide groove or dado. Numbers represent order of cuts.

the adjacent one(s) by at least 1/16 inch.

Cutting A Dado. The dado is cut using the miter gauge with or without an auxiliary face board in the same manner as a straight crosscut (Fig. 4-9). To cut regularly spaced dadoes, a yardstick can be clamped to the miter gauge as shown in Fig. 4-10 for setting various cuts.

A better method of making regular repeat cuts is to use the miter gauge with the stop rod as a stop (Fig. 4-11). To position the next dado, the stop rod can fit into the last groove made. The rip fence can also be employed with a stop block to control the location of the dadoes (Fig. 4-12). This is especially useful when cutting matching dadoes for cabinets, chests, or shelves.

A notched block is still another technique for cutting evenly spaced dadoes (Fig. 4-13). If the desired space is to be equal, the block steps are equal. If uneven spacing is needed, the steps are cut to the pattern desired.

Dadoes can also be cut at an angle (Fig. 4-14). This could be used to make sloping shelves and louvers, for example.

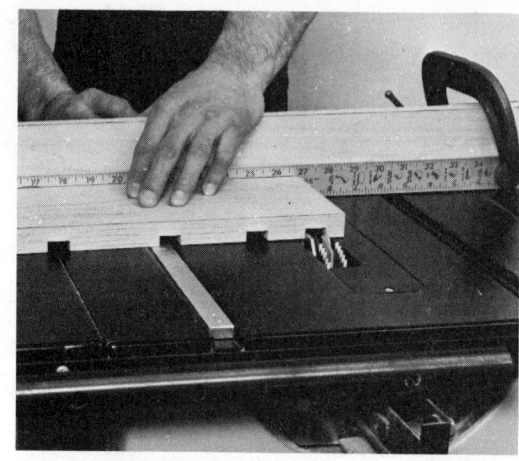

Fig. 4-10: Measuring regularly spaced dadoes.

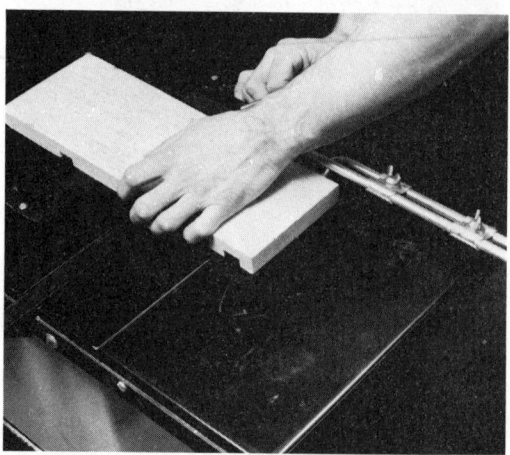

Fig. 4-11: Using a stop rod to space dadoes.

Fig. 4-12: The fence with a stop block as a guide for cutting several dadoes in a wide board.

Fig. 4-9: Cutting a dado.

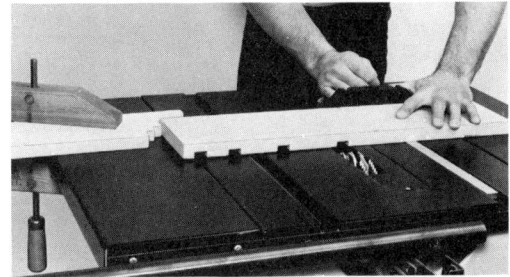

Fig. 4-13: Use of a notched stop block.

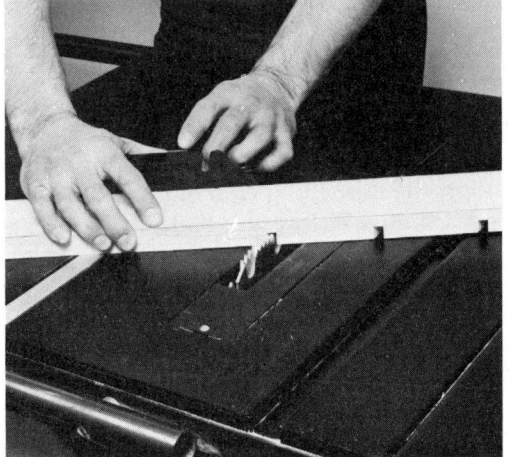

Fig. 4-14: Cutting a series of dadoes at an angle.

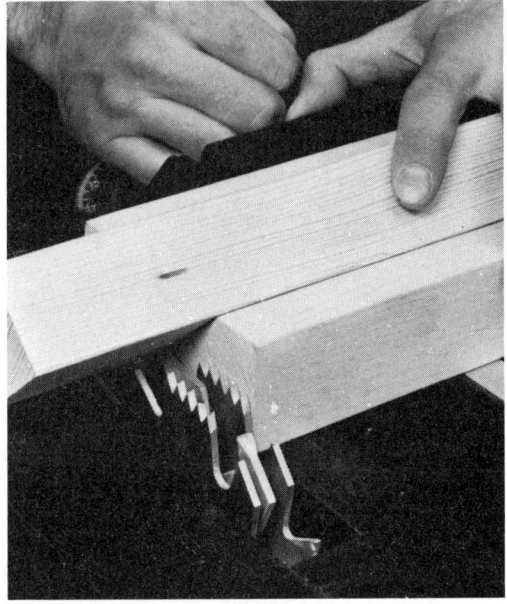

Fig. 4-15: Cutting a corner dado.

The corner dado (Fig. 4-15) usually is cut in a V-block held against the miter gauge.

Blind Grooving. A slot cut with the dado head which stops short of one or both ends of the work is called a blind groove or dado. Cuts of this kind are commonly used in making splined joints (see page 71). Clamps to locate the beginning and the end of the cut are necessary, the position of these being determined by holding the work alongside the saw in the required position. If the groove is in a long piece of work, clamp an auxiliary wood fence of suitable length to the regular fence, and then clamp the stop blocks to the auxiliary fence. To make this cut, determine the number of turns of the elevating control required to bring the dado to the desired height above the table. Lower the dado

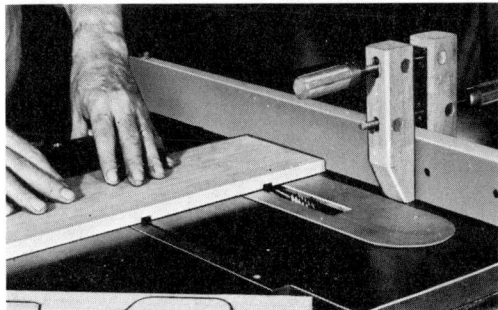

Fig. 4-16: Stop block can be used for both blind and stop grooves (above).

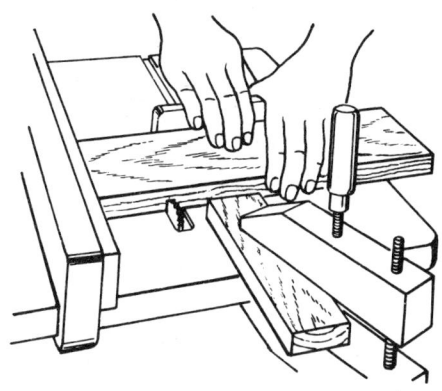

Fig. 4-17: Cutting a stop dado with a stop block clamped to the table to control the length of cut.

head flush with the table, place the workpiece in position, clamping a block over the workpiece to the fence, to hold the workpiece securely against the table surface. Turn on the saw, and raise the dado head the necessary number of turns while the cutter is running. Feed the workpiece to the backstop completing the cut, turn off the saw, lower the cutter, and remove the workpiece. *Under no circumstances should a workpiece be lowered into a rotating cutter.*

A stop dado can be cut by clamping a stop block to the fence or the saw table to control the length of the cut (Figs. 4-16 and 4-17). The dado corner will have to be squared with a wood chisel.

Edge Grooving. The long edge of a workpiece is grooved by using the same setup as for resawing. First, raise the dado head to the desired depth-of-cut. Then, position the rip fence and an auxiliary table, so the workpiece is positioned in its proper location (Fig. 4-18). Featherboards can also be used in place of the auxiliary table. This arrangement is also suitable for resawing, molding cutting and similar operations.

End Grooving. Because it is rather difficult to feed a long piece of stock (12 inches or more) on end, it is recommended that you use a tenoning jig (see page 9) to perform end grooving operations. Position the workpiece on this accessory so the bottom end just slides freely along the table; then raise the dado head to the proper height. Adjust the tenoning jig to align the cut, and lock it in position. Then feed the work into the dado head (Fig. 4-19) in the same manner as with a miter gauge.

Fig. 4-18: Arrangement for edge grooving.

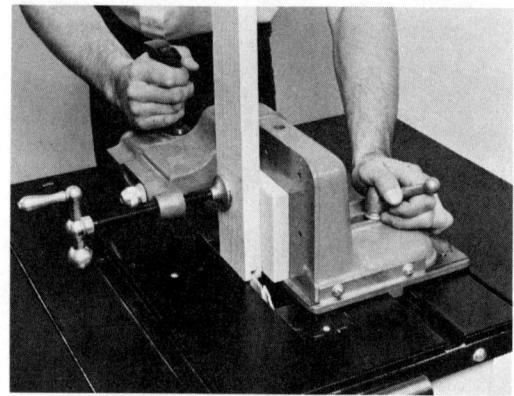

Fig. 4-19: Cutting an end groove.

Chapter 5

SPECIAL SAW AND DADO OPERATIONS *

Special operations performed on the table saw include chamfer cutting, rabbeting, pattern sawing, taper ripping, compound-angle sawing, cove-cutting, kerfing, and saw-cut moldings. These operations, as well as the others discussed in this chapter, are easy and safe to do as long as proper procedures are followed. While the nature of each one is different, the actual handling of the saw does not vary greatly from the basic techniques described in earlier chapters.

CHAMFER CUTTING

Chamfer cutting or chamfering is simply making bevel cuts along the top or bottom edges of stock (Fig. 5-1). The angle to which the blade is set depends on whether the work is set flat on the table or is positioned on edge or end.

If the angle between the stock top and chamfer is 45 degrees or more, the operation is done with the work flat on the table, using the basic bevel ripping or crosscutting procedure. When this angle is 45 degrees or less, the work should be positioned on edge or end. Whenever such edge cutting must be done, a wide wooden auxiliary fence should be fastened to the metal one to give plenty of support for the cut. Also make sure the table insert is in good condition so there is no chance the thin edge may slip into the opening. Hold the workpiece firmly down and against the auxiliary fence with both hands as the cut is made.

For end cutting use the tenoning jig in the slot on the left of the blade. Adjust the blade to the proper angle and elevation, then position the stock on the jig to make the cut as shown in Fig. 5-2.

The octagonal shape required for spindle lathe work can be cut in the same manner as described for chamfer cutting.

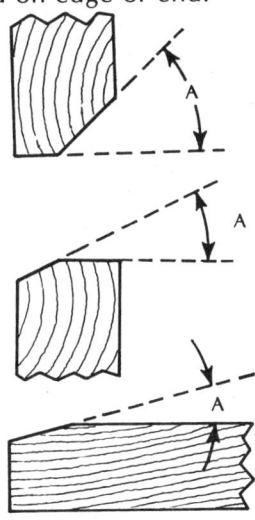

TABLE TOP

Fig. 5-1: Typical chamfering angles (A).

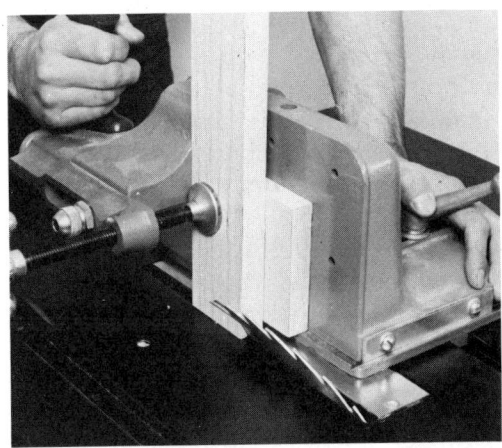

Fig. 5-2: Cutting a chamfer with a tenoning jig.

*NOTE: In order to clearly illustrate certain procedures described in this chapter, the blade guard and other safety devices have been removed. For safe operation of the table saw, guards and other safety devices must always be utilized.

RABBETING

Rabbeting is cutting a groove along the edge of a board by taking two saw cuts at right angles to each other so as to remove a corner down the length of the stock. There are several methods of making the cut; the two most common ways are described here.

In both methods, the cut should be pencil marked, and the fence and saw depth setting made to the marks before starting the saw (Fig. 5-3A). The cut which requires the work to be flat on the table is made first (Fig. 5-3B). Note that this is set a little shy of the pencil mark. The second cut (Fig. 5-3C) is run with the work on edge and this cut cleans the corner. This method of working produces a scrap piece, not trapped between the fence and the blade.

If done in the reverse order, a trapped piece, called an arrow, will be left between the blade and the fence, and can be thrown back with considerable force. The best way to avoid this is to follow the suggested procedure, so that the scrap piece is on the free side of the blade.

An alternate method which also avoids the trapped arrow is to make the cut from the face, Fig. 5-4A, first. The second cut would then be like Fig. 5-4B, with the scrap piece on the outside. As in the first method, the first cut should be a little short of the required depth, cleaning the corner with the second cut. This second system is suitable for most work. However, it should be noted that the final cut removes the supporting wood—be sure that enough stock remains to support the piece firmly without any danger of the work dropping onto the top of the blade. Also, downward pressure with a pushstick should be over the remaining solid wood and not over the part of the wood being cut away.

A bevel rabbet is cut in the same manner, except that the first cut is a bevel rip followed by a rip cut. Rabbets can be cut on the ends of a workpiece, too. This is a simple two-cut procedure following the

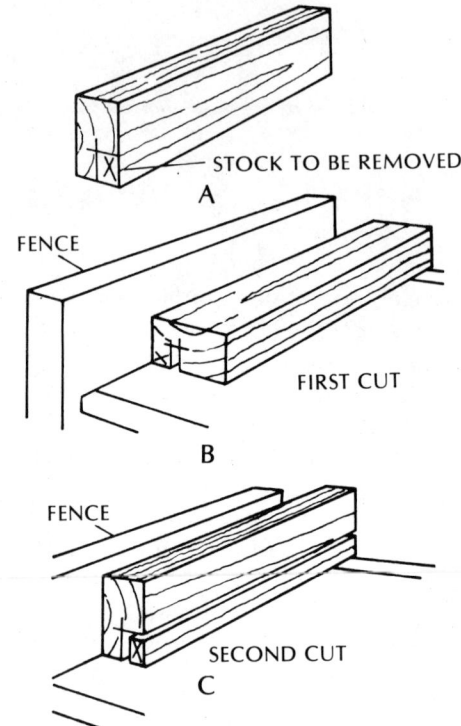

Fig. 5-3: First method of cutting a rabbet.

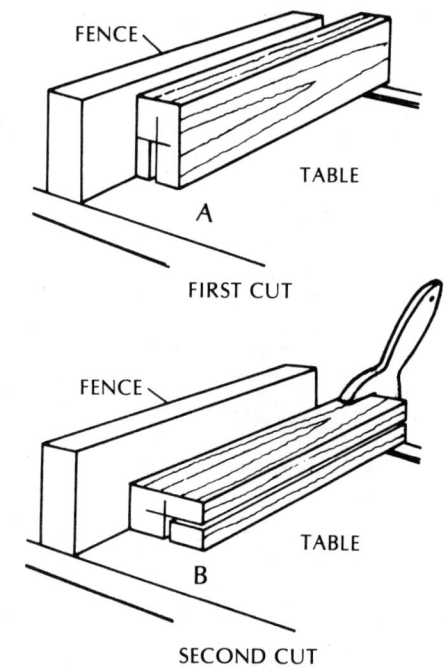

Fig. 5-4: Second method of cutting a rabbet.

same steps as for the edge rabbet.

Rabbets can be cut with only one pass by using the dado head. The dado head is made up to a width which will be more than enough to remove the required wood. The work—held against an auxiliary fence with a cutout for blade clearance—is then pushed into the head to cut the rabbet in one pass as shown in Fig. 5-5. This procedure is not recommended for large rabbets but it is fast and useful for small cuts. Rabbets can also be cut with molding cutters (see page 100).

Fig. 5-5: Cutting a rabbet with a dado head.

RAISED-PANEL CUTTING

Raised-panel cutting can add immeasurably to the beauty of a finished door project. Actually, raised-panel cutting is simply a combination of chamfering and rabbeting on all four sides of a stock. Whenever this work is done, a wide auxiliary fence should be fastened to the rip fence to give added support to the work. Hold the workpiece firmly against the auxiliary fence as the cut is made (Fig. 5-6). Where a design calls for a series of cuts, the edge and side cuts are made first and the the flat or face cuts are made last.

There are a variety of ways to decorate a raised panel (Fig. 5-7). Some cuts of this type end in a slight shoulder, which gives the bevel greater visual depth, while others do not. It is mostly a matter of taste. While raised-panel cuts can be accomplished completely with a saw blade, the use of a dado head reduces the number of setups.

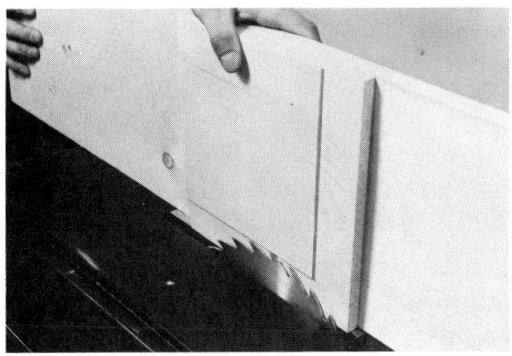

Fig. 5-6: Cutting a raised panel.

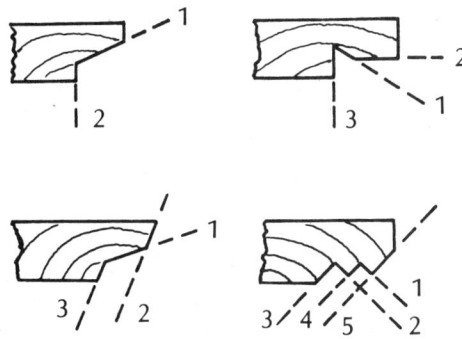

Fig. 5-7: Several raised panel designs. Numbers represent order of cuts.

V-GROOVE CUTTING

One of the most useful jigs you can make for shop work is a V-block. It can be made easily by bevel ripping. After placing the blade in the 45-degree position, raise the blade to the desired depth of the V. Position the fence and feed the stock past the blade in the same way as a basic bevel rip. Then reverse the stock, reduce the elevation of the blade so the cut enters only halfway into the first-cut kerf, and

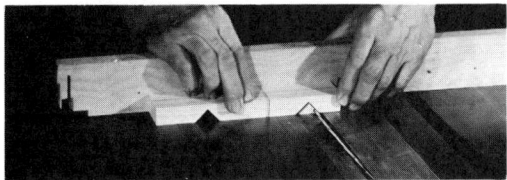

Fig. 5-8: Cutting V-grooves.

pass the work through the saw again (Fig. 5-8).

PATTERN SAWING

Pattern sawing on the table saw can be used to good advantage in production work for cutting any shape comprised of straight lines. It is extremely fast and its great advantage is that short pieces of waste stock can be worked quickly to size. In a typical setup, there is an auxiliary wood fence, which is clamped onto the regular saw fence (Fig. 5-9). This auxiliary fence clears the table sufficiently to allow the work to slip below it. The fence can be rabbeted on its outer, lower edge to house the blade, but this is not essential. The face of the blade must be exactly flush with the outer face of the fence. A pattern cut to the desired shape is necessary. This is fitted with any style of anchor point (nails are the

Fig. 5-9: Pattern sawing is an easy way of cutting odd shapes with straight sides.

Fig. 5-10: Example of typical pattern sawing operation.

simplest) to fasten it temporarily to the work as shown in Fig. 5-9. After the pattern is fastened to the work, it is a simple matter to guide each edge of the pattern along the fence, and cut the work to the same exact shape as the pattern.

Figure 5-10 here shows another common application of pattern sawing. In this particular case, no pattern is necessary

since the work itself is the pattern. The job is to cut off the cleats flush with the edges of the work. The cutting is done easily and quickly by running each edge of the work in turn along the fence. The same general method applies to trimming veneer edges flush with the main body of the wood to which it is applied.

TAPER RIPPING

Taper cuts, needed for many projects, call for a jig with one straight side for riding the rip fence and an angled side to gauge the taper. As illustrated in Fig. 5-11, various styles of tapered legs can be cut for furniture projects. Straight tapers, styles A, B, C, D, and G, are cut with the saw, while the spade foot, styles E and F, are worked on the shaper. The various shapes are often ornately carved, fluted or inlaid. Style B leg has the corners planed off, while C is rounded on the outer corner after sawing. Style A is tapered on two sides only. A planer combination blade is the preferable saw to use for this work since it cuts more smoothly.

Square table legs can be tapered by using a template, such as the one shown in Fig. 5-12. They are cut in the following manner.

1. Set the ripping fence at a distance from the blade equal to the combined width of the long template member and the leg stock, to just clear the blade with the leg when the stock is placed against the template (Fig. 5-13A).

2. Cut a taper on two adjacent sides with the end of the stock in the first notch (Fig. 5-13B).

3. Cut tapers on the two remaining sides with the end of the stock in the second notch.

It should, of course, be observed that the position in which the stock is placed depends upon the length of the taper desired. For example, if it is required to taper a 32-inch leg for a distance of 26 inches, the stock is fastened 26 inches from the end.

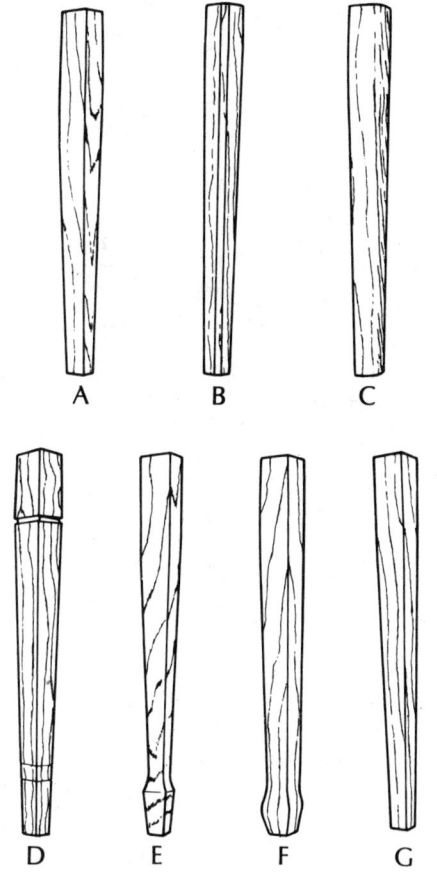

Fig. 5-11: Various examples of taper ripping.

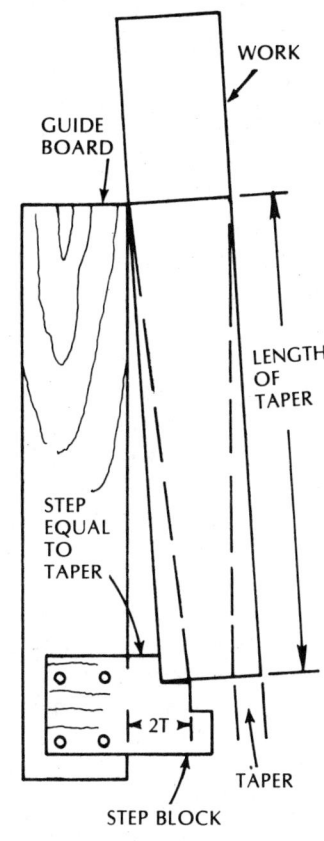

Fig. 5-12: Template for cutting square table legs.

Fig. 5-13: Using a template to make a taper cut.

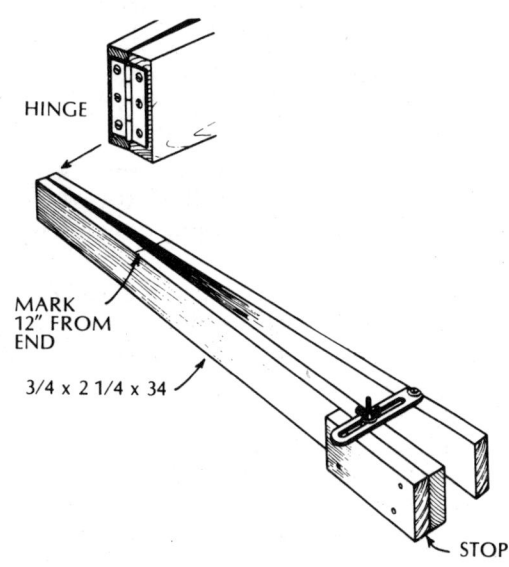

Fig. 5-14: A tapering jig suitable for production work.

When sawing tapers, the saw should project about 1/8 inch above the stock as in ordinary ripping. Use the splitter guard to prevent the stock from being caught on the back of the saw.

A special tapering jig suitable for production work is shown in Fig. 5-14. Such a jig is no more than two straight pieces of wood, hinged at one end and secured at the other by a crosspiece. When making the jig, keep the two pieces clamped together while you attach the hinge. The crosspiece can be made of sheet metal or hardwood. The method of calculating a symmetrical taper is shown in Fig. 5-15.

When the jig is complete, mark a line across both pieces, 12 inches in from the hinged end (Fig. 5-16). Set the jig by measuring between these two marks to determine the taper per foot. For example, if you are making a stool with legs that are 1 foot long, 3 inches wide at the top and 2 inches wide at the bottom, you would require a 1-inch taper per foot. By opening the jig 1 inch at the 1-foot mark you will have the right setting.

Square legs with a taper on each face are made by setting the fence to equal the combined width of the jig and the work. Make one pass (Fig. 5-17); then make the second pass on an adjacent face. Adjust the jig to twice the original setting and make the third and fourth passes on the next adjacent faces (Fig. 5-18). If the work is square, the rip-fence setting does not have to be changed.

Occasionally it is desirable to join a tapered workpiece to a mitered one. A good example of this is when it is necessary to fasten a tapered leg to a table skirt board. When the taper angle is known, the miter gauge can be set at this angle and the cut made. But if unknown, the angle of the miter cut can be determined using the following formula:

$$X = \frac{W - W_1}{2}$$

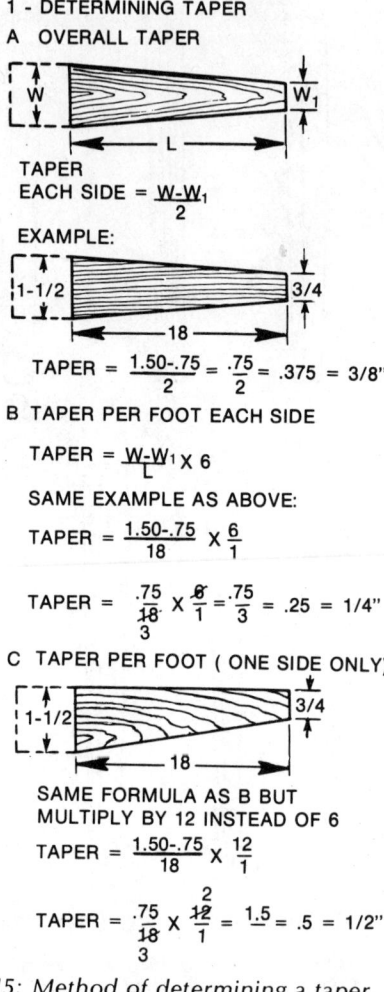

1 - DETERMINING TAPER
A OVERALL TAPER

TAPER EACH SIDE $= \frac{W - W_1}{2}$

EXAMPLE:

TAPER $= \frac{1.50 - .75}{2} = \frac{.75}{2} = .375 = 3/8"$

B TAPER PER FOOT EACH SIDE

TAPER $= \frac{W - W_1}{L} \times 6$

SAME EXAMPLE AS ABOVE:

TAPER $= \frac{1.50 - .75}{18} \times \frac{6}{1}$

TAPER $= \frac{.75}{\underset{3}{\cancel{18}}} \times \frac{\cancel{6}}{1} = \frac{.75}{3} = .25 = 1/4"$

C TAPER PER FOOT (ONE SIDE ONLY)

SAME FORMULA AS B BUT MULTIPLY BY 12 INSTEAD OF 6

TAPER $= \frac{1.50 - .75}{18} \times \frac{12}{1}$

TAPER $= \frac{.75}{\underset{3}{\cancel{18}}} \times \frac{\overset{2}{\cancel{12}}}{1} = \frac{1.5}{3} = .5 = 1/2"$

Fig. 5-15: Method of determining a taper.

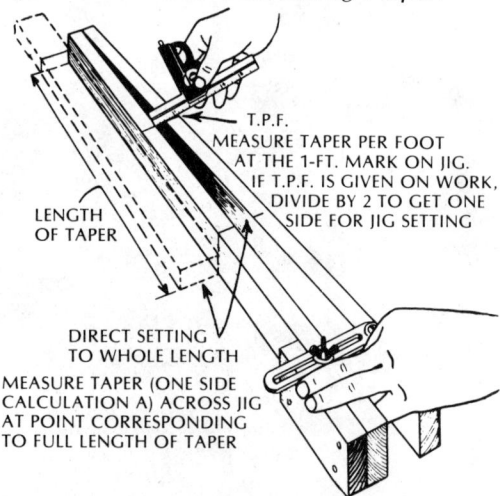

Fig. 5-16: Method of setting the tapering jig.

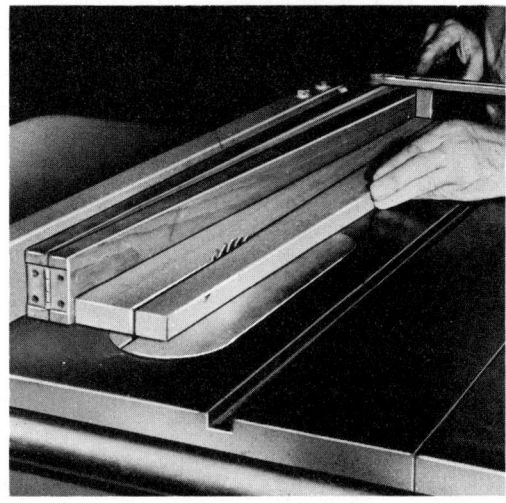

Fig. 5-17: The tapering jig in use.

Line A in Fig. 5-19 is at 90 degrees to the leg top starting at W and Line B is parallel to the line starting at W_1. Use the distance X to draw the cut-line on the workpiece that requires the crosscut. It is accepted practice to make a trial cut on a scrap piece of the same dimensions first, to insure a proper fit.

Dovetail Tapers. Wide pieces of solid lumber are often fitted with dovetail keys to prevent warping. Figure 5-20A shows the general detail of the joint. Both the groove and the key can be cut with a tapering jig on the table saw. The taper should be about 3/8 inch per foot or as little as 1/16 inch per foot if appearance is important. Some taper is always required, since it is impossible to drive a straight key for any distance. The groove is cut by tilting the saw blade as shown in Fig. 5-20B. Other methods of cutting the keyway are illus-

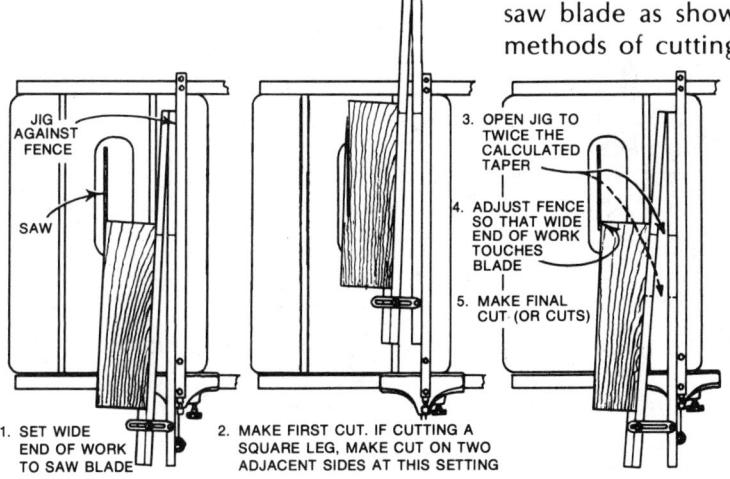

Fig. 5-18: The saw setting when using a tapering jig.

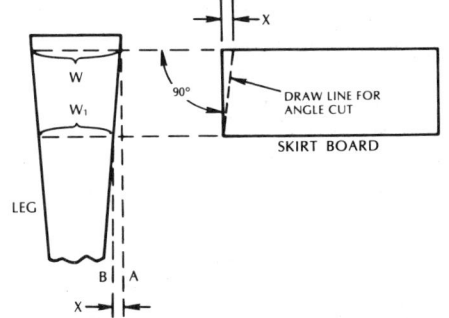

Fig. 5-19: Method of mating a crosscut miter to a taper.

trated in Fig. 5-20C and Fig. 5-20D. Figure C shows the work as done on the shaper, while Fig. D shows the use of a dovetail router bit on a portable router. Both these methods give a clean cut in the keyway but require rematching of the taper when the keys are cut on the saw. If both groove and key are cut with the saw, the same setting is used for both operations, ensuring a good fit. A disadvantage of cutting the keyway

51

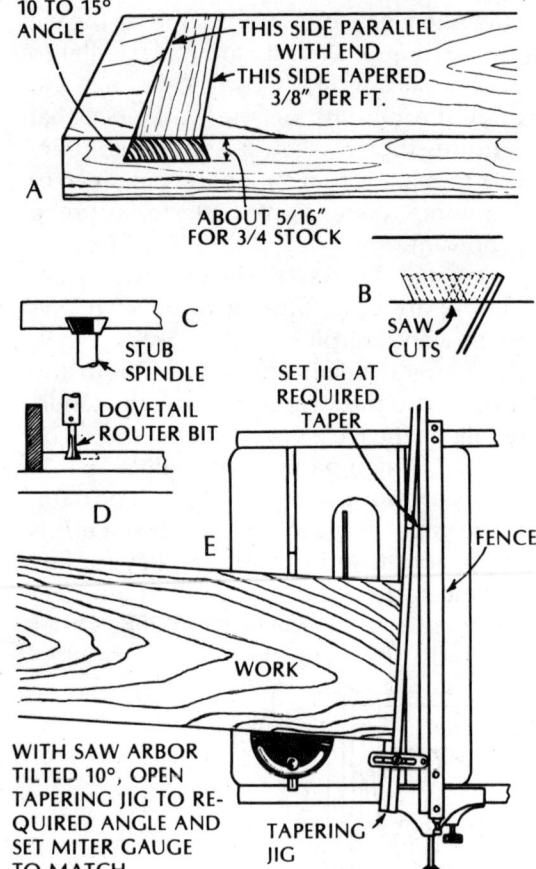

Fig. 5-20: Steps in making a dovetail taper.

on the saw is the slight roughness made by the saw blade in the tilt position. This, however, is usually of no consequence as regards appearance, and it makes a good gluing surface for the final assembly.

The setup for work done on the table saw is illustrated in Fig. 5-20E. The tapering jig is opened to the required taper, and the saw arbor is tilted about 10 degrees. With the end of the work placed against the tapering jig, the miter gauge can be set at the same angle to cut the tapered side of the keyway. Successive cuts across the work clean the slot on one side. The opposite, untapered edge will have been cleaned previously with the miter gauge at the zero position. The keys are cut without any change in the arbor tilt, using the tapering jig at the angle previously set. The keys should be made a little longer than necessary and cut off flush after they have been fitted in place. A heavy driving fit should be avoided, since this in itself will cause warping.

MITERED AND BEVELED POLYGON JOINTS

A polygon is a figure of any number of equal sides. To make a proper joint of any figure other than a square, miters of some angle other than 45 degrees are needed. Mitered polygon segments (Fig. 5-21A) are cut with the use of the miter gauge. The angle setting is made according to the table in Fig. 5-22, as required for the polygon being cut. The second cut can generally be made by flopping the segment end-for-end.

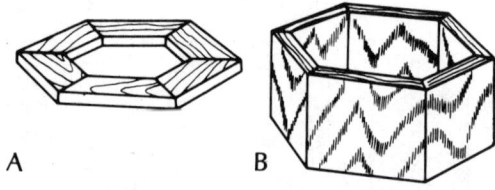

Fig. 5-21: (A) Mitered polygon segments and (B) beveled polygon segments.

When the sides of an on-edge polygon (Fig. 5-21B) are to be constructed, the beveled segments are cut by tilting the saw blade to the required angle given in the table (Fig. 5-22). The method of calculating the size of the segments is given in Fig. 5-23.

COMPOUND-ANGLE SAWING

A compound angle made on the table saw requires both a tilt of the blade and a swing of the miter gauge. In other words, a miter and a bevel are cut in one pass. Cuts of this kind are required for making boxes with tilted sides, sawhorses, pedestal stands, and similar work. Compound cuts are also required in making tables with splayed legs if the outward tilt is more than 10 degrees. The basic figure is a box

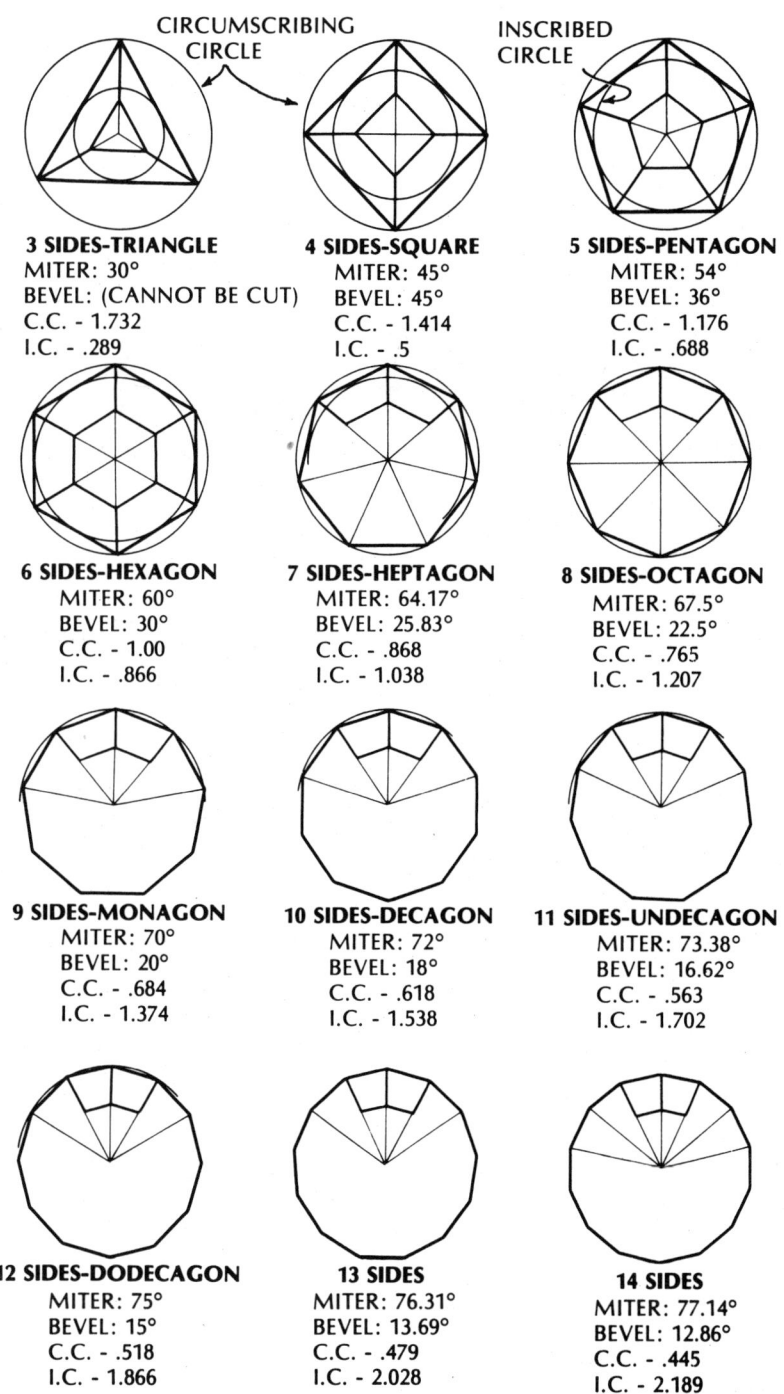

Fig. 5-22: Cutting angles and size factors for polygons.

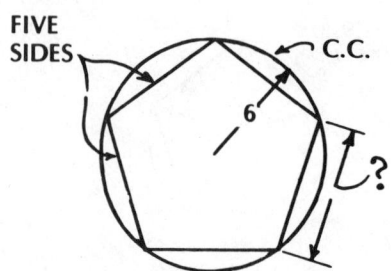
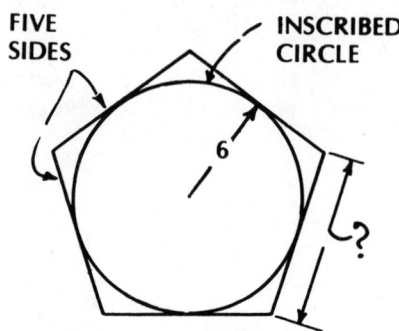

GIVEN: RADIUS OF CIRCUMSCRIB-
ING CIRCLE (CC) AND
NUMBER OF SIDES
FIND: LENGTH OF SIDE
RULE: MULTIPLY RADIUS OF
CC CIRCLE BY CC FACTOR
EX. — FIVE SIDES, 6" RADIUS
1.176 x 6" = 7.056"
7.056" = 7 1/6" LENGTH OF SIDE

GIVEN: RADIUS OF INSCRIBED
CIRCLE AND NUMBER
OF SIDES
FIND: LENGTH OF SIDE
RULE: DIVIDE THE RADIUS OF
INSCRIBED CIRCLE BY
THE IC FACTOR
EX. — FIVE SIDES, 6" RADIUS

$$.688 \overline{)6000} = 8.72" = \text{LENGTH OF SIDE}$$

IV DETERMINING SIZE

Fig. 5-23: Method of determining the size of polygon segments.

(Fig. 5-24), which can have four, six, or eight sides, all equally tilted. The chart gives the saw settings at 5-degree intervals, so the work should be planned to match. Joints for a four-sided figure can be either butted or mitered. Six- and eight-sided figures are always mitered because on such work a butt joint would be poor construction.

The actual sawing is as simple as a common miter. All you do is refer to the table, and set the miter gauge and blade tilt to the figures given for the type of box and amount of slope required. Large work can be cut from individual boards, but, if the job allows, it is better to cut all parts from one board (Fig. 5-25), turning the work over for alternate cuts. If the edges of the board are square, any miter-gauge position can be used. For general work of this kind, the closed (zero) position is best for the tilting arbor.

As mentioned previously, legs on tables and chairs are sometimes splayed outward. This construction demands a compound cut at top and bottom. Work of this kind

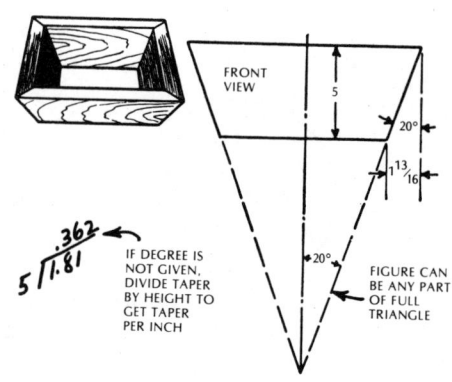

Fig. 5-24: A four-sided miter box with side tilted at 20 degrees.

TABLE OF COMPOUND ANGLES

Tilt of Work	Equivalent taper per inch	Four-Sided Butt		Four-Sided Miter		Six-Sided miter		Eight-Sided Miter	
		Bevel Degrees	Miter Degrees	Bevel Degrees	Miter Degrees	Bevel Degrees	Miter Degrees	Bevel Degrees	Miter Degrees
5°	0.087	1/2	85	44 3/4	85	29 3/4	87 1/2	22 1/4	88
10°	0.176	1 1/2	80 1/4	44 1/4	80 1/4	29 1/2	84 1/2	22	86
15°	0.268	3 3/4	75 1/2	43 1/4	75 1/2	29	81 3/4	21 1/2	84
20°	0.364	6 1/4	71 1/4	41 3/4	71 1/4	28 1/4	79	21	82
25°	0.466	10	67	40	67	27 1/4	76 1/2	20 1/4	80
30°	0.577	14 1/2	63 1/2	37 3/4	63 1/2	26	74	19 1/2	78 1/4
35°	0.700	19 1/2	60 1/4	35 1/2	60 1/4	24 1/2	71 3/4	18 1/4	76 3/4
40°	0.839	24 1/2	57 1/4	32 1/2	57 1/4	22 3/4	69 3/4	17	75
45°	1.000	30	54 3/4	30	54 3/4	21	67 3/4	15 3/4	73 3/4
50°	1.19	36	52 1/2	27	52 1/2	19	66 1/4	14 1/2	72 1/2
55°	1.43	42	50 3/4	24	50 3/4	16 3/4	64 3/4	12 1/2	71 1/4
60°	1.73	48	49	21	49	14 1/2	63 1/2	11	70 1/4

usually has less than 10 degrees tilt, and for these small angles, direct setting to the work tilt gives a satisfactory joint. At 10 degrees tilt and equal, the saw is tilted 10 degrees and the miter gauge is swung 10 degrees. At 5 degrees tilt as seen from the front and 10 degrees as seen from the end, the saw arbor is tilted for one of the angles and the miter gauge is swung for the other. The cut surfaces are parallel, so both cuts are made at the same setting by simply sliding the work along the miter gauge facing, as shown in Fig. 5-26. The example is a round leg, which should be aligned with a mark on the miter-gauge facing to guard against twisting. The work must not turn when shifted from one end to the other. It should be noted that square table legs of more than 10 degrees tilt must be backed off and otherwise treated the same as a corner block.

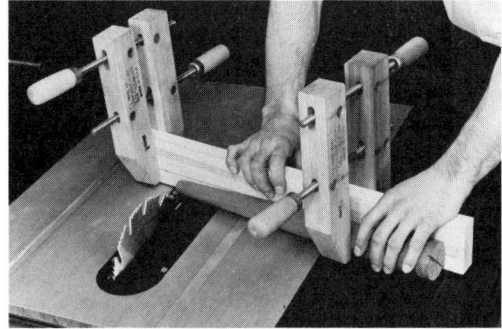

Fig. 5-25: Continuous cutting of compound angles.

Fig. 5-26: A compound cut being made on a table leg.

Corner Blocks. Corner blocks are sometimes used to brace four-sided figures (Fig. 5-27). The stock is first bevel ripped, setting the saw tilt the same as for a four-sided butt joint (chart on Page 55). The same block will also fit a box assembled with miter joints since the shape of the box is the same. The tops and bottoms of corner blocks are leveled with a compound cut, using the miter gauge setting given in the chart on page 55. The saw blade is tilted to the same angle as the box sides (not taken from the table). If the sides of the box (Fig. 5-27) are removed, it can be seen that the cutting angles used for corner blocks apply equally well to splayed legs on tables and sawhorses.

COVE CUTTING

You can create cove molding for decorative and other purposes with a table saw. The work is done by clamping a straight guide fence to the saw table, out of parallel with the blade, and then running the stock against this fence, making a number of light cuts until the desired

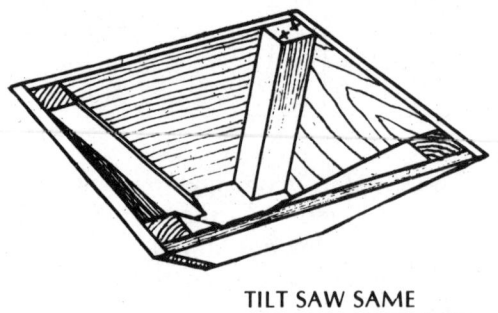

TILT SAW SAME
AS GIVEN IN CHART
FOR FOUR-SIDE BUTT
(SEE PAGE 55)

SAW BLADE

Fig. 5-27: Corner blocks.

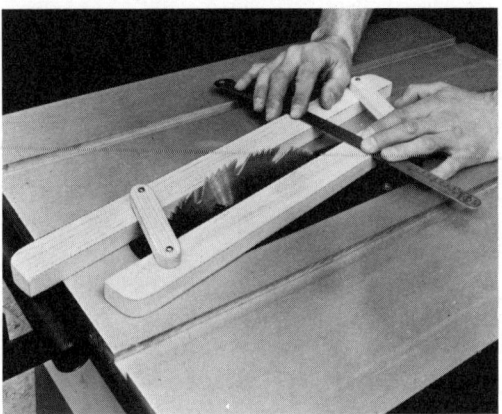

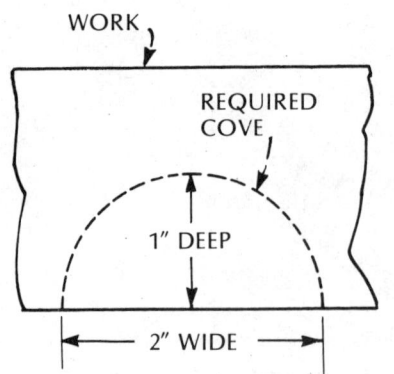

Fig. 5-28: Wood frame jig.

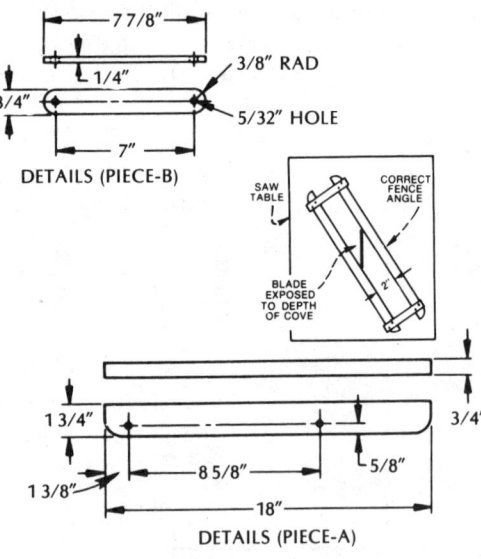

Fig. 5-29: A parallel rule makes cove cutting easy.

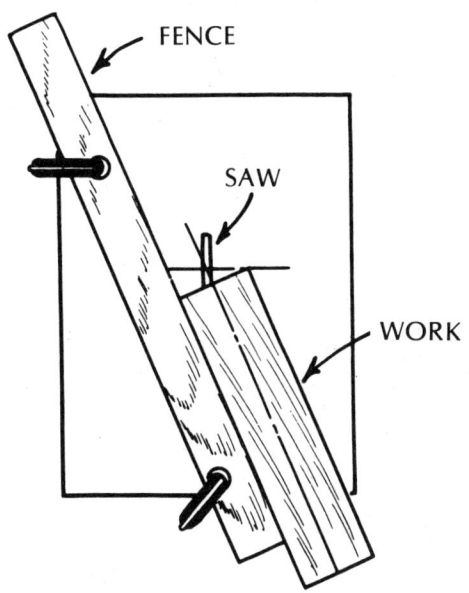

Fig. 5-30: How the cove is set out with the jig.

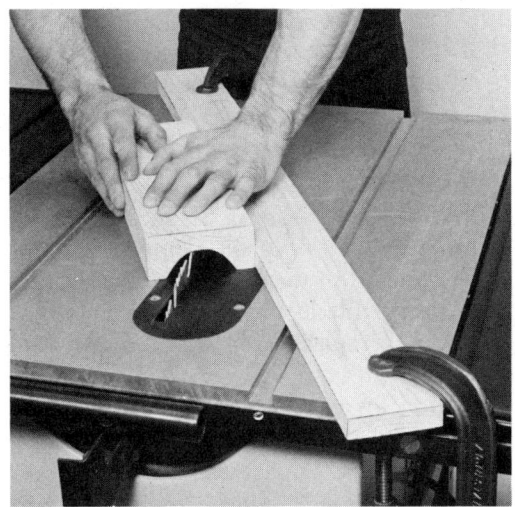

Fig. 5-31: How a cove cut is made.

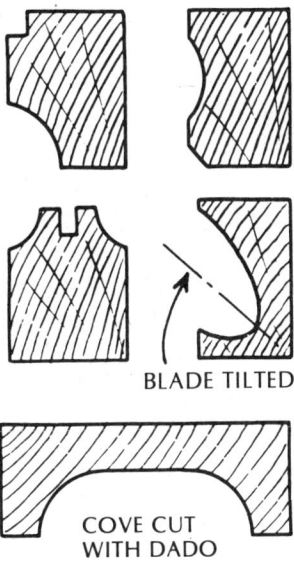

Fig. 5-32: Different cove molding shapes.

depth is obtained. The proper fence angle is determined by using a parallel rule or four strips of wood nailed up to make a frame. Figure 5-28 shows a sample job, in which a cove 2 inches wide by 1 inch deep is to be cut. First, set the saw at the required projection of 1 inch. Then make a frame (for setting the parallels) with the sides 2 inches apart. Next, place the wood frame or parallel rule (Fig. 5-29) over the saw and turn it until it just touches the front and rear teeth of the exposed blade. Rotate the saw by hand to make sure the teeth will just nick the setting-out frame. The setting-out frame determines the proper angle for the fence, and the fence itself is located by measuring to intersect the centerline of the work with the centerline of the saw blade, (Fig. 5-30).

When cutting the cove shape, the blade is set so that it projects no more than 1/8 inch above the table, and the first cut is made. The saw is then raised about 1/8 inch, and a second cut is made. This operation is repeated to the required depth; never raise the blade more than 1/8 inch in any one cut. On deep cuts, however, time is saved by roughing the work with a number of straight-saw or dado-head cuts. The shape produced is an ellipse, as indicated in Fig. 5-31, which must be sanded with paper held over a suitable round if a true circle is required.

Different cove shapes and moldings (Fig. 5-32) can be formed by varying the angle at which the stock meets the blade, as well as the final elevation of the blade. Twin coves are formed by turning the stock end-for-end after each pass, but the auxiliary fence must be properly offset for the desired spacing of the twin coves.

The preferred saw for cove-cutting is a combination or ripping blade with a good amount of set. A carbide-tipped blade is also popular for this operation. But regardless of the blade used, it must be sharp. The best circular shape is obtained with a small saw. It is sometimes practical to finish the cut with a 6-inch dado saw; although this saw should not be used for rough cutting. Similar work can be done with the full dado head. Cuts of the same nature can be produced with a molding head in one or two passes of the work. Such a setup is most practical if a large number of shapes are to be made.

KERFING

It is often necessary to bend wood. When the problem of curved surfaces arises, you have a choice of three methods: (1) bending the wood by steaming it (this calls for special equipment); (2) building the curve up by sawing thick segments of the circle on a saber or band saw (which means that a great deal of expensive wood would be wasted); or (3) cutting a series of saw kerfs to within 1/8 inch of the outside surface to make the material more flexible for bending. The latter—called *kerfing*—is the most practical method.

The distance between these saw kerfs determines the flexibility of the stock and the radius to which it can be bent. To form a more rigid curve, the saw kerfs should be as close together as possible. To determine the proper spacing, the first step is to decide on the radius of the curve or circle to be formed. After the radius has been determined, measure this same distance (the radius) from the end of the stock and make a saw kerf at this point. The kerf can be crosscut, with the blade raised to within 1/8 inch of the top of the stock. It is usually best to saw kerfs at right angles to the grain. While this may make bending a little more difficult, there will be less chance of the thinned stock splitting. Remember that the closer the kerfs are spaced, the more sharply the wood can be bent. But, making too many kerfs needlessly wastes time and weakens the workpiece.

After the first cut is made, clamp the stock to the table top with a C-clamp. Raise the end of the stock until the saw kerf is closed (Fig. 5-33). The distance from the underside of the stock to the top of the table will determine the correct kerf spacing required to form the desired curve.

Since most bending operations require many saw kerfs, it is a good idea to make a miter-gauge face board (Fig. 5-34) that can be used as a jig to space the cuts automatically. All you have to do is run a saw slot through the face board, and then use a nail as a guide, spacing it away from the saw slot a distance equal to the kerf spacing required. The first cut is made with the end of the work butted against

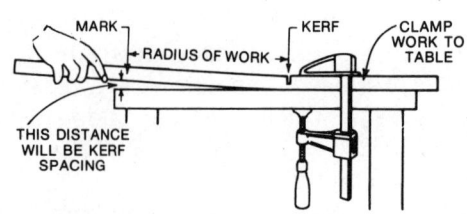

Fig. 5-33: Guide to figuring kerf spacing.

Fig. 5-34: A miter-gauge face board jig that can be used for kerf spacing.

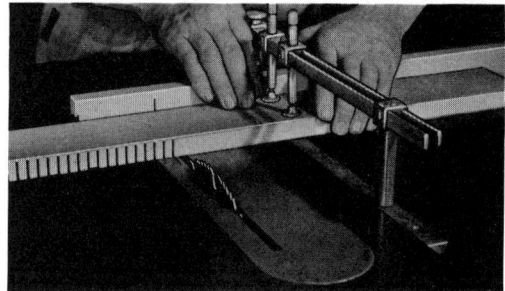

Fig. 5-35: Using the extension jig to cut kerfs.

the pin. The remaining cuts are gauged by placing each new kerf over the guide pin (Fig. 5-35). When the kerfs must be cut in an area away from the end of the stock, make the first cut without the jig. Where only a few kerfs are to be made, a pencil mark on the table insert may be used (Fig. 5-36).

When the kerfing is complete (Fig. 5-37), the stock is slowly bent until it matches the required curve. Wetting the wood with warm water will help the bending process, while a tie strip tacked in place will hold the shape until the part is attached to the assembly. Even compound curves may be formed in this manner by kerfing both sides of the work. When kerfing is exposed, veneers may be glued in place to hide the cuts.

When bending wood for exterior work, the kerfs should be coated with glue before the bend is made. After making the bend, wood plastic and putty may be used to fill the crevices. When properly finished, only a close examination of the wood will show the method used to make the bend.

If kerfs are cut at a miter angle (instead of straight across), work can be bent in a spiral curve (like a coil spring). The miter angle determines the "looseness" of the spiral, which increases with the angle.

SAWCUT MOLDINGS

Several attractive moldings can be made with cuts similar to those used for kerfing. The zigzag shape shown in Fig. 5-38 is commonly called a "dentil molding," although this term has broad application

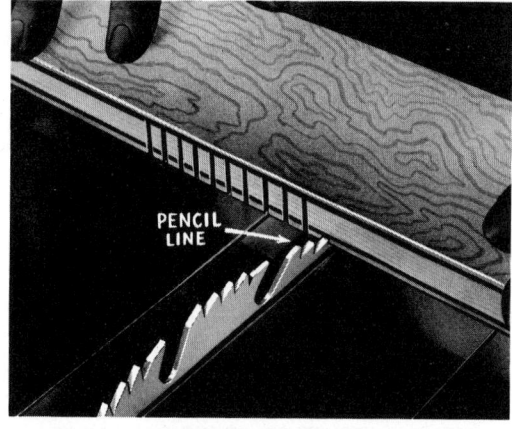

Fig. 5-36: A pencil mark on the table can be used to mark the kerfs.

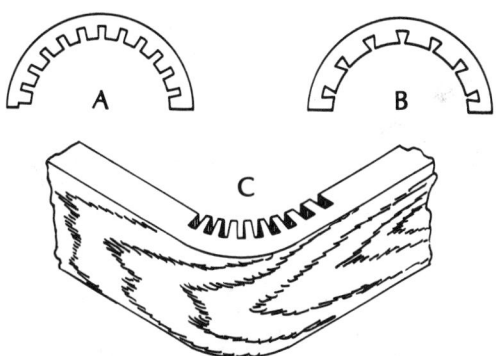

Fig. 5-37: Wood being bent at a kerf: (A) The closer the kerfs the smoother the contour, but remember the open kerfs are weaker. (B) While the shorter tangents must be sanded, the closed kerfs are stronger. (C) Kerfs are best if they are together at the bend.

and can include many different shapes. The setup is made by fastening a wood facing to the miter gauge. A nail is driven into the wood auxiliary facing to act as a guide pin—as when kerfing (Fig. 5-34); the distance from nail to blade determines the spacing of the saw cuts (Fig. 5-39).

To complete the moldings, the saw is set at a suitable projection, and repeat cuts are made by ripping narrow strips from the work (Fig 5-40). But ripping work as narrow and delicate as this demands a special setup, both for clean work and for safety. The best method is to fit the saw table with an auxiliary wood table to give the work full support. If this is not done the narrow work might be pulled down through the opening in the table insert. To rip the molding to a desired thickness (actually thinness), proceed as follows.

1. Cut the auxiliary table to size to fit the saw table.
2. Lower the blade beneath the table.
3. Clamp the auxiliary table to the saw table.
4. Set the rip fence a distance from the blade equal to the thickness of the strips desired.
5. Raise the blade to cut its own slot in the auxiliary wood table.
6. Be sure to use a push stick when cutting the work. Once the setup is made, the same auxiliary table may be used with different thicknesses of molding. These should be cut to exact desired thicknesses. Incidentally, when this ripping method is used with a hollow-ground blade, it is possible to cut strips as fine as 1/64 inch thick.

Other attractive sawcut moldings (Fig. 5-41) can also be designed if you use a little thought.

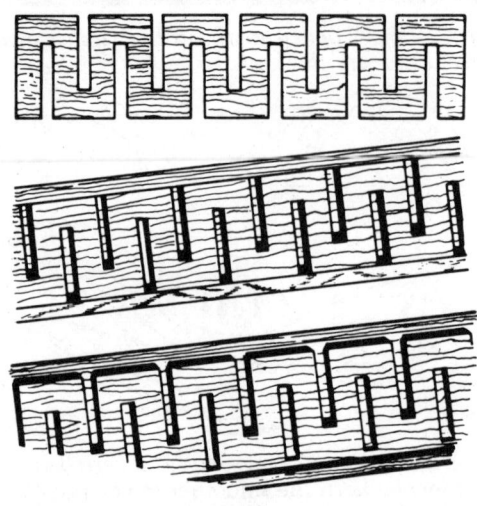

Fig. 5-38: Variations of dentil moldings.

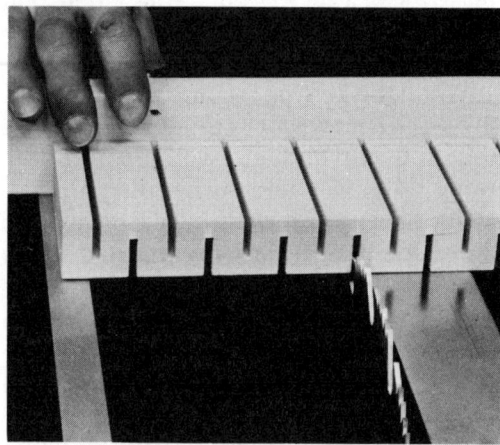

Fig. 5-39: The spacer pin and how the dentil molding is cut.

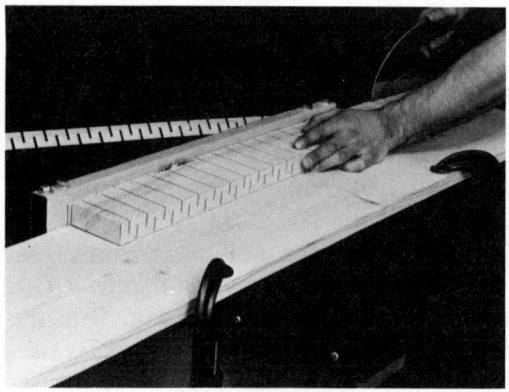

Fig. 5-40: Ripping the dentil molding.

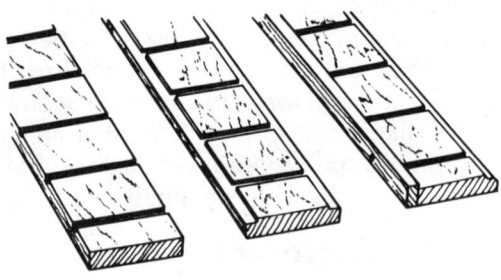

Fig. 5-41: Other attractive sawcut moldings.

Chapter 6

SPECIAL JIGS AND HOW TO USE THEM *

As illustrated throughout this book, numerous jigs are used in table saw work. A few of these such as the tenoning jig are so universal in application as to be considered an essential part of the saw. Other devices, while less extensive in scope, are often extremely handy in doing some particular job.

MITERING JIGS

Perfect miters, as stated earlier, are difficult to cut because the work tends to creep along the miter gauge. Another difficulty is that right- and left-hand cuts are required, which frequently do not match when the miter gauge is swung from one side to the other or used in both table grooves.

These problems are eliminated by various types of mitering jigs, a good style being shown in Fig. 6-1. The mitering jig in Fig. 6-2 consists of a 3/4-inch plywood table, about 16 by 24 inches, for a 10-inch saw. The top, triangular piece is worked to an exact 90 degrees and screwed in place. The metal clamps—available at most large hardware dealers—are screwed into place. Cutouts on the base allow easy working of the clamp screws. The jig is guided by hardwood or metal bars which slide in the table slots. A little adjustment may be required to get the jig lined up properly, but once set up it will cut a perfect miter every time.

Additional simple jigs are shown in Figs. 6-3, 6-4 and 6-5. They do not have the clamp feature, but they provide good

Fig. 6-1: Mitering jig prevents creep and permits cutting right- or left-handed as needed.

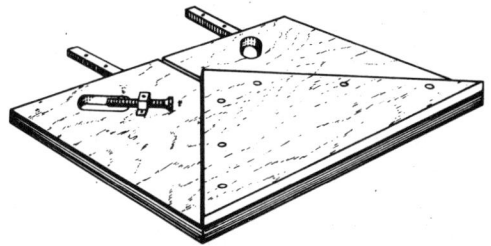

Fig. 6-2: Details of the mitering jig.

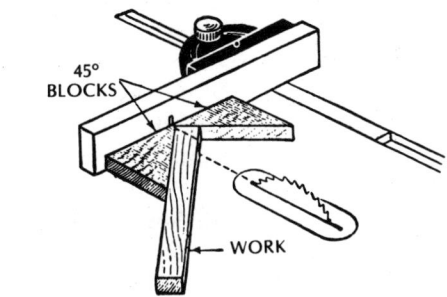

Fig. 6-3: A simple mitering jig.

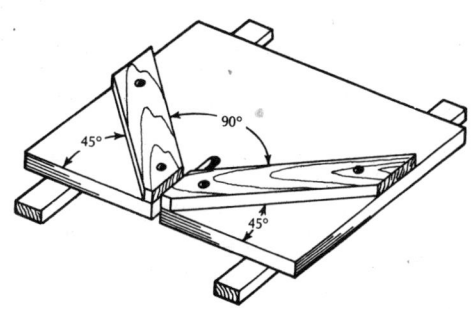

Fig. 6-4: Sliding table mitering jig.

*__NOTE:__ *In order to clearly illustrate certain procedures described in this chapter, the blade guard and other safety devices have been removed. For safe operation of the table saw, guards and other safety devices must always be utilized.*

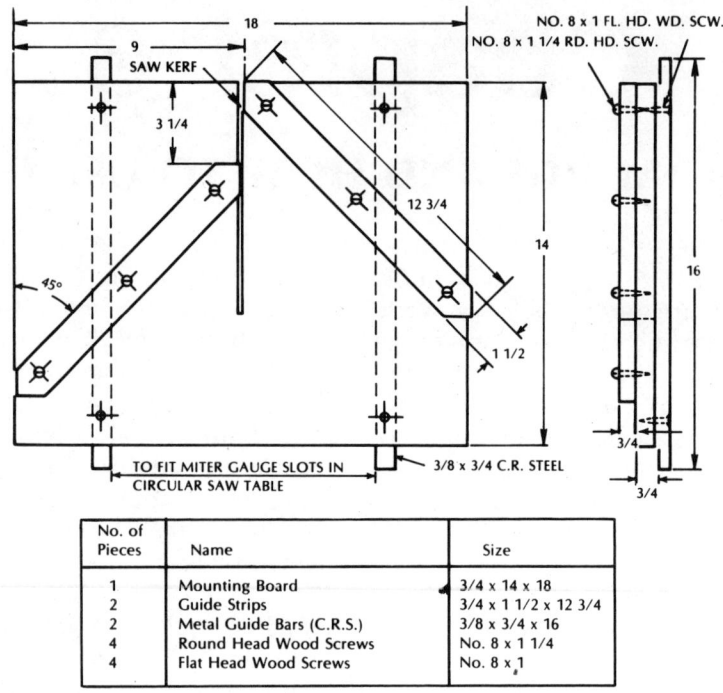

No. of Pieces	Name	Size
1	Mounting Board	3/4 x 14 x 18
2	Guide Strips	3/4 x 1 1/2 x 12 3/4
2	Metal Guide Bars (C.R.S.)	3/8 x 3/4 x 16
4	Round Head Wood Screws	No. 8 x 1 1/4
4	Flat Head Wood Screws	No. 8 x 1

Fig. 6-5: A different version of the sliding table mitering jig.

support for the work and cut right and left with constant accuracy after once being adjusted. Both require that the work be cut square to net length. When this is done, the miter cut is set by butting the square end of the work against the jig guide to make the cut. Duplicate parts are cut accurately and will be accurate in length if the initial square cutoff length is correct. The jig illustrated in Fig. 6-3 normally requires its own miter gauge. However, the auxiliary facing and blocks can be removed and replaced by merely adding a small block to the back of the facing, so positioned as to butt against the miter gauge. Some moldings that have a narrow base must be supported upright to prevent wobbling when being cut. To avoid this, use suitable scrap pieces of wood to hold the molding upright.

The miter gauge jigs shown in Figs. 6-3 and 6-4 have the following additional other uses: cutting across the diameter of circular work; cutting a true diagonal across opposite corners of a square; and cutting diametrical slots across the end of a cylinder or turning square for mounting on the spur center in lathe work.

The sliding tables shown (Figs. 6-2, 6-4, and 6-5) are, of course, limited to the miter cut determined by the angle of the guides, in this case 45 degrees. In production work, when a special job calls for numerous miters at a specific angle, it pays to make a special table with the guides set at the angle required

Jigs of this type—in fact, all permanent-type jigs—should be protected from dampness. Sand them carefully and apply three or four coats of shellac, starting with a wash coat and ending with full-strength applications. Or you can use a resin-type sealer.

MITER GAUGE CLAMP ATTACHMENT

The miter gauge clamp attachment is excellent for holding work which cannot be guided with the fence or the miter gauge alone. Figure 6-6 shows a typical operation. It is quite easy to duplicate this

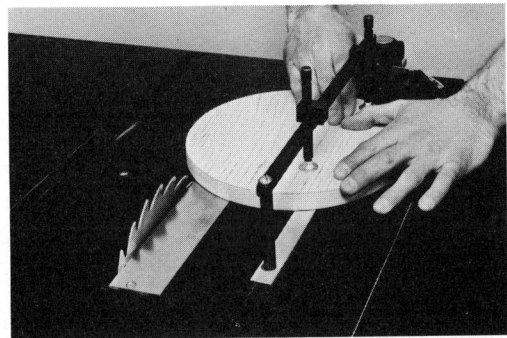

Fig. 6-6: The miter gauge clamp attachment is useful for holding odd-shaped work.

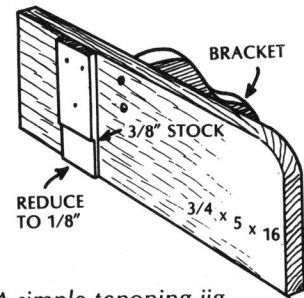

Fig. 6-7: A simple tenoning jig.

in wood if desired, using a wood table and suitable hold-downs. An alternative to hold-downs is the use of a double board. One board is the regular sliding table part and is fitted with a bar to work in a table groove. The second board is the same size and is loosely fastened to the table board by means of two carriage bolts and wing nuts. Work to be cut is sandwiched between the two boards and clamped by turning the wing nuts.

TENONING JIG

The commercial tenoning jig is described on page 9. Practical substitutes can be made as shown in Figs. 6-7, 6-8 and 6-9. A jig of some kind should always be used when cutting tenons (Fig. 6-10). Do not attempt this operation by simply pushing the work on end along the fence. Variations of the simple jig board can be made as needed to support miters and odd-shaped work; for example, a V-shaped support is used for keying miters.

HOLD-DOWN

A good hold down for thin stock can be fitted to an auxiliary wood fence which has been screw-fastened to the regular fence. This device is a block or something similar, which is clamped to the auxiliary fence, directly over the blade and over the top surface of the workpiece. It will resist the tendency of the workpiece to lift or buck when pushed into the blade. The same device is useful for various molding-head

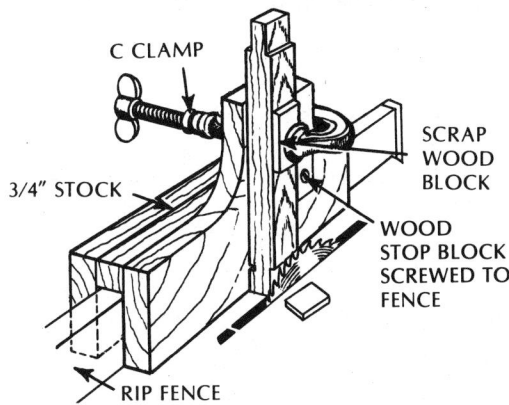

Fig. 6-8: Another style of sliding tenoning jig. It is made to fit over rip fence.

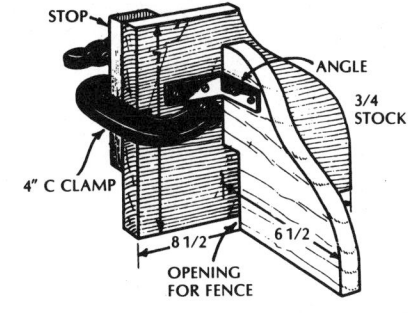

Fig. 6-9: This tenoning jig can be easily made.

Fig. 6-10: The simple tenoning jig in use.

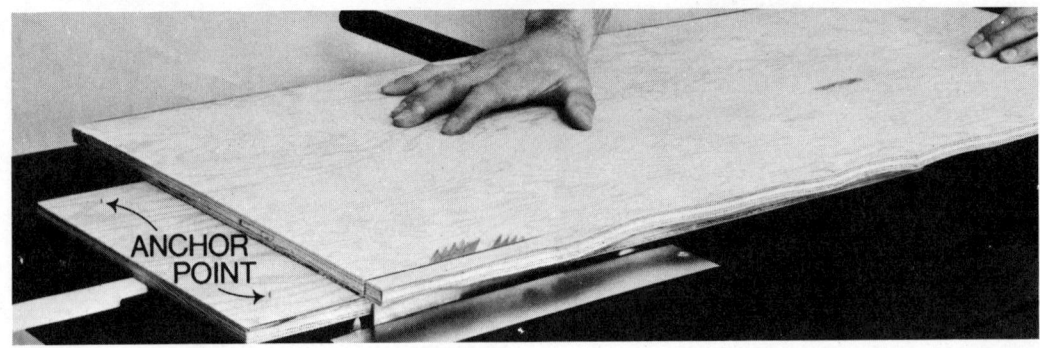

Fig. 6-11: The sliding table idea plus anchor points to hold the work makes a good set-up for ripping raw edges.

Fig. 6-12: The platform and the stop is made from 3/4-inch lumber or plywood. The hardwood slide should be slide-fit in the table slot.

jobs to assure uniform contact of the work against the table.

SQUARING BOARDS

There are times when it is necessary to cut a piece of stock which does not have a straight edge to use against the rip fence. The stock may be a piece that has been jig-sawed or band-sawed on both edges or it may be a rough piece of lumber.

Four methods of ripping raw edges are shown in Figs. 6-11 through 6-14. The first (Fig. 6-11) is a variation of the sliding table idea, but instead of hold-downs, the table is fitted with several projecting pins or anchor points. The work to be cut is pressed down on the wood table over the

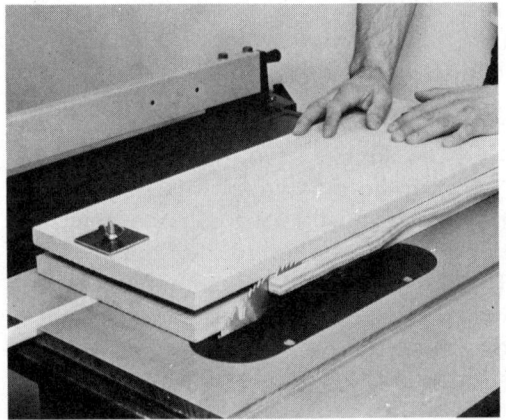

Fig. 6-13: The cut-off board is handy when stock has no straight edges.

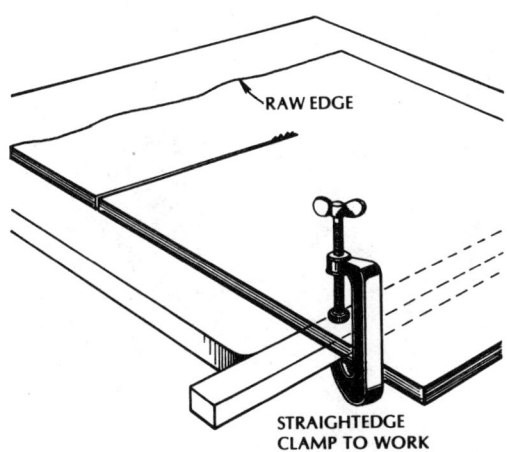

Fig. 6-14: The straight edge clamped to work rides against edge of saw table.

anchor points, making it secure for the ripping cut.

Another variation of the sliding table idea (Fig. 6-12) consists of a squaring board with a guide to fit the miter-gauge slot fastened to its underside. A cleat or stop is fastened to the forward edge of the sliding table at right angles to the saw blade. The work to be sawed is butted against the cleat and the whole assembly is fed past the saw blade. (Fig. 6-12). Another variation of this is the cut-off board shown in Fig. 6-13. The top board of the jig acts as a clamping device.

The fourth method (Fig. 6-14) is especially useful for cleaning up a raw edge on a large sheet of plywood. All you do here is clamp a straightedge to the underside of the work in the proper position. The straightedge rides against the side of the saw table and guides the work into the blade. This will not work on every saw because it is dependent on the side of the table being parallel with the blade. However, in most cases the required alignment is sufficiently exact.

Another method is to nail a straightedge to the top surface of the work, and then guide the job as described for pattern sawing, on page 48. This system is excellent for plywood, and good for long taper cuts which cannot be handled with a tapering jig. Pattern sawing in this manner is advantageous for handling large work because the guide furnishes a hold-down which helps to keep the work in place.

NOTCHED JIGS

There are times when a part cannot be sawed accurately or safely using the miter gauge or rip fence only. The part may be too small to be held safely or too oddly shaped to be done conventionally. A notched jig is often the solution (Fig. 6-15).

This jig is a piece of wood with parallel sides. The notch can be the shape of the part you wish to keep, or it can be the shape of the waste piece. Usually, the jig will ride the rip fence and act as both carrier and gauge (Fig. 6-16). It allows you to position the work precisely, even when unusual shapes are involved.

Making generalizations about the use of notched jigs is difficult because, in most cases, they are employed for very special jobs. In a few general situations, however, notched jigs can be very helpful. Safe operation calls for using them whenever the part is so small or so oddly shaped that it cannot be safely hand-held, whenever the cut is such that the piece cannot be held in the normal manner with the rip fence or the miter gauge, or whenever you need many identical parts so that making a special setup is justified. Of course, the jigs

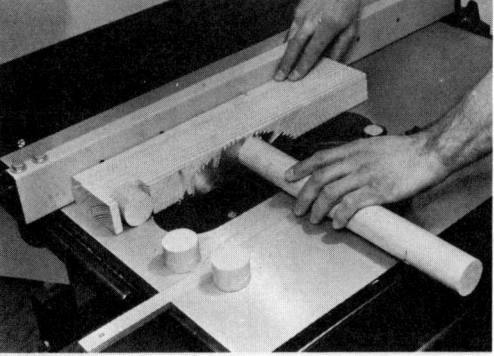

Fig. 6-15: A simple jig facilitates cutting duplicate disks from a wood rod. Depth of notch determines width of disk.

must be made accurately. This may be too much trouble when you need only a piece or two. At such times, if accuracy is really critical, it may be better to lay out the work piece, cut just outside the line and then finish the job on a belt or disk sander.

The stake pointing jig (Fig. 6-17A) is typical of a special function notched jig. Instead of making a separate jig for various angle stake points, this angle board is made to fit your miter gauge bar, and is easily adjusted for any suitable angle. When using a hardwood, like birch or maple, make a 1/4 inch pivot hole for a machine screw (Fig. 6-17B). A hole must be drilled and tapped 4 1/2 inches from the pivot point in the miter gauge bar.

Fig. 6-16: Jobs like tenon cheek-cuts can also be accomplished with notched jigs.

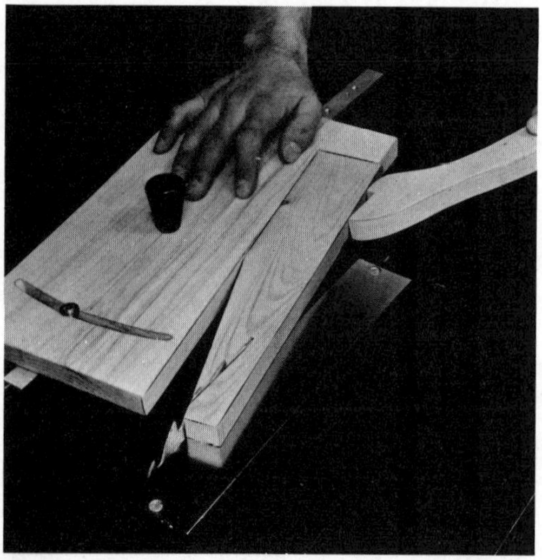

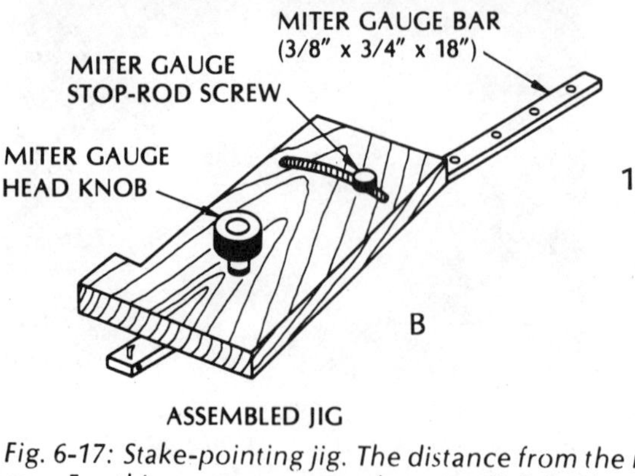

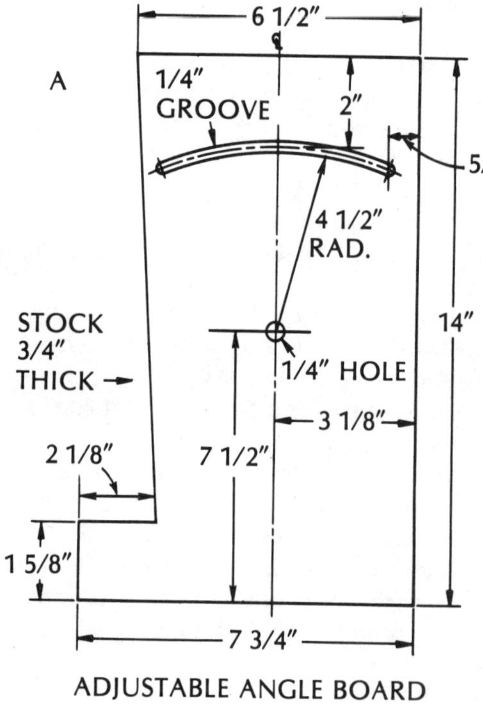

Fig. 6-17: Stake-pointing jig. The distance from the miter gauge slots to the blade varies from saw to saw. For this reason you may have to slightly change the dimensions given above to fit your saw.

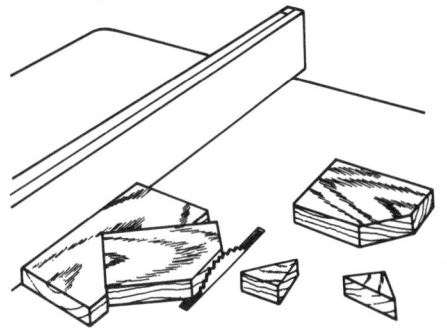

CORNER CUTTING JIG

A simple jig for removing corners from a square workpiece is shown in Fig. 6-18.

WEDGE CUTTING JIG

Some joints call for a wedge to spread a tenon, or other projection, in a cavity made for it. The end of the projection is slotted and the wedge is driven into the cut, spreading the halves tightly against the sides of the cavity.

If you must cut a number of wedges, the job can be accomplished with a notched template such as shown in Fig. 6-19, A, B. and C. The jig is notched to suit the desired

Fig. 6-18: A notched template pushed along a fence provides an easy way to remove corners from square workpieces.

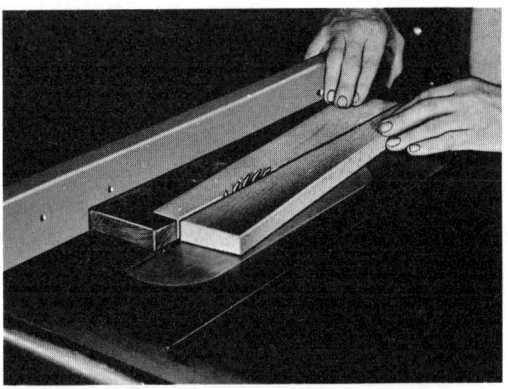

A

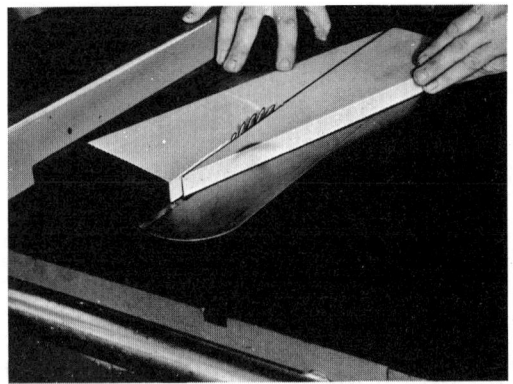

B

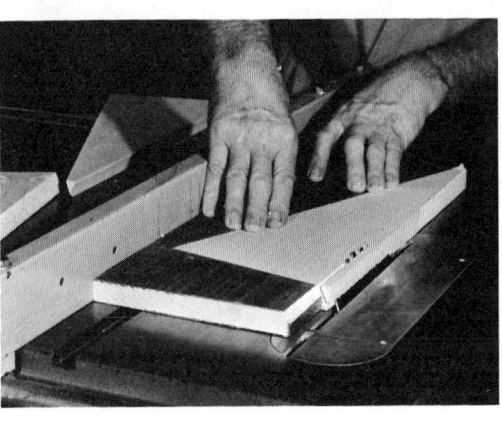

C

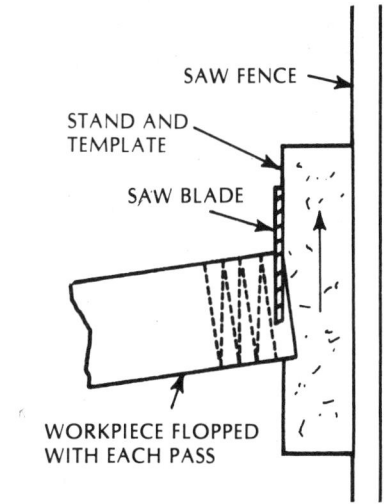

D

Fig. 6-19: The notched board is cut to suit desired wedge shape.

taper, and the saw fence is set so the blade just clears the jig as it is passed along the fence. Sawing is done with the grain after the stock is first crosscut from wide material. In Fig. 6-19 D as each wedge is cut, the stock is flopped in the notch. Like slicing cheese, the jig is pushed forward, then withdrawn with the wedge in the notch. Select stock free of knots and with a straight grain. If you use a hollow-ground combination blade, there will be no need to sand the wedges. Width of the stock from which the wedges are cut must equal the length of the notch so the wedges will have chisel points. If blunt points are wanted, make the notch in the board deeper.

While a standard template can be made easily for individual wedges, an adjustable jig (Fig. 6-20) makes more sense. A bolt, which can be seen at the front of the jig, is turned in or out as required to set the taper. The bolt head rides against the fence, and should be ground and polished to prevent marring of the fence. For occasional work of this kind it is more practical to make up a jig from solid lumber. This can be visualized by imagining the wedge formed by the bolt to be solid wood contacting the fence. Never attempt to cut wedges freehand; always use some type of jig.

ADJUSTABLE CUT-OFF STOP

Frequent use is made of a stop in doing cutoff work. Many workers favor an adjustable stop instead of hunting for a block and clamp for every job. A unit of this kind is shown in Fig. 6-21. As can be seen, it is simply a sliding block which works in a groove cut in the miter-gauge facing. This jig should preferably have its own miter gauge since the stop may sometimes interfere with plain cutoff work. Some craftspeople house a yardstick in the lower face of the facing to make it possible to set the stop block without the need of measuring and pencil marking the work.

Fig. 6-20: Adjustable jig for cutting wedges.

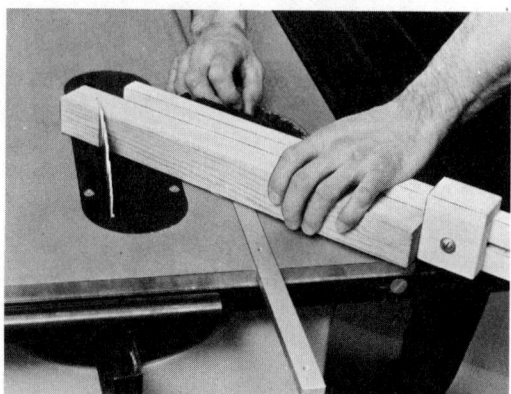

Fig. 6-21: Adjustable stop is a worthwhile convenience.

Chapter 7

POPULAR WOOD JOINTS *

Saw cuts needed to fashion wood joints compose a large part of all table saw work. The best blade for this type of work is the hollow-ground blade because it makes a cleaner cut and can be set more accurately to guidelines than spring-set blades.

BUTT JOINTS

The butt joint is the simplest of all joints (Fig. 7-1). Though it is extremely simple to make, the edges to be joined must be tested for absolute squareness before the pieces are fitted together. The squareness can be assured if the crosscutting operation is performed carefully.

If an exceptionally strong joint is required, dowels and splines are preferred over nails or countersunk screws. Dowels are, of course, hardwoods—generally birch or maple. They are available in diameters from 1/8 to 3 inches, with either a plain or grooved surface. The latter surface allows the glue to run more freely into the joint. The grooves are generally cut on a band saw or lathe.

When selecting the size of a dowel rod to use, a general rule is that the diameter should be no more than half the thickness of the stock. The depth of the hole will vary with the type of joint. Remember that a dowel inserted in the drilled holes of a joint adds considerably to the strength of the joint. The dowel's hardness and the fact that it is used with the grain at right angles to the materials joined are the reasons for this added strength.

Actually, there are two methods used in doweling, the open method and the blind method. In the open method (Fig. 7-2A), a hole is drilled completely through one

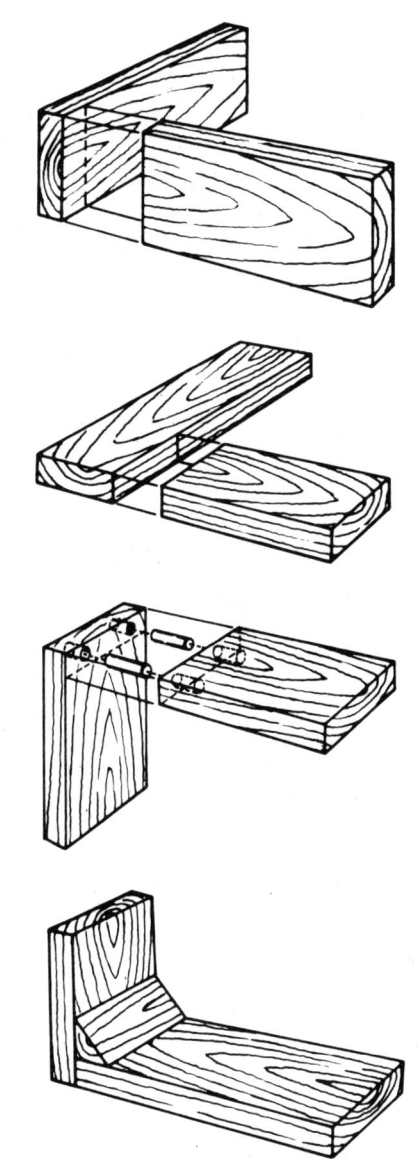

Fig. 7-1: Butt joints and ways to strengthen them.

*NOTE: In order to clearly illustrate certain procedures described in this chapter, the blade guard and other safety devices have been removed. For safe operation of the table saw, guards and other safety devices must always be utilized.

piece of wood and deeply into or through the piece to be joined. The dowel is coated with glue and pushed completely through the drilled holes, joining the pieces. The remainder is then sawed off flush with the outer surface. Thus, dowel stock for open doweling is kept long to allow for a flush cut after the joint is made.

In the blind method (Fig. 7-2B), holes are drilled part of the way into each piece from the joined faces. a rule of thumb is to drill the holes in each piece to a depth of approximately four times the diameter of the dowel. A dowel is then glue-coated and inserted in one hole, and the second piece pressed onto the protruding dowel end. The length of the dowel rod should always be cut about 1/4 inch shorter than the total of the two holes. Cut the ends of the dowel pins with a bevel. To ensure adequate glue on a snug-fitting dowel, some are spiral-grooved and others are provided with a lengthwise slot. When filled with glue these indentations assure a firm grip. In most joints two or more dowels are used instead of one to prevent the pieces from twisting on the dowel.

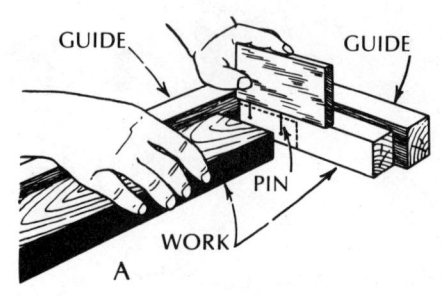

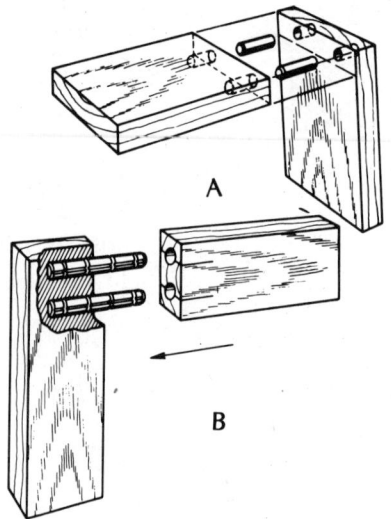

Fig. 7-2: (A) An open dowel joint; (B) a blind dowel joint.

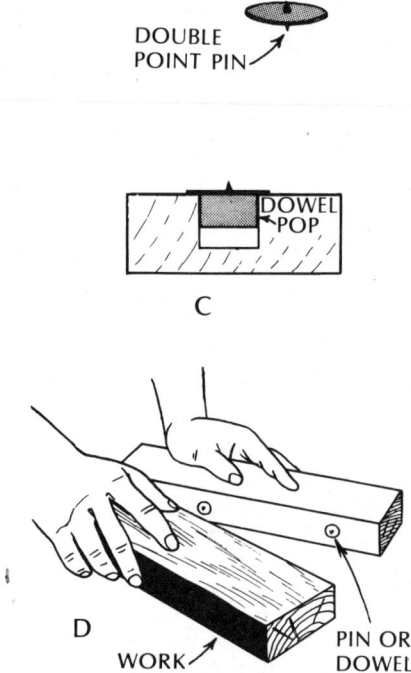

Fig. 7-3: Methods of laying dowel holes.

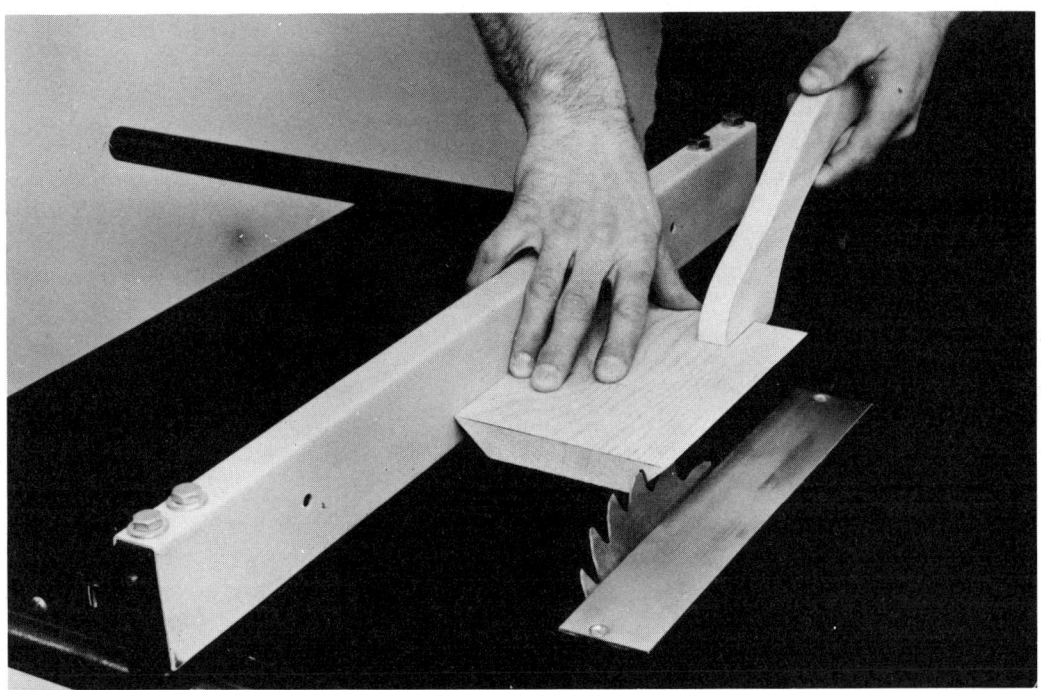

Fig. 7-4: Cutting a spline groove with a saw blade.

Various methods are used for laying out the hole positions. The pin method shown in Fig. 7-3A is made with two ordinary pins stuck in a block of wood which is placed between the joining members of stock. When the pieces are pushed together, the pin heads make an impression on each piece, and this serves as a center point for the hole to be drillled. Double point thumb tacks can be used in the same manner (Fig. 7-3B). A standard method is to use dowel pops or points as shown in Figs. 7-3C and D. Here one hole is drilled first. The dowel point is placed in the drilled hole which locates the exact position of the mating hole in the second piece. Holes can also be marked with the use of templates (Fig. 7-3E).

When using the open method of doweling, the problem of aligning drilled holes does not occur. Even when poorly centered, the holes match and the dowel can be driven through both holes. In the blind system, however, two separate holes must be drilled—and here trouble can develop unless a jig is used.

In some instances the drilling device is clamped into position and the wood is guided to it along measured channels to ensure proper centering of the holes. In others the wood is clamped and the drilling device is guided along identical channels for all holes drilled. In either case the guide is actually a jig. Furthermore, it is also possible to arrange the jig so as to control the depth of the hole drilled.

To further insure that dowels do not turn or become loose, thereby permitting the joint to crack or spread as the surrounding wood shrinks, small finishing nails or brads may be set through wood surfaces into the dowels.

Splines are used to strengthen all types of joints from plain butt to fancy miters. The spline itself is a thin strip of hard-wood or plywood inserted in a groove cut in the two adjoining surfaces of a joint. The groove is cut with a saw blade or dado head (Fig. 7-4) to a specific width and depth. (The groove for the spline is commonly run in with the dado head, 1/4 inch being usual for 3/4- to 1-inch stock, although a 1/8-inch spline, a single saw cut, is sometimes used, especially for miters.) A thin piece of stock is then cut to fit into this groove. The spline stock should be cut so that the grain runs at right angles to the grain of the joint (Fig. 7-5).

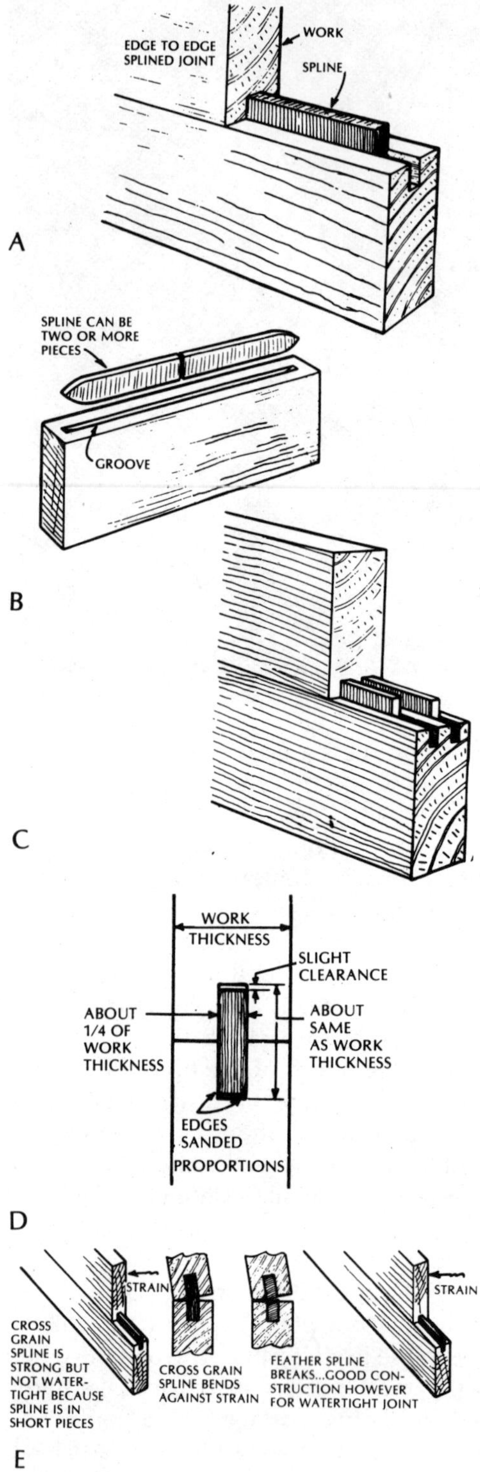

Fig. 7-5: Details on spline joints.

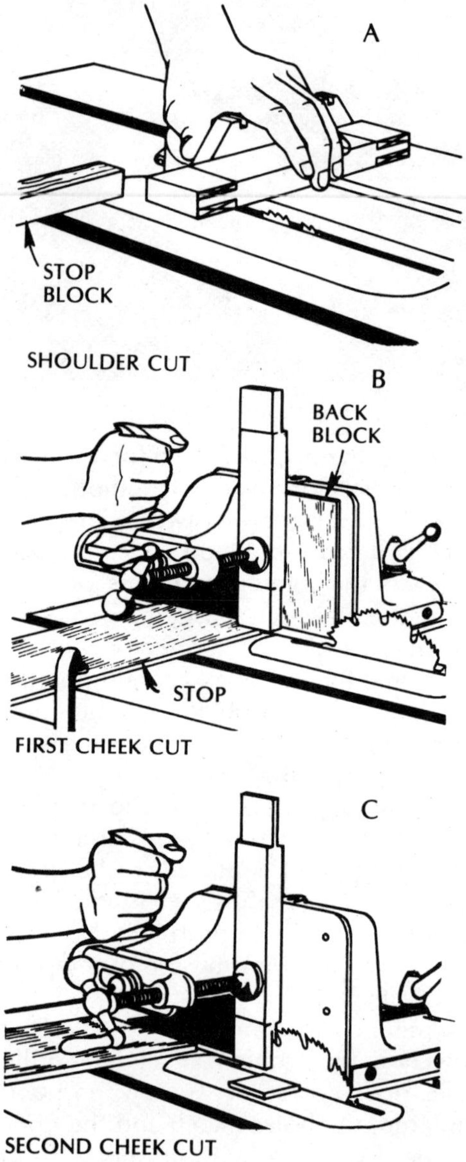

Fig. 7-6: Cutting a tenon with a saw blade.

A very simple way to produce splines is to cut up scrap pieces of 1/8-inch plywood. A supply of these can be kept on hand. The advantages of the plywood is its strength in each direction and its constant thickness. Quite probably your saw blade cuts a 1/8-inch kerf which is just right. Various types of joints employing splines are illustrated in this chapter.

In addition to dowels and splines, angle irons, mending plates, or a T-strap are used to strengthen butt joints.

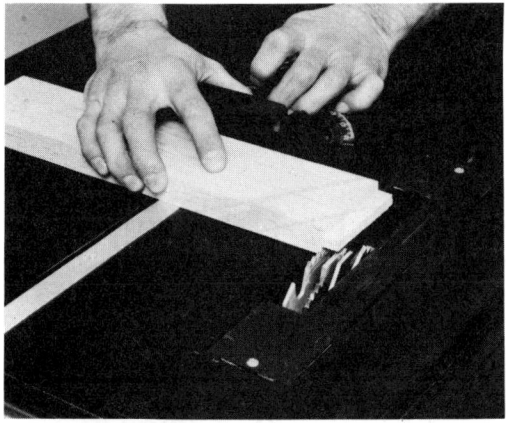

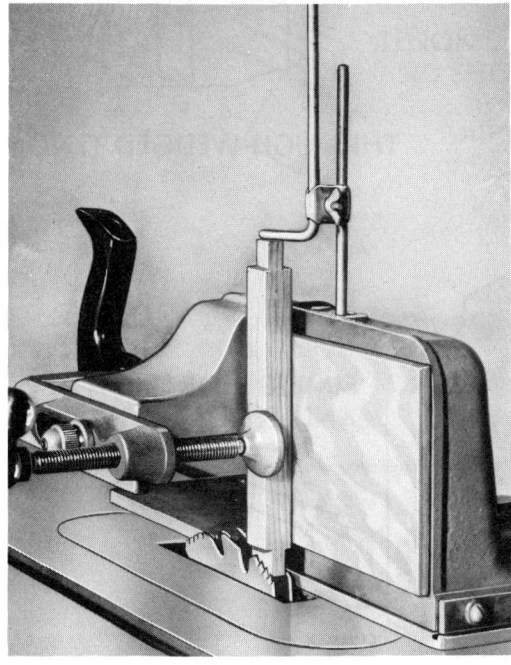

Fig. 7-7: Cutting a tenon with a dado head.

MORTISE-AND-TENON JOINTS

The mortise-and-tenon is a very good joint, stronger and more widely used than the butt joint. It is one of the best techniques used in fine furniture making. All enclosed mortises (those with material on four sides) should be cut with a mortising attachment on a drill press, or with a router.

The tenon for the mortise-and-tenon joint can be cut in a number of different ways, depending on the equipment available and the nature of the joint. One of the easiest ways is shown in Fig. 7-6. This method makes use of a base stop and a backing block, both of which should be made up and kept as regular fixtures. The shoulder cuts are made first (7-6A). The first cheek cut is then made, using a backing block of a thickness equal to the thickness of the tenon plus the thickness of the saw blade (7-6B). After the first cheek cut is made, the backing block is removed and the second cheek cut is made (7-6C), keeping the same face of work against the jig. The base stop shown in (7-6C) is the same thickness as the baseplate of the tenoning jig. This system of cutting eliminates any possible errors because of variations in work thickness. If only one or two joints are to be made, the simpler procedure of working to pencil lines and turning the work over for the two cheek cuts can be used, eliminating the base and backing blocks.

Tenons are also made easily and quickly with the dado head (Fig. 7-7). Adjust the dado head to a height equal to the thickness of the stock to be removed on one side of the tenon. Then make one or more passes to cut half the tenon. Reverse the stock and cut the other side. The work is held against the miter gauge and a stop block or stop rod to the length of the tenon. The feed should be slow, to prevent a natural tendency for the work to creep away from the saw. Where the tenon is longer than the width of the dado head, the inside cut should be made first. Then, the work is stepped over to make the necessary extra cuts. Speed in making wide tenons or grooves can be obtained by using a notched stop block. Each of the steps in the block advances the work 11/16 inch, permitting the maximum width of cut to cover the required area in the least number of passes.

As described on page 100, tenons can also be cut with a molding head. When joining a mortise and tenon, apply plenty of glue and hold in clamps until the glue sets.

Some of the more popular variations of the simple mortise and tenon (Fig. 7-8) are described below.

The *haunched tenon* is employed where added tenon strength is needed and where partial exposure on top is not objectionable.

The *concealed haunched tenon* gives the needed extra strength to the joint without showing a break at the end.

The *mitered tenon*, frequently utilized in table construction, is used to secure the maximum length of tenon. Each joint is a simple mortise and tenon with the tenon end mitered at 45 degrees as shown. The two mortises meet at 90 degrees inside the vertical (leg) member. Mitering of the tenon ends allows for deeper tenons.

The *bare-faced tenon* has but one shoulder and it is used when a tenoned piece is thinner than a mortised piece.

The *through-wedged tenon* is useful where both added strength and resistance to pulling apart is required. The two ends of the mortise are sloped outward to provide room for the wedges, which are about half the tenon in length.

The *blind-wedged tenon* is used in the same way as the through-wedged tenon but can be employed in locations where the through-wedged cannot be used.

The *tenon with splines* can only be used when work is 1 3/8 inches or more in thickness. The splines guard against the work twisting out of line.

The *tenon with long and short shoulders* is used in a framework or sash where a rabbet is required.

The *stub tenon* is not a true mortise-and-tenon joint, but it is made easily and is useful for light framing.

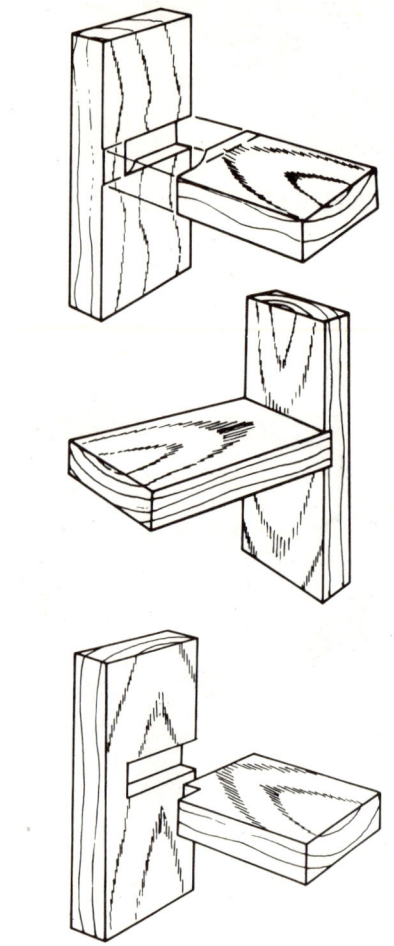

Fig. 7-9: Common variations of dado joints.

DADO JOINTS

A dado joint is formed when one piece of wood is set into a groove or dado cut into another. There are many variations of a dado joint (Fig. 7-9) used in cabinetwork and furniture making. For instance, a *standard or housed dado* joint is a groove that is cut in one piece of wood to the exact thickness of the second piece to be joined.

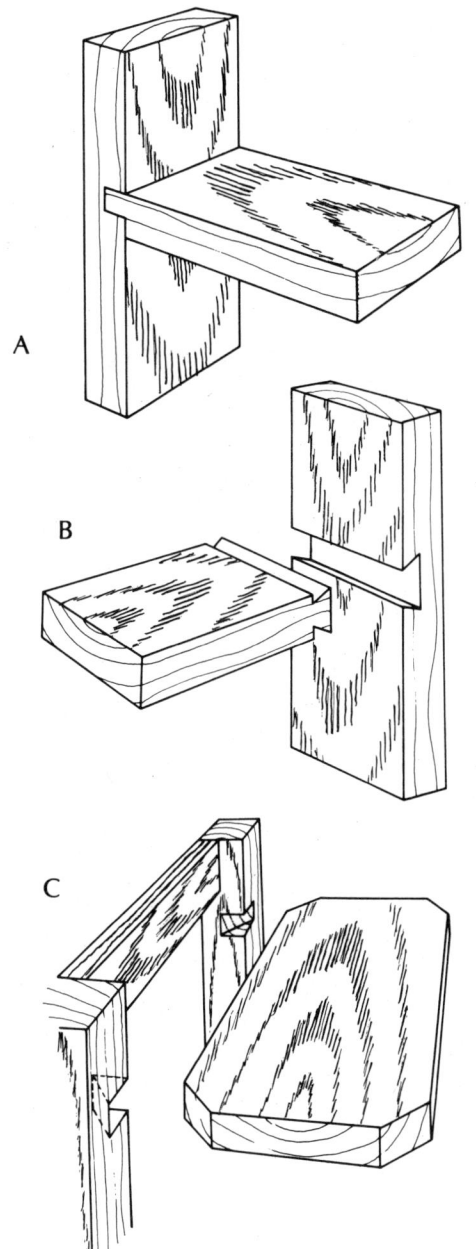

Sometimes a dado is also stopped on one or both sides. This is done by clamping one or two stop blocks to the rip fence following the procedure as described on page 43. The dado tongue-and-rabbet accomplishes the same purpose as the drawer joint but is used when it is desirable to expose the cross grain at the side rather than at the end. If the two grooves and the end lap are all of equal thickness, this gives a strong, serviceable joint.

The *dado-and-rabbet* can be used for drawer joints, but is also used extensively in shelf construction as shown in Fig. 7-10A.

The *full-dovetail dado* (Fig. 7-10B) is made by first cutting a mortise or slot. Cut a dado to the narrowest width. Then replace the dado head with a single blade and adjust to an angle of 15 degrees. Make the angle cut on both sides to clean out the mortise. The tenon is cut in two steps with a single blade. First cut the kerfs in the faces. Then adjust the blade to a 15-degree angle and make the two shoulder cuts. The *half-dovetail dado* is cut the same way except that the angle cuts are made on only one side of the joint.

Fig. 7-10: (A) Rabbet-and-dado; (B) full-dovetail, and (C) corner dado.

All standard dadoes are best cut with a dado head, set to exact width (see page 42). They can also be cut by making several passes with a single blade, then cleaning out the waste with a chisel. The dado can be cut at any angle to the edge.

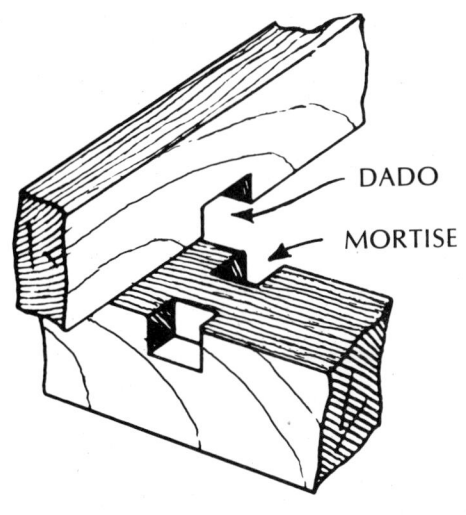

Fig. 7-11: Cogged dado joint.

The corner dado shown in Fig. 7-10C is another popular joint, but it generally needs the added support of dowels.

The *cogged dado joint* (Fig. 7-11) has an uncut portion that is fitted into the main frame member as follows: Using a dado head, cut the groove in the reinforcing strip, then rout out the slots in the frame member and square their corners with a hand chisel.

The *tongue-and-groove joint* (Fig. 7-12), can be cut with a dado head. The groove is cut in a single pass with a head of the correct thickness. The matching tongue can be cut by placing a spacer collar between the blades of the dado head, with a chipper on the outside of each blade to remove waste stock. The tongue-and-groove joint is most frequently used to join flooring or siding.

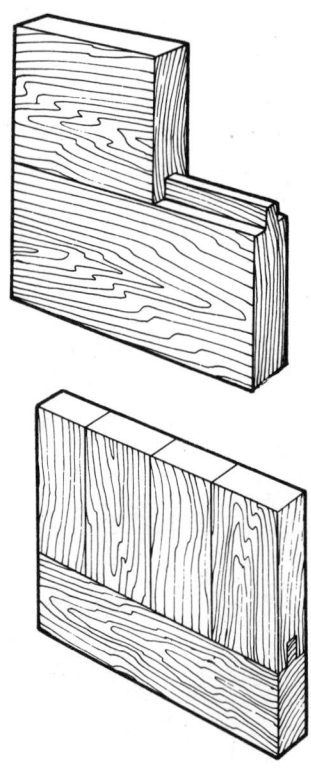

Fig. 7-12: Tongue-and-groove joints.

Dado joints can be secured in several different ways. Adhesive can be used by itself or in combination with dowels, nails, corrugated fasteners, angle irons, or screws.

LAPPED JOINTS

Bring two workpieces together, notch them equally where they overlap, and you have either a cross- or middle-joint, a half-lap joint (end-to-end, at right angles), or a tee half-lap joint (end-to-side, at right angles). The desired visual effect of such joints is that the two thicknesses overlap within a single thickness. Figure 7-13 illustrates various lapped joints.

The first step in making a lapped joint is to set the saw projection equal to one-half the work thickness, testing on a piece of scrap stock. The width of the cut is usually set off by pencil lines, although a stop block and spacer can be used to advantage for repeat work. A single joint is commonly cut by working to pencil marks, walking the saw across in successive cuts to obtain the required width.

The use of a dado head will reduce the number of passes needed. But remember to limit your dado passes to a 1/4-inch depth-of-cut at a time. For instances a 1-inch groove in 2-inch stock should take you four passes. Never overload the dado head with any deeper cut. There is no limit to the width of any groove you can make. All you have to do is keep repeating the basic cut until you are finished.

The fit of the two pieces should be snug. Test for surface evenness of the lap with a steel straightedge. If screws are to be used, preparatory to assembling, drill pilot holes for the screws, then glue and clamp the parts, inserting the screws after the lap has been positioned.

The End-Lap or Corner-Lap. The end or corner-lap joint is made by halving and shouldering the opposite sides of the ends of the workpieces and then joining them at right angles. When one of the cuts is made at a point other than the end of the workpiece, you have a center, or middle, lap. This joint is used most commonly when joining a rail to an upright.

The Edgewise Cross-Lap or Middle Half Lap. The edgewise cross-lap is another joint that is made by halving the two pieces at right angles, but in this case the notches are cut in the edges rather than the surfaces of the two members. This is particularly useful when making framing or partitioning, and often both cuts can be made at the same time.

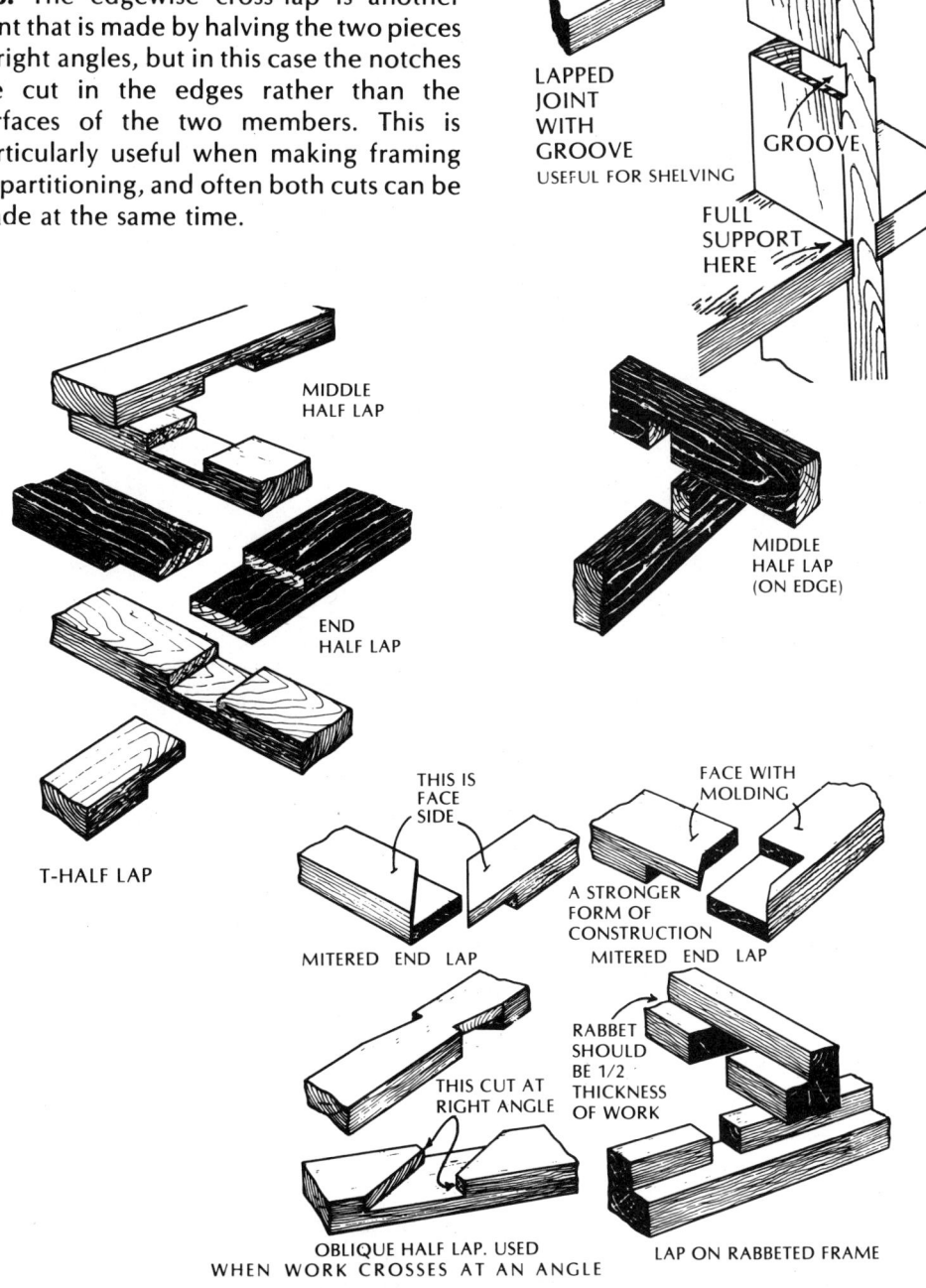

Fig. 7-13; Various forms of lapped joints.

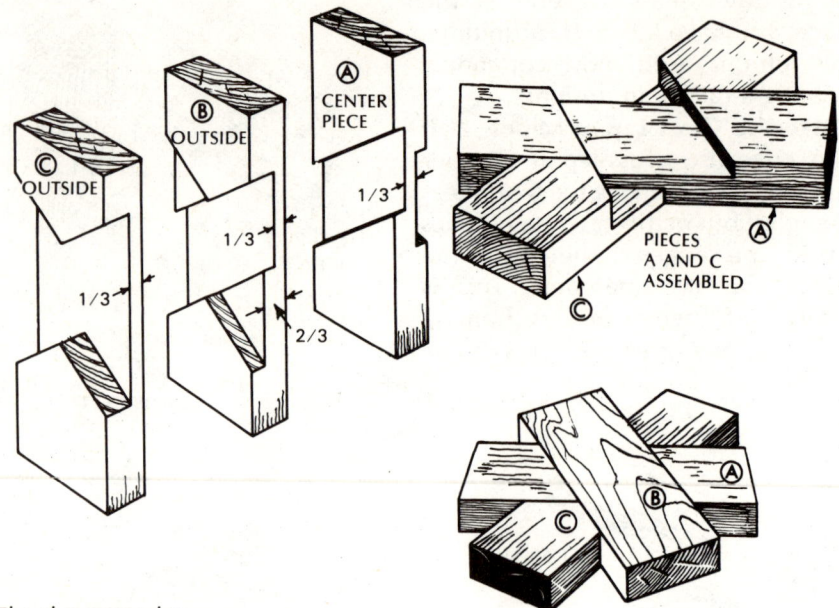

Fig. 7-14: The three-way lap.

The Three-Way Lap. This joint (Fig. 7-14) is accomplished by making all three cuts with the miter gauge set at 60 degrees. It is used for joining three pieces of wood while retaining a single thickness.

The Open Mortise-and-Tenon. This arrangement, which makes a corner joint a bit stronger than the corner lap, is used on the corners of cabinet-door frames. A variation of the open mortise-and-tenon can be used in place of the middle lap to join rails and crosspieces or uprights.

The Full-Dovetail Half Lap and the Half-Dovetail Half Lap. These fancier versions of the corner and cross-lap are often seen in old cabinetwork. In both these joints the dovetail is half-lapped into a rail, crosspiece, or upright, and the two pieces are joined at right angles. The main difference between the two is that the half-dovetail lap is not as difficult to make.

Where a T-half-lap with strong resistance to separation is required, the dovetail is a logical form of construction. Piece B, Fig. 7-15, is cut first. Where the work permits, it is best to make the angle of

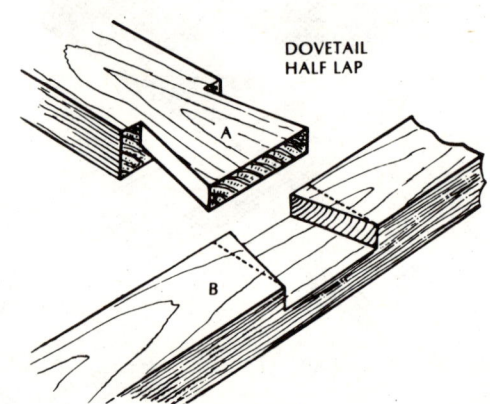

Fig. 7-15: Parts of dovetail half-lap.

the dovetail equal to half the thickness of the work, since this eliminates one setting of the saw. For example, if 3/4-inch stock is being worked, the dovetail should be 3/8 inch. The angle setting for piece B is obtained by holding the work against the miter gauge and rotating it until a measurement taken off the end of the work measures 3/8 inch, as shown in Fig. 7-

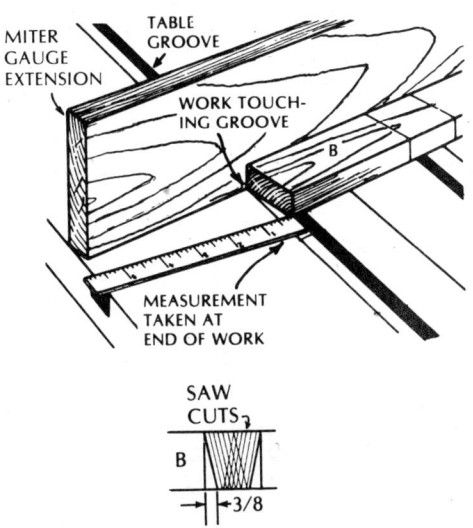

Fig. 7-16: Laying out of dovetail half-lap.

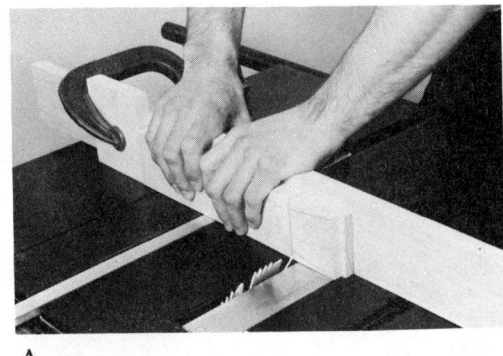

A

B

Fig. 7-17: Cutting a half lap.

16. The saw is set to cut half the thickness of the work; many saw cuts are made to clean one side of the joint. The opposite side is worked the same way, with the miter gauge set to the same degree on the opposite side. Piece A is made by cutting the shoulder cuts on three sides, as shown in Fig. 7-17A. Surplus wood can be removed by walking across the cut. Alternately, the wood can be removed in one pass if it is mounted in the tenoning jig, as shown in Fig. 7-17B. The sloping shoulders of the tenon are cut last, tilting the arbor the same number of degrees as previously used for the miter-gauge setting. The same joint is satisfactory with only one side dovetailed, leaving the other edge square, as in the common lap joint.

The half-dovetail half-lap shown in Fig. 7-18 has only one side of the tongue and slot cut at an angle.

DOVETAIL JOINT

A single dovetail joint can be cut on a table saw as illustrated in Fig. 7-19. The saw blade is set at an angle of 5 to 7 degrees to cut both the tongue and dovetail slot. The groove is completed by cleaning out the stock between the angle cuts with the blade in a vertical position. When making dovetail joints, remember that the accuracy of the cut and depth-of-cut setting are most important.

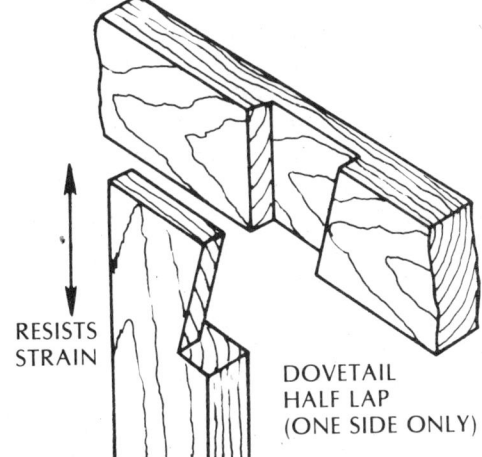

Fig. 7-18: The dovetail half-lap on one side only.

Fig. 7-19: Cutting a dovetail joint on a table saw. A tenoning jig or similar device should be used to hold the workpiece.

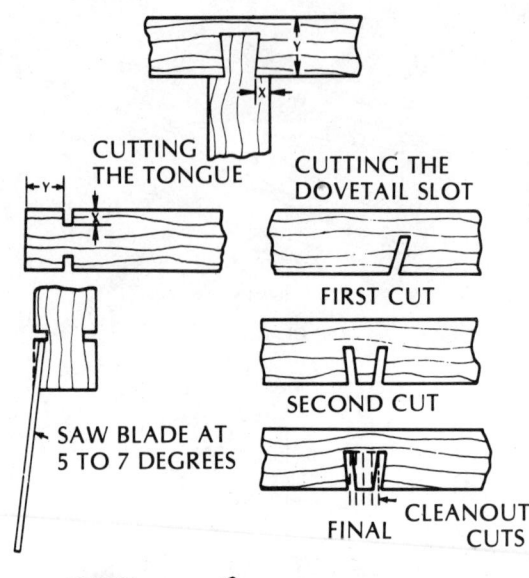

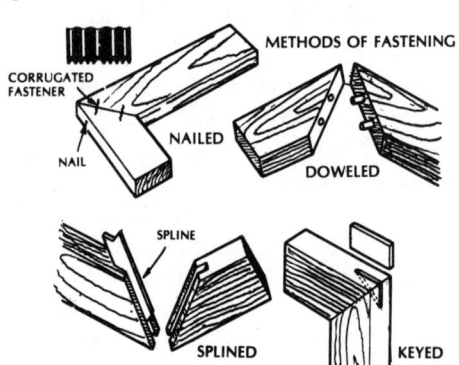

Fig. 7-20: Methods of fastening miter joints.

MITER JOINTS

The miter joint is primarily for show. For example, it may be used for an uninterrupted wood grain around edges (side to top to side of a cabinet) or at corners (a picture frame). The joining ends or edges are usually cut at angles of 45 degrees, then glued, clamped, or otherwise fastened (Fig. 7-20). Cuts slightly less than 45 degrees are often necessary when fitting new moldings on settled window casings, but the differences are hardly noticeable once they are up and painted. In other words, there is a definite finished look to a mitered joint, whether it is left natural or painted.

The miter joint is worked flat or on edge. The setting of the blade or miter gauge, as required, is commonly a full 45 degrees and should be checked for accuracy on scrap stock before cutting the joint.

The Splined Miter Joint. The splined joint is simply a plain miter with a spline (Fig. 7-21) to give it added strength. The spline, which can be hardwood, hardboard, or plywood, should always run the full length of the joint. The miter is cut with the saw blade tilted to 45 degrees, using either the rip fence or the miter gauge to guide the workpiece. Use the tenoning jig to cut the slot for the spline.

Leave the blade at the same angle but adjust it for height. The spline groove must be perpendicular to the bevel. When both pieces are mitered and slotted, the spline is glued in place. Reinforced in this manner, the miter joint is very strong. Where appearance is not too important, corrugated fasteners can be used across the miter joint.

There are several jigs that will help to assure good spline miter joint cuts. The slotted jig shown in Fig. 7-22 is designed to hold the workpiece at the proper bevel angle. Two other simple jigs are illustrated in Fig. 7-23. The tenoning jig (Fig. 7-24) can also be used to cut spline grooves. The

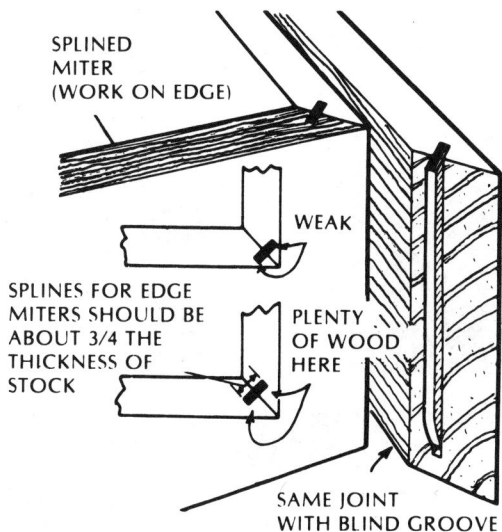

Fig. 7-21: Splined miter joint.

important point to keep in mind when cutting a spline groove is that it must be perpendicular to the bevel.

The Blind Splined Miter Joint. In a blind splined miter joint there is one edge, as seen in the open view of the joint. Stop blocks are needed to control the length of the spline groove. A test block of the same thickness and width as the work provides an accurate means of setting the stops and also shows the exact shape of the spline sawed apart. The complete schedule for cutting the joint, as shown in Figs. 7-25 and 7-26, is described here.

1. Cut the work to the net length for a plain miter, Miter the test block about 6 inches long. Arrange the work four-square and number the joints.

2. Cut the groove on the test block, using the straddle stop mounted on the fence, to locate the workpiece at the end for the proper depth of cut.

3. Split the groove using the band saw or some other convenient means. Make pencil marks 1/4 inch from the edge.

4. Use the test block to determine the starting point and the forward travel of the miter gauge. Clamp the stops in place.

5. Cut joints 1, 3, 5, and 7. Also make the

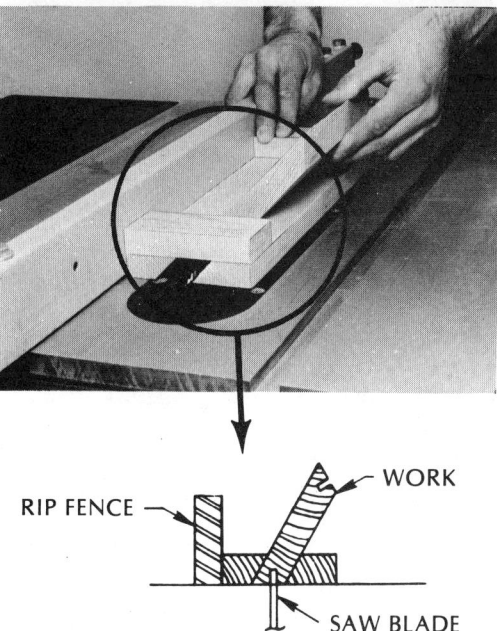

Fig. 7-22: A slotted jig for cutting splined miter joints.

same cut on opposite end of the test block.

6. Lower the blade flush with the table surface. Using the first-cut end of the test block, count the number of turns and partial turns required to raise the blade to the original depth of cut on the test block.

7. Lower the blade flush to the table top. Clamp joint 2 in the miter gauge against the straddle stop, with the miter gauge against the front stop block. Turn on the saw, and raise the blade into the work the required number of turns and partial turns. Feed the

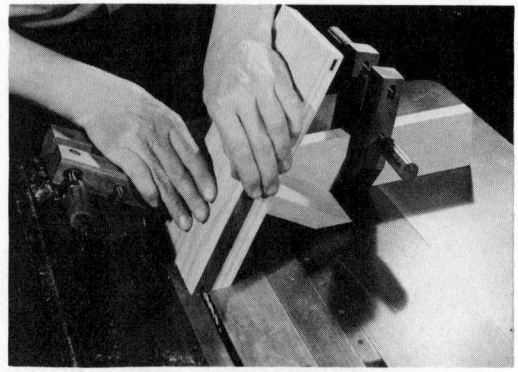

Fig. 7-23: Other jigs for cutting splined miter joints.

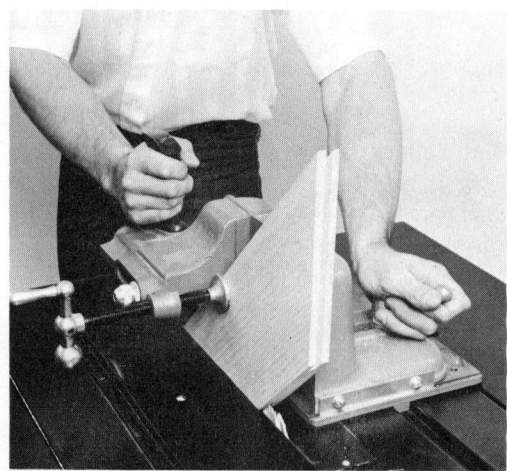

Fig. 7-24: Using a tenoning jig to cut a spline.

workpiece to the backstop. Turn the saw off and lower the blade.

8. Repeat step 7 for joints 4, 6, and 8.
9. Cut the spline to shape and assemble.

The Slip-Feather or Keyed Miter. Similar to the splined miter, except that the splines are placed in the outside edge of the corner, a slip-feather miter joint (Fig. 7-27) is generally used when making something wide and flat. The two miters are cut in the conventional manner, then the pieces are clamped together in a tenoning jig and one or more slots are cut across the end of the joint. The slip feathers or keys (triangular splines of plywood) are then secured in the slots and sanded smooth. This gives a strongly reinforced miter joint.

The Lapped Miter. The lapped miter joint (Fig. 7-28) is also used when jointing

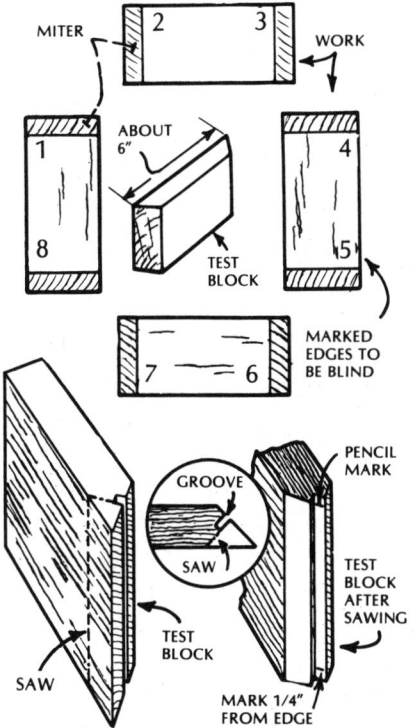

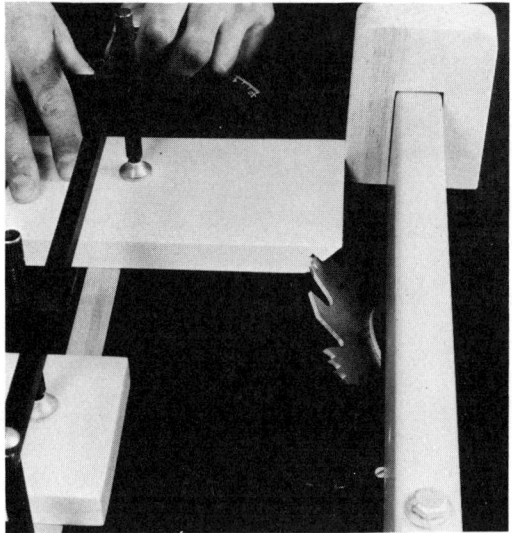

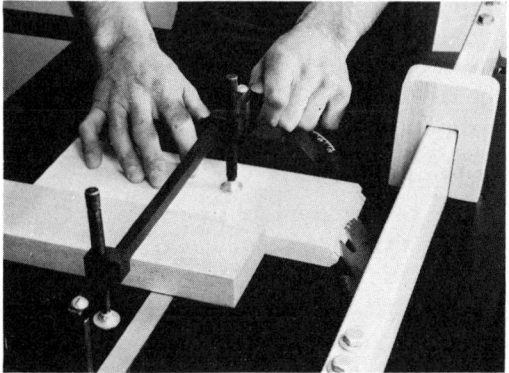

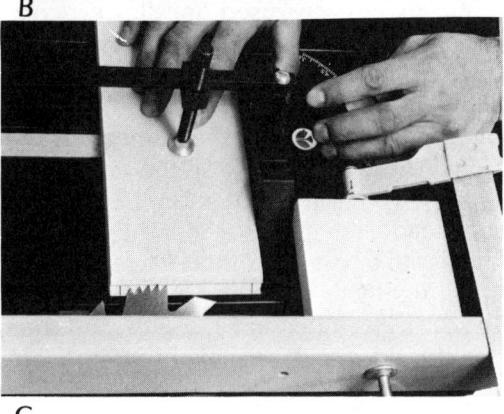

Fig. 7-25: Steps in making a blind splined miter groove.

frames, but only if it is desirable to have the miter show on one side only. This joint will give the appearance of a conventional miter from one side, yet will be considerably stronger because of the increase in the area of contacting surfaces.

In every mitered construction, always use corner clamps, web clamping devices, or rope to hold your workpiece square while drying after gluing. Mitered articles, more than any other jointed project, have a tendency to shift without your knowing it, so you have got to take extra care to maintain the position of the joints.

Compound Miter Joints. To cut compound miter joints, adjust the blade and the miter gauge to the correct setting as described on page 52. If you wish to use a splined joint (this joint can also be used for polygon miters) keep the saw blade at the same bevel angle used to cut the joint. Then, groove each piece staying closer to

Fig. 7-26: Cutting a blind splined miter joint: (A) making the first spline slot in the test block; (B) using a cut-away test block to locate the rear stop; and (C) using the test block to locate the front stop.

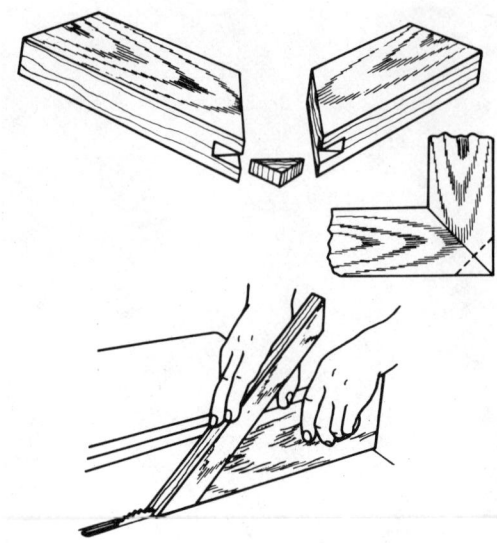

Fig. 7-27: The slip-feather miter joint detail and how it can be cut by a beveled pushboard.

the heel than to the point and do not make the cut too deep. Make the spline to fit the mating grooves exactly.

RABBET JOINTS

The rabbet joint is similar to a dado except that it has only two surfaces (a bottom and one side) and therefore has to be made at the edge of your workpiece (unlike the rabbet, the dado occurs anywhere, except along an edge). This simple joint, extensively used in drawer construction, is pictured in Fig. 7-29. A fair standard with 3/4 inch front stock is to allow 1/4 inch for the lip. It can be seen that all of the work on the rabbet is at the front. There is no work on the side of the drawer. To cut the rabbet, mount the 1/4 inch dado combination on the saw. Set the depth of cut at 1/2 inch. Place the front stock tightly against the side of the dado head, as illustrated in Fig. 7-30A, and then use the side stock as shown to determine the position of the stop block. Clamp the stop in place and make the cut (Fig. 7-30B). Clean out the surplus stock by moving the work over, as shown in Fig. 7-30C. You can also use a notching technique with a single blade as described on page 46.

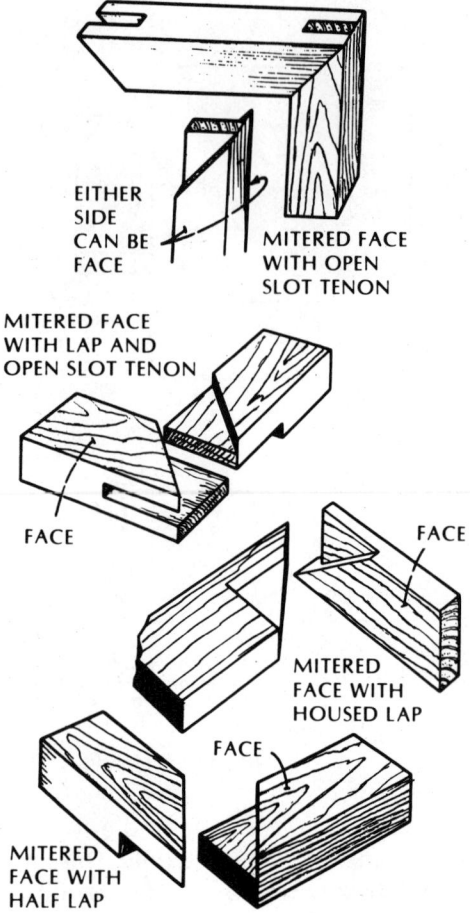

Fig. 7-28: Lapped miter joints.

Rabbeted Miter Joint. A rabbeted miter joint is excellent for cabinet bases and can be cut easily by following the schedule given here. The square-cut section simplifies gluing or nailing operations. As a cabinet base joint (Fig. 7-31), piece B should be the end or side, and nails, if used, should be entered from this piece. In heavy work the joint is sometimes assembled with dowels fitted across the square step in the same position as the nails that can be seen here. A more complicated variation of the joint is the lock miter, described on page 92, which is sometimes used for drawer or furniture box work. This construction is usually worked with

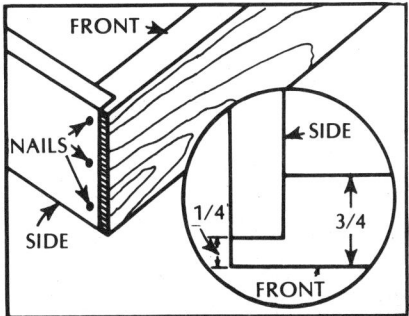

Fig. 7-29: A simple drawer rabbet joint.

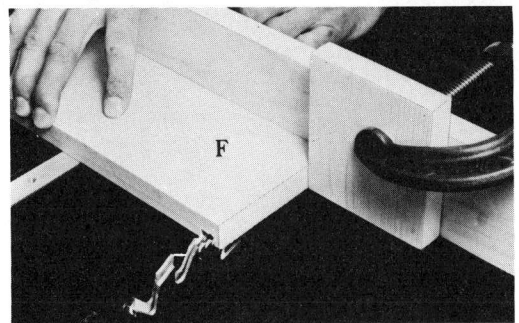

A

B

C

Fig. 7-30: Making a simple drawer rabbet joint.

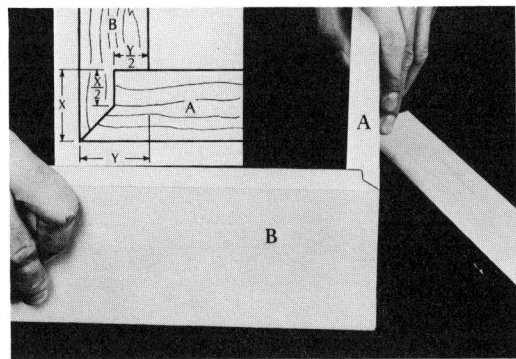

Fig. 7-31: The rabbeted miter joint and its formula.

the use of the dado head. However, for most work, the simpler rabbeted miter is both neat and strong. But before attempting this joint, be sure to study the dimensional relationships shown in Fig. 7-31.

The following is the cutting schedule (shown in Figs. 7-32 through 7-36) for the rabbeted miter joint.

Fig. 7-32: Step 1.

1. Set the saw projection at half the thickness of the work, checking on a piece of scrap stock. Next, using a scrap piece of stock or one of the workpieces, set the fence at a distance equal to the thickness of the stock, as measured from the free side of the blade. In other words, the saw blade is flush with the face of the work, as shown. Be sure both adjustments, saw height and fence setting, are exact.

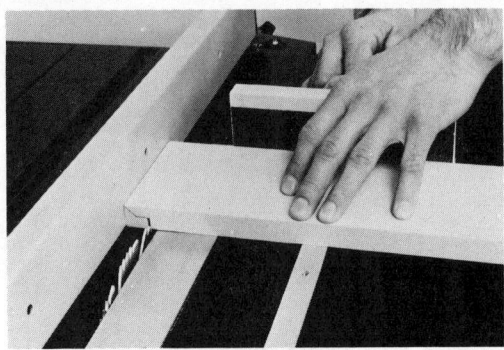

Fig. 7-33: Step 2.

2. With the depth and fence setting made, make the first cut. Pencil marks on the work are not essential as far as actual cutting is concerned, but they are useful to identify each piece. If more than one joint is required, all similar pieces should be cut before advancing to the next step. Using pencil marks to identify the face surface and edge is always a good practice as it will ensure more accurate work.

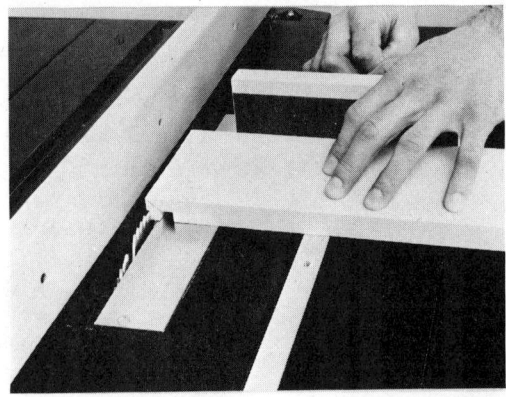

Fig. 7-34: Step 3.

3. With the saw blade at the same depth, walk across the joint with about four saw cuts. The exact width of the groove cut in this manner is immaterial so long as it extends a little more than halfway to the end of the work. Also, on the first piece, make a single saw cut at the extreme end. This cut, which serves as a guide in the next operation, is not essential and can be omitted if desired.

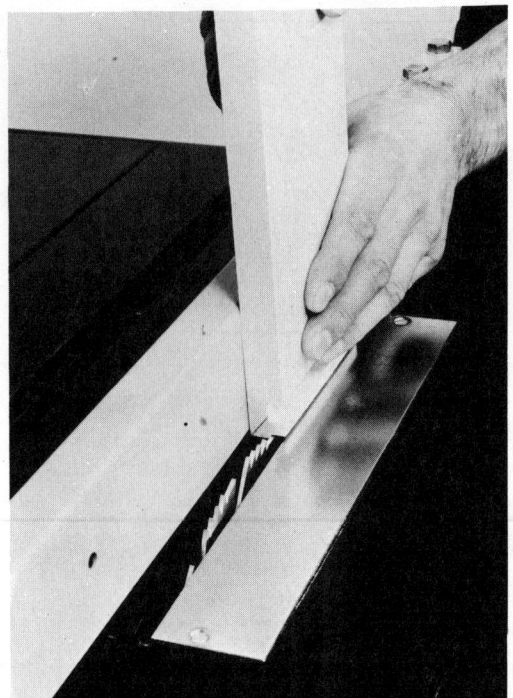

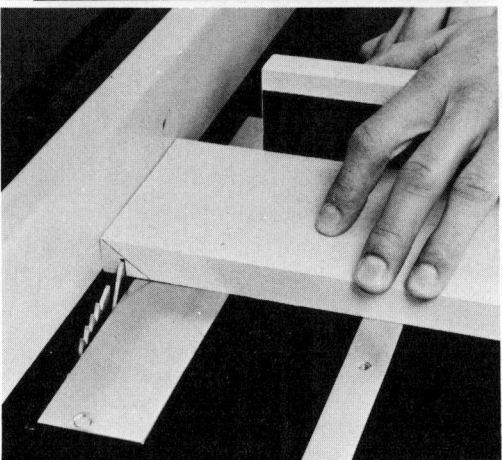

Fig. 7-35: Step 4.

4. Using the step at the end of the work as a guide, set the fence so that the distance from the fence to the open side of the blade is equal to half the thickness of the work. Measure the distance by holding the work in contact with a raker tooth. Piece B is used to make the saw setting, but the operation is on piece A, as previously described.

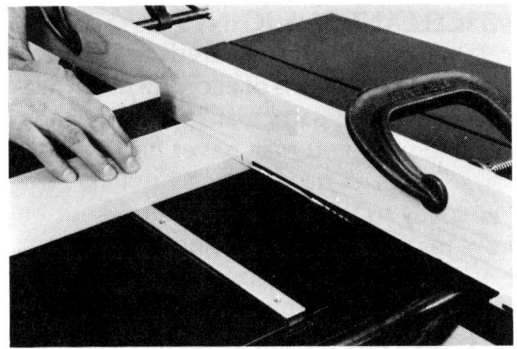

Fig. 7-36: Step 5.

Fig. 7-38: Adjusting the tenoning jig.

5. Fasten an auxiliary wood fence in place and adjust the fence so that the saw cut will come exactly to the corner of the work. Make the cut, raising the saw blade as required. Run the same cut on piece B to complete the joint.

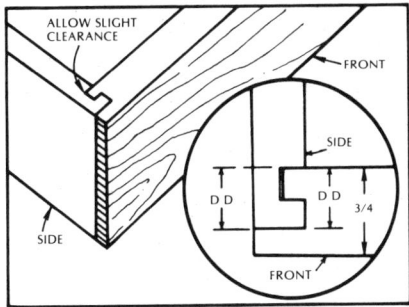

Fig. 7-37: Rabbet-and-groove joint.

The Rabbet-and-Groove Joint (as used in drawer construction). Stronger and neater than the plain rabbeted joint, the rabbet-and-groove, or milled joint, is popular for drawer construction. The joint with average dimensions is shown in Fig. 7-37. The dimension DD means double dado and represents a distance equal to twice the width of the dado combination being used. The 1/4-inch dado combination is commonly used, making DD equal to approximately 1/2 inch (dado saws are usually a trifle scant of their named size). The fit of the joint depends on getting the dado groove exactly DD distance from the inner face of the front, and the same DD distance from the end of the side. This is best accomplished by using the same stop block for both cuts. Start by mounting the 1/4-inch dado combination in place. Use a thin metal collar or several paper collars behind the innermost saw so that the outer edge of the combination will be DD distance from the edge of the tenoning jig base plate, as shown in Fig. 7-38. Set the depth of cut to a trifle less than one-half the thickness of the side stock. Using the edge of the tenoning jig baseplate as a stop (Fig. 7-39A), cut the groove in the side piece, as shown in Fig. 7-39B. This completes the side. Reset the depth of the cut to the same depth as the thickness of the side stock. Mount the front stock in the tenoning jig, with the inner side of the front against the base plate (Fig 7-39C), and cut the groove in front. You can now assemble the joint as shown in Fig. 7-39D. You need only to cut off the tenon to bring it to a perfect fit. A slight amount of clearance at the tenon should be allowed.

Both drawer joints—straight rabbet and rabbet groove—are sometimes worked with the front overhanging the sides by about 1/32 inch, as illustrated in Fig. 8-16. This is easily managed by varying the saw setting slightly. The purpose of the overhang is to allow a neat closing fit of the drawer without binding the sides.

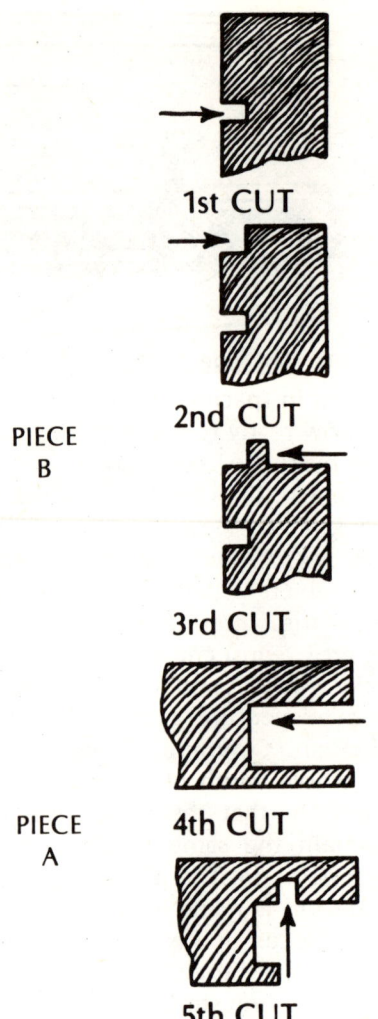
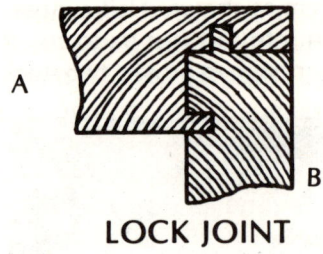

LOCK JOINT

is recommended for all-around work, since it permits any width of dado-cutter to be used. Another feature is that any box joint can be made either with a driven or with a loose fit by simply setting the auxiliary facing a fraction of an inch one way or the other.

The Lock-Corner Joint. The lock-corner joint shown in Fig. 7-44 is one of the better joints to use on chests and special boxes. Box side B is made with a single blade or dado as shown in the 1st, 2nd and 3rd cuts. Side piece A is made in two operations as shown in Fig. 7-44. Allow a little tolerance between tongues and grooves so that you can assemble the joint by sliding the pieces together.

A popular variation of this joint is the so-called "lock-miter." It combines the neat appearance of a mitered corner with the strength of a dado corner (Fig. 7-45). The mitered portion should not exceed half the

Fig. 7-44: The lock-corner joint.

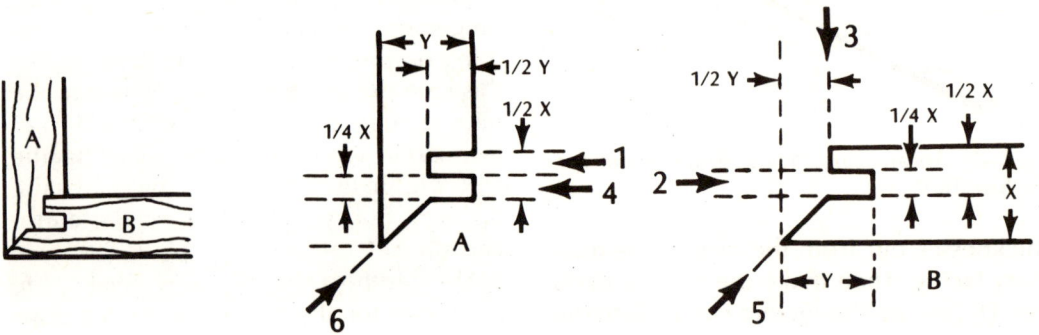

Fig. 7-45: The lock-miter joint. Numbers represent order of the cuts.

joint, as shown. Do cuts 1 and 2 with a dado and 3 through 6 with a regular blade (making 5 and 6 at a 45-degree bevel angle, with boards on end).

Another similar joint is the housed rabbet miter which is used for joining pieces that are different in thickness as shown in Fig. 7-46. The following steps are involved in making the rabbet miter:

1. Start with the thicker piece. The blade projection should equal the thickness of this piece minus that of the thinner one. The distance from the fence to the blade's outer surface should equal the thickness of the thinner stock.

2. The miter cut on the thick stock starts exactly at the corner and just meets the bottom inside corner of the shoulder cut. The blade projection is critical.

3. The final cut, on the thinner piece, is a simple miter.

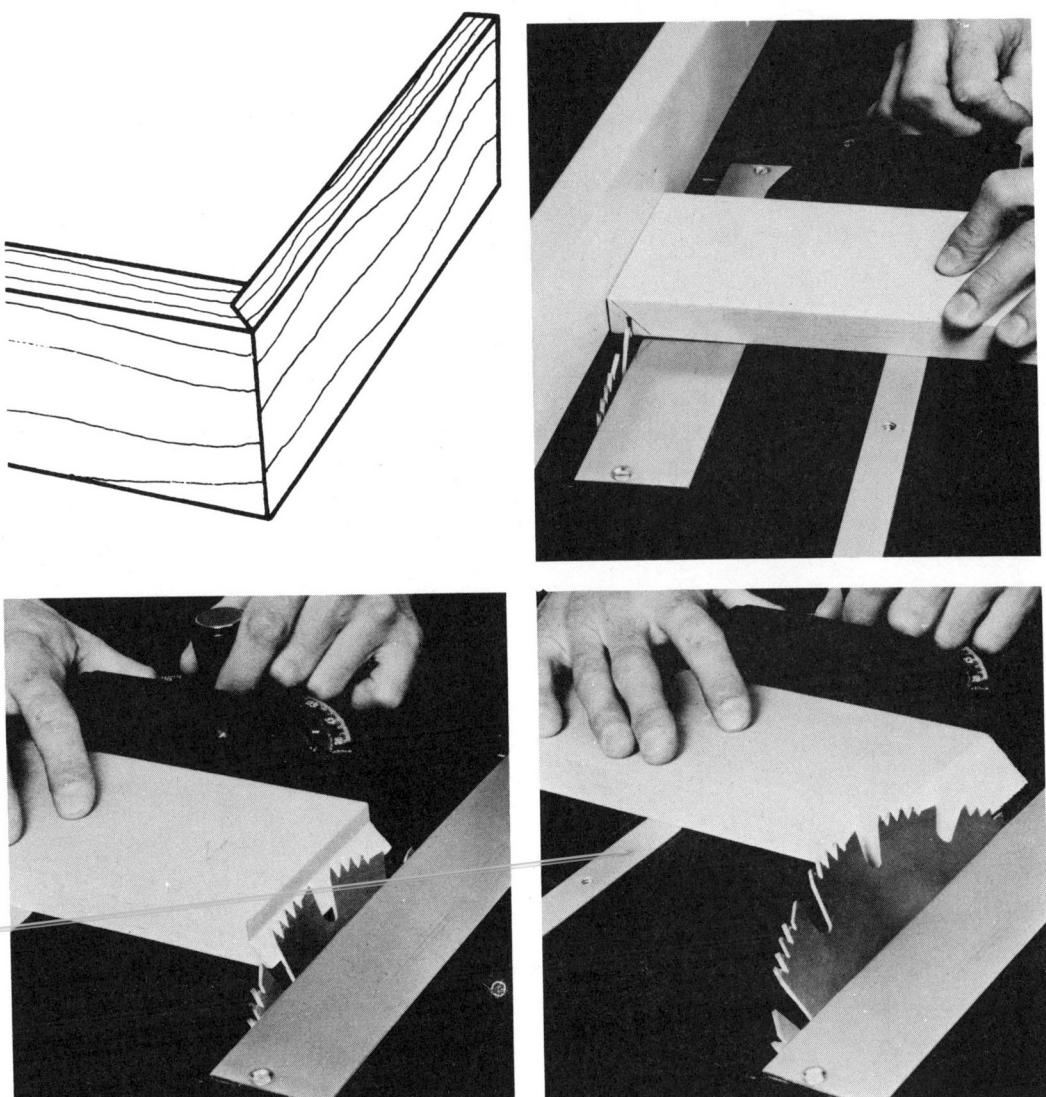

Fig. 7-46: The housed-rabbet miter joint and how it is made.

In this chapter, we have described and shown numerous wood joints. These are commonly used today in modern woodworking. But, many other joints do exist. Museums and antique shops offer an excellent source for studying the various uncommon and previously employed methods of wood joinery. Regardless of the joint, however, practice in making it is very important.

Although the illustrations and explanations in this chapter might make the joints appear simple, it is extremely easy to spoil expensive material by making such common mistakes as cutting through or on the wrong side of the layout lines, not properly identifying mating surfaces, and/or not following the proper sequence of steps. Therefore, when attempting a joint for the first time, it is wise to practice on scrap material of the same size to check settings, fits, and final results. Sometimes it might be necessary to make the same joint several times before obtaining satisfactory results. remember, when woodworking, "practice makes perfect."

Chapter 8

USING THE MOLDING CUTTERHEAD *

Molding is cutting a shape on the edge or face of a workpiece. Cutting moldings with a molding cutterhead in the table saw is a fast, safe, and clean operation. The many different knife shapes available make it possible for the operator to produce almost any kind of molding, such as the various styles of corner molds, picture frames, table edges, and so on.

MOLDING-CUTTER OPERATION

The molding head consists of a cutterhead in which various shapes of steel knives can be mounted. Each of the three knives in a set is fitted into a groove in the cutterhead and securely clamped with a screw. The knife grooves should be kept free of sawdust which would prevent the cutter from seating properly.

The molding cutterhead is assembled on the saw arbor in the same manner as the saw blade. The guard, splitter, and anti-kickback finger assembly cannot be used when molding and must be removed from the saw (Fig. 8-1). Therefore, extra care must be taken. Also, the accessory molding cutterhead table insert must be used in place of the standard table insert.

Always turn the cutterhead manually before turning on the power to determine if (1) the head is running true and (2) all head parts clear all saw parts. Check and double-check to be absolutely sure the cutter knives are secure in the head. Read the manufacturer's mounting instructions most carefully.

Auxiliary Fence. It is necessary when using the molding cutterhead to add wood-facing to one or both sides of the rip fence. As shown in Fig. 8-2, the wood-

Fig. 8-1: The molding cutterhead in place on the arbor.

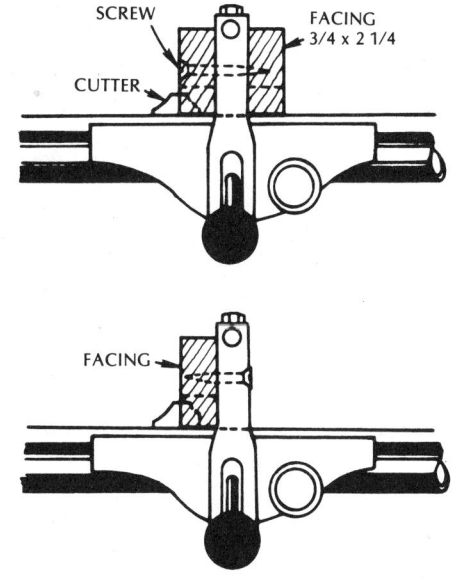

Fig. 8-2: Wood-facing attached to rip fence.

*NOTE: In order to clearly illustrate certain procedures described in this chapter, the blade guard and other safety devices have been removed. For safe operation of the table saw, guards and other safety devices must always be utilized.

facing is attached to the fence with wood screws through the holes provided in the fence. Three-quarter inch stock is suitable for most work, although an occasional job may require 1 inch facing.

The auxiliary double-faced fence illustrated in Fig. 8-3 slips over the regular rip fence and does not need to be screwed in place. Vary the dimensions, if necessary, to fit your saw.

Application of Cutters. With a molding cutterhead and an assortment of cutters, you can make an almost unlimited number of designs on both edge (or end) molding and surface decoration (like grooving with a dado head). Since most table saw molding cutters are identical with standard shaper cutters, any mold made with the same-shape cutter on the shaper can be duplicated on the table saw. In addition to

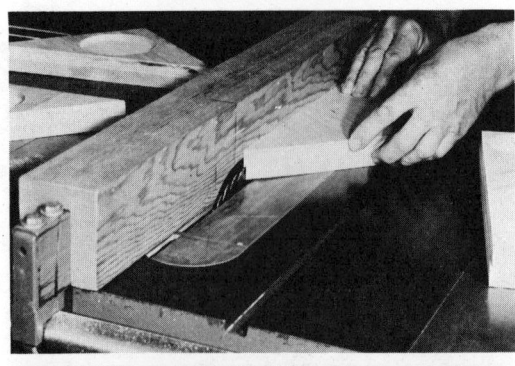

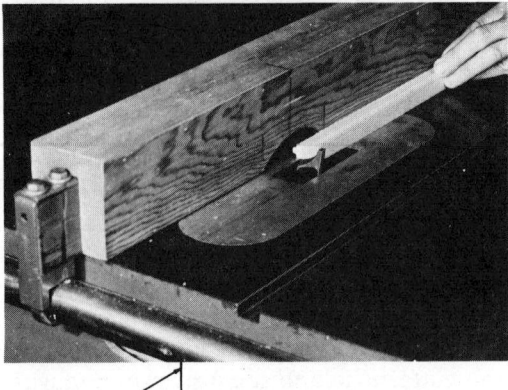

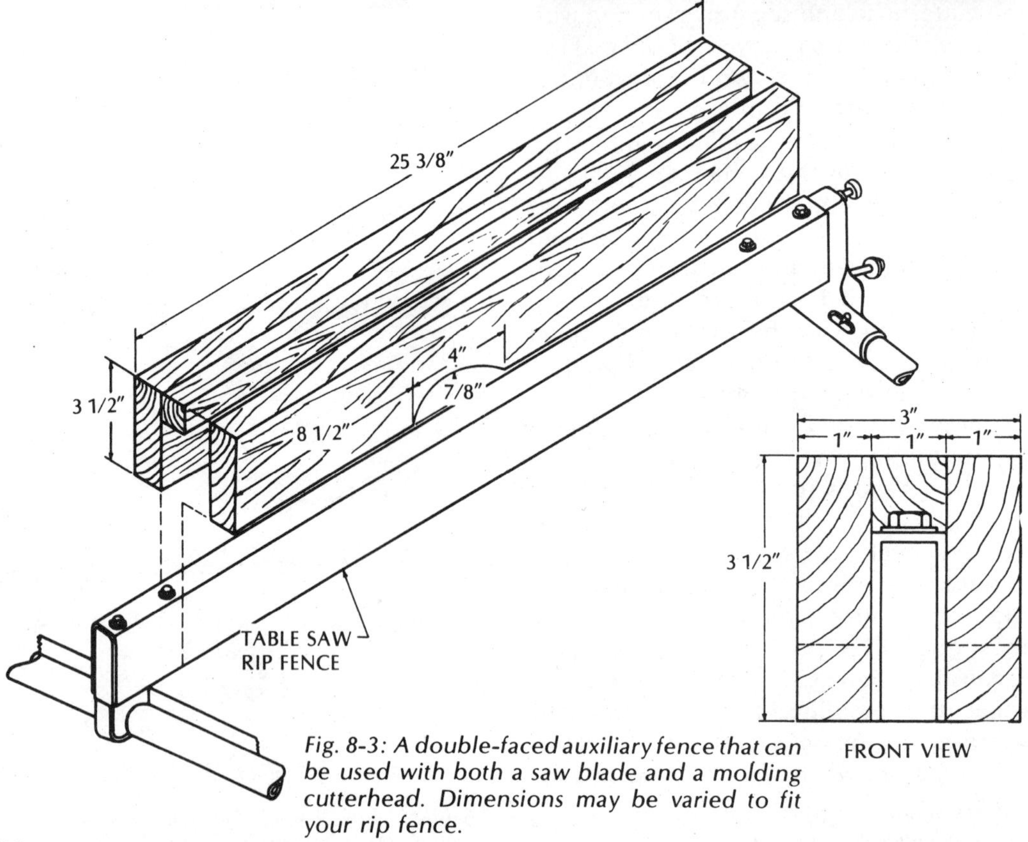

Fig. 8-3: A double-faced auxiliary fence that can be used with both a saw blade and a molding cutterhead. Dimensions may be varied to fit your rip fence.

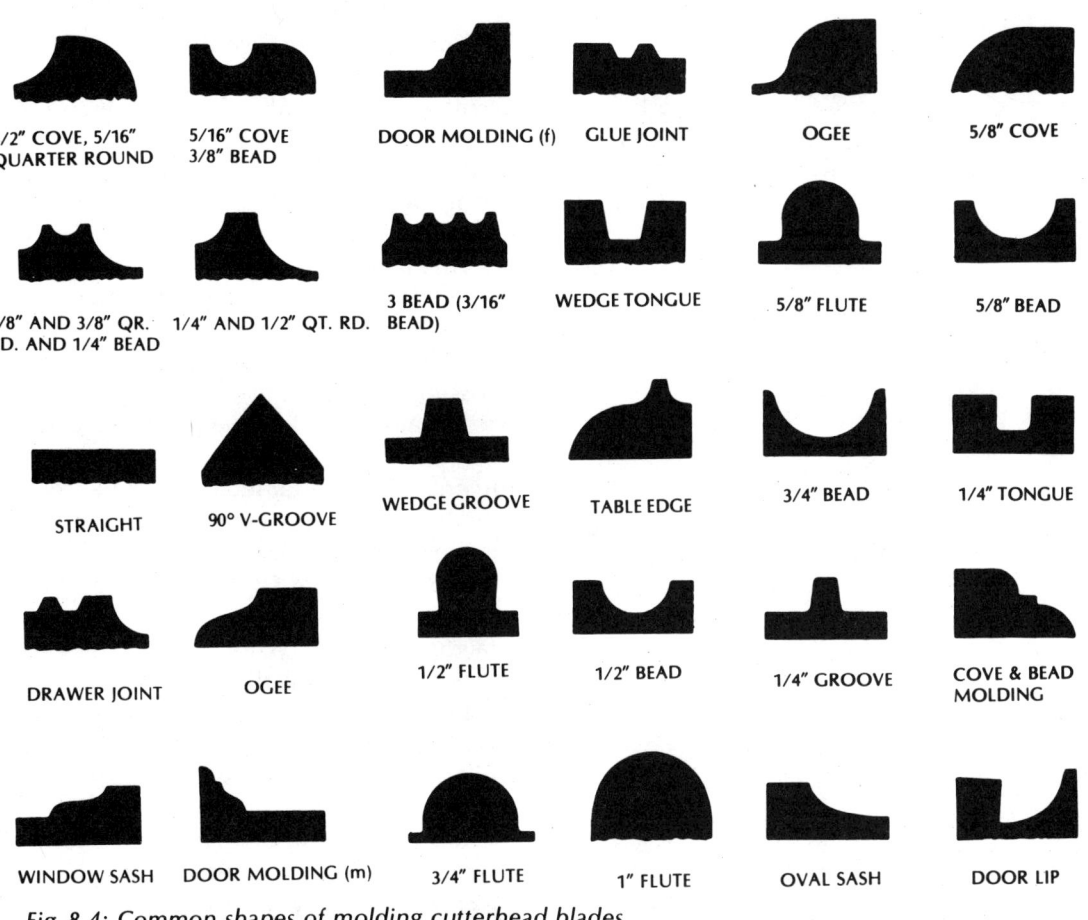

Fig. 8-4: Common shapes of molding cutterhead blades.

cutting full profile shapes (Fig. 8-4), the knives can be used for partial cuts or they can be used in combination to produce almost any original molding design.

Cutters for the cabinet-door lip, wedge tongue-and-groove glue joint, three-bead molding and so on, are designed to do a specific job and are usually set to cut the full profile. Other knives, like the 1/4- and 1/2-inch quarter-round, can be described as *combination cutters,* and they are usually set to cut a portion of the profile. This portion may constitute the entire operation, or it might be just one part of an edge that can be completed by making passes with different cutters.

Cuts can be planned to just meet, to be spaced, or to overlap (Fig. 8-5). To help in planning, it is advisable to make a file record of each cutter shape. This can be traced from a piece cut in scrap wood. The profile, or section of the profile, which fits in with the design can be marked off for reference when you make the cuts. You will find that molding knives, since many of them are classic forms, can be very useful when planning lathe turnings.

Like a dado head, the molding cutterhead removes a considerable amount of stock, so it is not wise to cut too deeply or too fast, especially in hardwoods. Deep cuts can be accomplished, but make them in stages, adjusting tool projection after each pass. If the molding cutterhead slows up or if the work begins to chatter, you are cutting too fast or too deeply. Stop feeding the workpiece, let the head attain full speed, then resume cutting at a slower

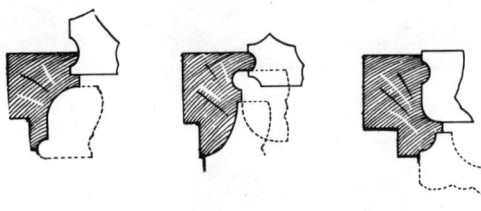

PICTURE FRAMES

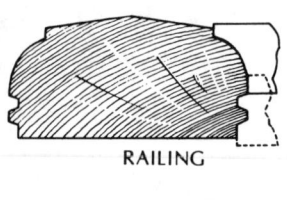

RAILING

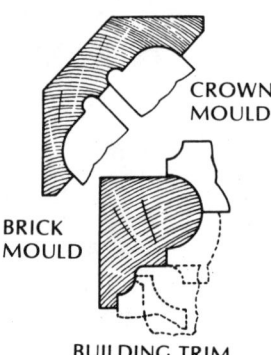

CROWN MOULD

BRICK MOULD

BUILDING TRIM

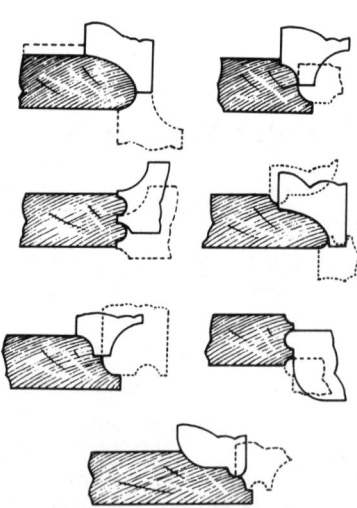

EDGES SUITABLE FOR TABLES

Fig. 8-5: Molding made with two or more cuts.

feed rate and/or reduce the depth of cut. As a general rule, it is best to limit your cuts in softwoods to depths of no more than 1/4 to 3/8 inch and to 1/8 to 1/4 inch in hardwoods.

Cuts made with the grain are always easier and smoother than cross-grain cuts. Cuts made with the grain, whether they are at the edge or somewhere along the width of the work, are made like rip cuts, with the work riding the rip or auxiliary fence. Cross-grain cuts are usually made with the work against the miter gauge if the stock is narrow in width. If it is 6 inches or wider, the end or cross-grained cuts can be made exactly the same as with the grain, using the auxiliary fence to guide the workpiece.

Molding Straight Edges. A large portion of all work done with the molding cutters is straight line work. Where the cut is along the side of the work, the operation is much the same as using a saw or dado head, the fence being adjusted to the proper width while the cutterhead is adjusted to the right height. Work can be shaped flat on the table (Fig. 8-6), or it can be stood on edge and fed into the cutter (Fig. 8-7).

Fig. 8-6: Molding cut flat on the table.

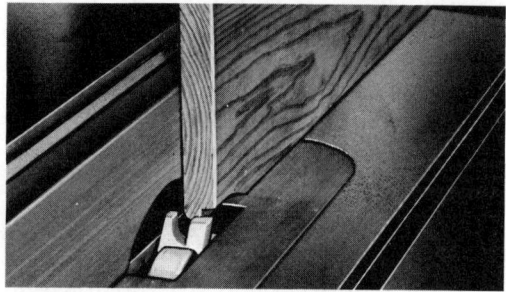

Fig. 8-7: Molding cut on edge.

The cut should always be made on the side nearest the fence since it is not then affected by variations in the width of the stock. A hold-down clamped to the auxiliary fence will prevent the work from lifting or bouncing, and will assure a uniform depth of cut.

Molding End Grain. When molding end grain, use is made of the miter gauge. As in crosscutting with the shaper or jointer, the feed should be slowed down at the end of the cut to prevent splintering. Where the mold is completely around the piece, the ends should be worked first so that the final with-the-grain cuts will remove any splintered edges. For all cuts, attention should be given to the grain. Make the cut in the same direction as the grain whenever possible.

Strip Moldings. The usual manner of working strip moldings is to mold the edge of a wider board, and then rip off the molded portion. Another method is to use a strip jig (Fig. 8-8). The jig is made according to the drawing, the channel opening being of the required height and width to accommodate the work. The piece which is bradded to the main body of the jig is cut away at the center to permit the passage of the knives. In use, the jig is clamped against the saw fence, and the strips are run through. A cloverleaf molding, such as the one used on screen doors, can be cut with one pass of the work with the proper knife. Moldings which require combination cuts are run through the jig as often as necessary to produce the needed shape.

Table Inserts. When cutting certain moldings which require only a small portion of the knives to project above the table, it is best to make a special wooden table insert piece which fits up close to the knives. Such an insert is usually necessary when molding thin work on edge to prevent the stock from dropping into the opening around the cutterhead. Inserts are made from plywood to the required shape to fit the table opening. With the wooden insert clamped in place, the machine is started and the molding cutterhead gradually raised so that the knives will cut their own opening in the insert.

Caution. *Do not attempt to hold the insert in place with your hand as you make this cut.* The cutterhead should be elevated a scant fraction of an inch further than necessary in order to give the cutter clearance, after which the cutterhead is again lowered to the level required for the work.

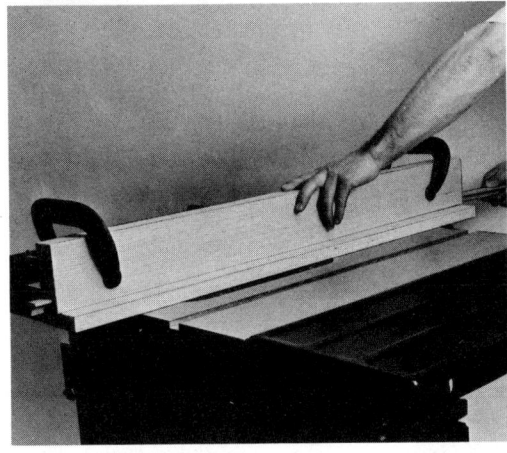

Fig. 8-8: The strip jig is used when making large quantities of any particular molding, especially a clover-leaf mold.

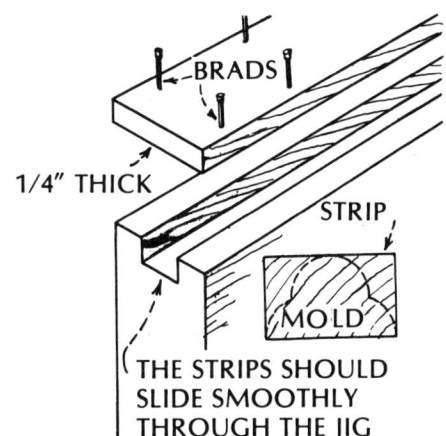

RABBETING

Rabbeting is done easily and quickly with a straight knife. This method is a great deal easier than making two saw cuts, and is especially useful for shallow cuts (Fig. 8-9A).

Fig. 8-9: Straight knife set-up used for shallow rabbets and tenons.

TENON CUTTING

Straight knives in the molding cutterhead offer a quick and clean method of cutting tenons. Tenons up to 1-inch wide can be made in one pass of the work (Fig. 8-9B), while longer tenons are cut by simply walking across the work to the width desired. Where more than one cut is to be made, the first cut should be made on the inside to form the shoulder.

PANEL RAISING

With the saw arbor slightly tilted, the same application of straight knives as for tenoning will enable the operator to do panel raising. One, two, or three cuts can be made entirely around the work in order to make up any required panel. As in other cuts where the work is molded all around, the end cuts should be run in first so that the final cuts with the grain will clean up the work.

CUTTING DOWELS

Dowels of various diameters can be cut with standard molding cutters. Figure 8-10 shows the 3/8-inch size being cut. The stock should be about 1/32 inch more than 3/8 inch thick. A cut is first made on one side of the piece after which the work is turned over for the final cut on the opposite side. A light edge will be left connecting the dowel with the main body of the work. This is easily broken off with the fingers.

GLUE JOINTS

Glue joints are made with the knife illustrated in Fig. 8-11. This knife makes both cuts for the joint, the shape of the cutter being such that the tongue and the groove fit perfectly by reversing the stock. To get good results, the setup must be very accurate. The guide fence must be set so that the centerline of the work is exactly in line with the centerline of the knives. The cutterhead must be adjusted so that the lowest cutting part of the knives will just touch the stock lightly. After these adjustments have been made, two pieces of scrap stock which are the same thickness should be run over the knives. After cutting, one piece is reversed end for end and fitted over the other piece. The joint should fit perfectly. If one side projects more than the other, make the necessary adjustments to center the joint. Do not make any glue joint in this manner without first checking the setup on scrap stock. If not properly adjusted, one piece will be offset from the other, necessitating the job of resurfacing.

CUTTING COVES

Oblique feed with molding head knives produces large cove moldings of exceptional smoothness. The maximum depth of

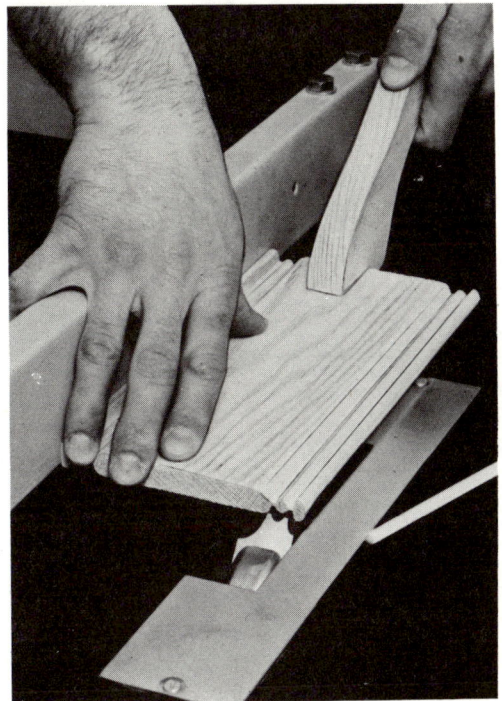

Fig. 8-10: Cutting dowels on the table saw.

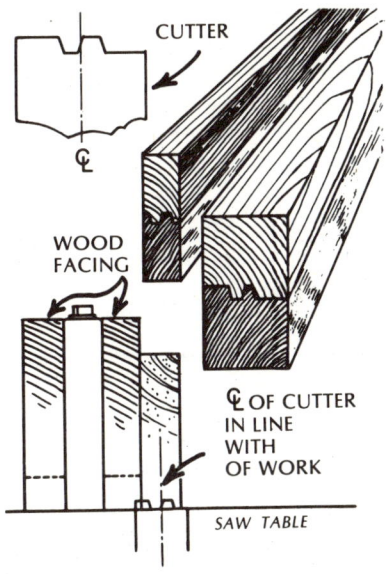

Fig. 8-11: The accurate setting of the fence is essential for making good glue joints.

cut is about 11/16 inch. The width of the cove is controlled by the angle of feed. In Fig. 8-12, the smallest cove was cut with a 1/2 inch knife in the usual position, that is, straight into the cutter. The mold is 1 inch wide—the full width of the cutter being used. The middle sample was cut with a 30-degree feed. The depth is the same as before, but the width of cut is increased to about 1 1/4 inches. With a 60-degree feed, the width of the cove increases to about 1 5/8 inches. This is the maximum width. All cuts can be made in one pass, although two passes would be preferable if working on dense cabinet woods. After cove cutting, the molded portion can be ripped on the saw to any width.

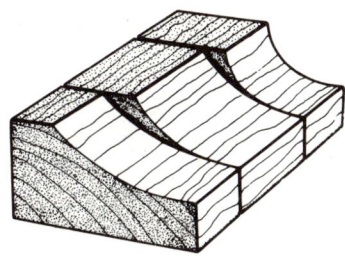

Fig. 8-12: Three different size coves.

DRAWER JOINT

Although several drawer joints were discussed in Chapter 7, the drawer joint made with a molding cutterhead is one of the best (Fig. 8-13). To cut the front of the drawer, mount the work in a tenoning jig (Fig. 8-14). Set the cutterhead with paper washers (Fig. 8-15), so that the knives will cut an approximate 1/8 inch lip when the workpiece is mounted alongside the jig baseplate. Use a backing block behind the work, making sure to set the cutting depth to the thickness of the side stock. The dimensions for the front overhang are given in Fig. 8-16.

To cut the sides, set the workpiece against the stop so that the mark on the knife (Fig. 8-17) is exactly in line with the end of the work. Use a backing block to prevent tearing. Remember that the miter gauge (Fig. 8-18) must be set at an exact 90-degrees.

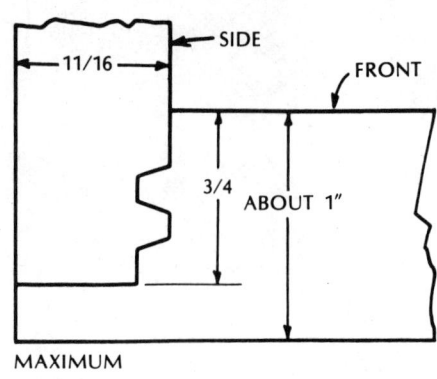

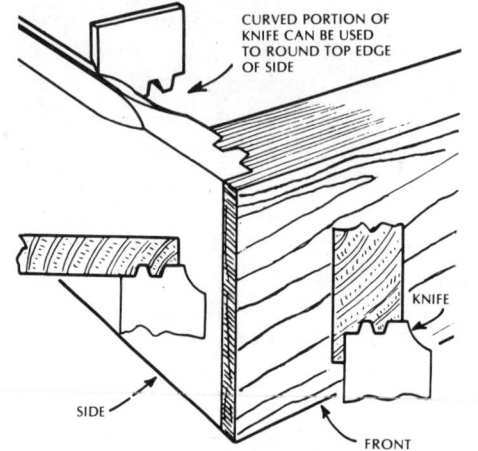

Fig. 8-13: General construction of drawer cut with a molding cutterhead.

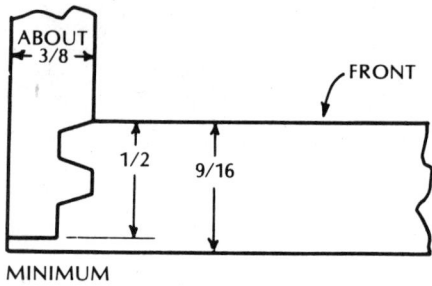

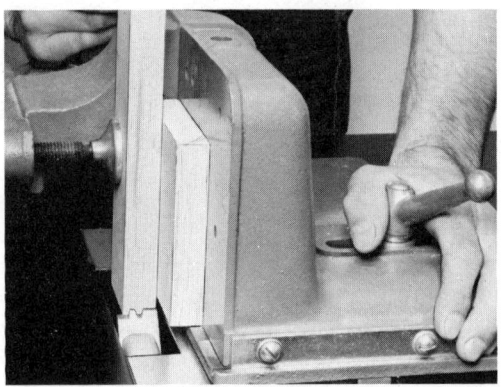

Fig. 8-14: Holding the work in a tenoning jig.

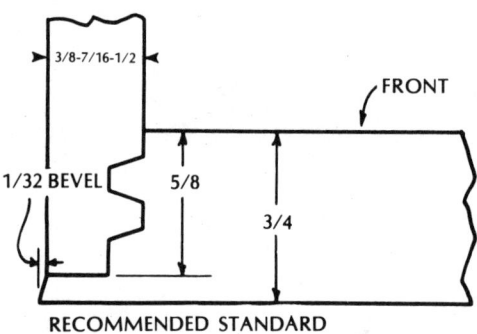

Fig. 8-15: Installing washers.

Fig. 8-16: Work dimensions.

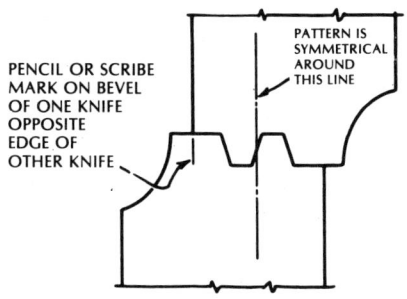

Fig. 8-17: Match the two knives as shown above, and make a mark on one knife.

Fig. 8-18: Use the miter gauge when cutting side pieces.

JOINTING AND PLANING

Where a jointer is not available, good jointing and planing can be done with straight knives in the molding head. To joint an edge, clamp the work to a guide board known to have a true edge. The work should be entirely inside the straight edge, as shown in Fig. 8-19. The work is advanced to the knives, as illustrated in Fig. 8-20. It can be seen that the straight edge serves as a guide and insures an accurate edge on the work. The cutterhead should be set so that a small rabbet is cut in the guide board at the same time as the operation is being done. In the planing operation, runners are nailed to each edge of the work, as in Fig. 8-21. As in the jointing operation, the work surface must be entirely inside the projection of the runners, as indicated by the straight edge across the work in Fig. 8-22. The first cut is

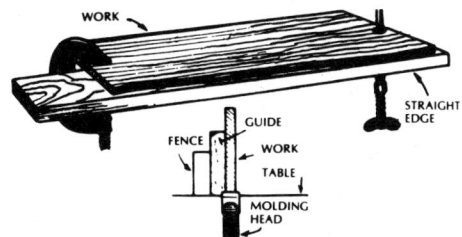

Fig. 8-19: Guide board arrangement for jointing an edge.

Fig. 8-20: The edge jointing operation.

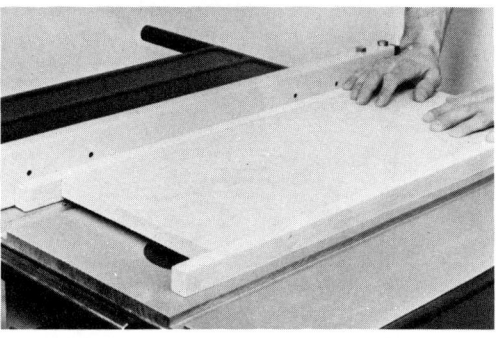

Fig. 8-21: Planing a board with straight molding cutterhead knives.

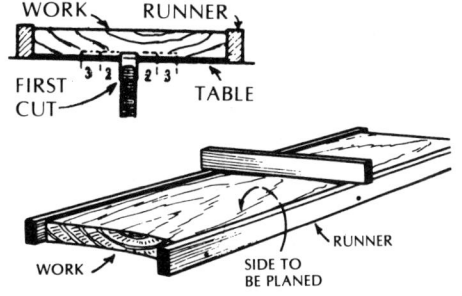

Fig. 8-22: Guide board arrangement for planing. Numbers represent order of cuts.

made at the center of the work, then successive cuts are taken on either side by setting the fence more than 1 inch for each new cut. When the surface being planed is true and smooth, the runners are not required since a narrow strip of uncut wood at either side will serve the same purpose. If the board is evenly warped, it can be worked without runners. However, if there is a twist in the work or unequal warping, the runners must be nailed in place.

ORNAMENTAL MOLDINGS

A wide variety of ornamental moldings giving the appearance of hand-carved work can be made with molding cutters. Typical examples are shown in Fig. 8-23. The work is simply a repetition of any suitable molding cut, the cuts being spaced by means of a guide pin or guide board. A guide board makes the best setup because many of the shapes cannot be spaced accurately with a pin set to the work itself. Figure 8-24 is an example of a bead molding cut with a bead molding cutter. The guide board is a separate saw cut strip, made as described on page 59 and nailed to the edge of the work. The saw kerfs should be spaced a strong 5/8 inch apart for this particular cutter, as shown in Fig. 8-25. The guide pin is a nail driven in the miter-gauge faceboard, as can be seen in Fig. 8-24. The pin can be located at any position because the spacing is determined by the guide board and not by the work itself. It is obvious how the cuts are made, being merely a matter of cutting and spacing until the full length of work is machined. The projection of the cutter should be high enough to assure a full round.

After the wide molding is complete, it can be ripped into suitable strips and further ornamented, if desired, by running molding cuts lengthwise on the strip in the ordinary manner. In Fig. 8-23, molding C is a thin slice of the bead shape. Shapes D, E, G, and L are thicker slices with lengthwise

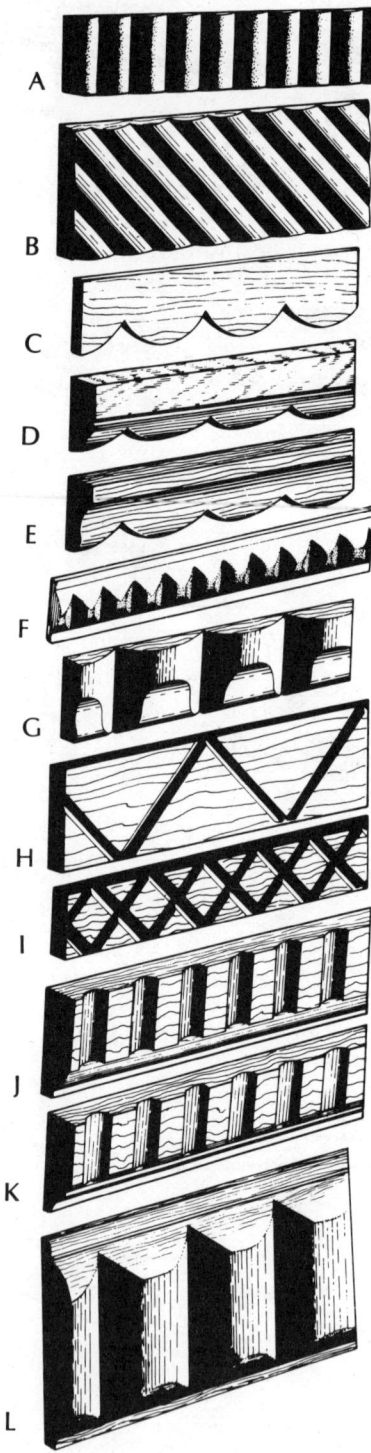

Fig. 8-23: Various ornamental moldings.

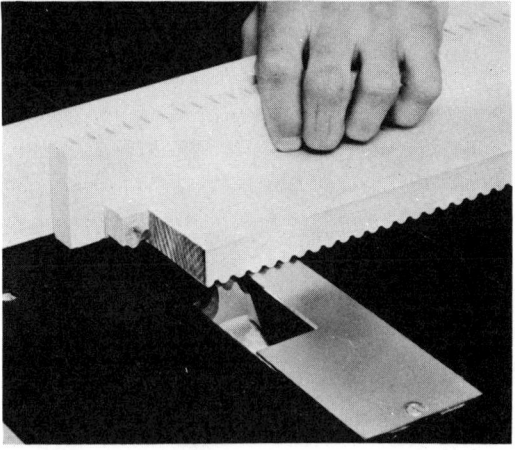

Fig. 8-24: Using repeat cuts set by a guide board.

molding cuts added. Molding B is a small bead shape cut with the miter gauge at 45 degrees. Molding F is a small bead shape with the same cut returned along the edges to produce a rounded diamond similar to a sharp diamond as produced with a flute cutter. Molding H is worked with the flute cutter. I, J, and K are cut with the cove-flute cutter, and a running molding added at the bottom. All molds shown are worked in the same general manner; that is, first a wide strip is formed and then it is ripped into suitable narrow moldings.

Another method of using the guide board is to fasten it to the top of the work, as illustrated in Fig. 8-26. This type of guide board is especially useful for production work since it is not touched by the molding cutter. Each edge of the guide board can have a different spacing of saw cuts to suit some specific molding.

Molding cutters must be sharp for this type of work because the work involves cross-grain cutting. Like other cuts of this nature, the end of the cut will tend to splinter out, especially when the guide-on-top method is used, since this method does not offer a fresh backing for each cut.

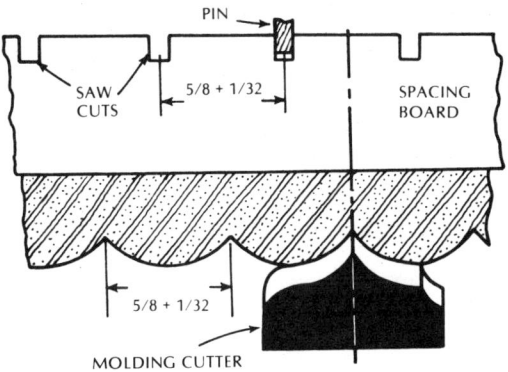

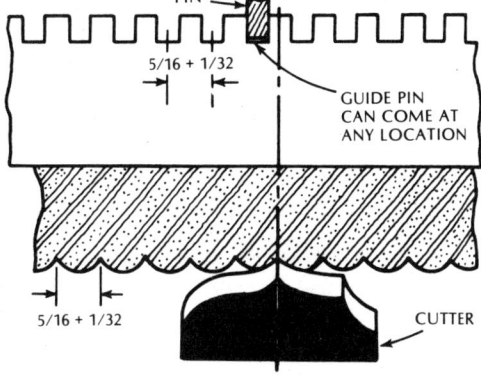

Fig. 8-25: Diagram of bead moldings.

105

Another method of spacing which is sometimes useful for occasional work is a waste board, as illustrated in Fig. 8-27. After each molding is cut, the waste board is run over the jointer to slice off 1/4 inch or whatever spacing is needed. Other set-ups can be made with stops and spacing strips. As well as making moldings, the same general methods described can be used for working up imitation carved panel effects, the only difference being the size of the work. When combined with ornamental cuts run on the drill press and shaper, the possibilities are almost endless.

A necessary safety measure when handling small work is using a special wood insert let into the saw table to provide full support for the work (see page 99).

Fig. 8-26: Guide board on top of the work.

Fig. 8-27: Spacing molding cuts with the use of a waste board.

Chapter 9

OTHER USES OF THE TABLE SAW *

Two types of abrasive wheels—the cutoff wheel and the sanding disk—will make a table saw even more useful in your shop.

CUTOFF WHEEL

Cutoff or abrasive wheels can be used for cutting metals, tile, brick, porcelain, and other materials. The wheel commonly used is reinforced, resin bonded, 8 inches in diameter and 3/32 inch thick. Nonreinforced wheels tend to be brittle and should never be used. The feed should be firm and continuous to prevent glazing of the wheel. On the other hand, the work should not be forced too strongly since this will greatly shorten wheel life by tearing the abrasive grains from the bond before they have done their full share of cutting. Because cutoff wheels are mounted on the saw arbor as a saw blade, the guard should be used. Be sure the area is properly ventilated.

Cutting Thin-Wall Tubing. One of the most common uses of the abrasive cutoff wheel on the circular saw is the cutting of thin-wall tubing to exact lengths. In this operation, it is advisable to hold the tubing in a suitable V-block, the block being held to the miter gauge by means of the miter-gauge clamp attachment, as shown in Fig. 9-1A. The tubing can project beyond the block, or the block may be cut away partially to permit the passage of the wheel. As in similar operations in cutting wood, various stop blocks and stop rods can be used to gauge accurately the exact length.

Cutting Solid Stock. Solid metal or other stock in bars or sheets is cut to size with cutoff wheels in much the same manner as wood is cut with the table saw. Some form

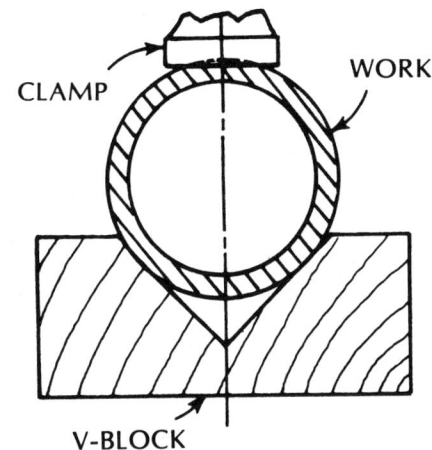

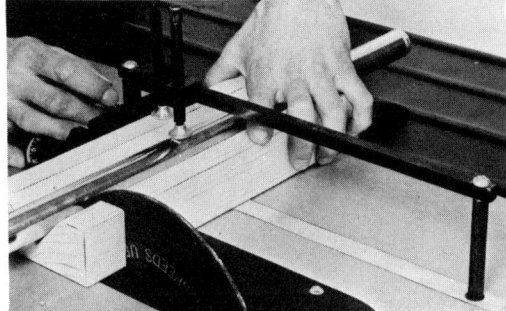

A

B

Fig. 9-1: (A) Cutting thin-wall steel tubing with an abrasive wheel; (B) truing a wheel with an abrasive stick.

---

*NOTE: In order to clearly illustrate certain procedures described in this chapter, the blade guard and other safety devices have been removed. For safe operation of the table saw, guards and other safety devices must always be utilized.

of guide is always necessary. Also, since heavy material will become quite hot some distance from the point of cutting, it is necessary to use clamps or other devices to hold and feed the work.

When cutting masonry materials, it is advisable to score 1/8 inch deep with the cutoff wheel, then break clean with a mason's hammer or a brick chisel.

True Wheels Essential. A balanced wheel with a clean edge is necessary for successful cutting. If the wheel should get a little out of round, it will start to vibrate. This will result in a cut considerably wider than the thickness of the wheel. Wheel life is shortened, and precision cutting off is impossible. If the wheel should get out of round or chip, it can be brought to a true edge with the use of a suitable abrasive stick (Fig. 9-1B).

SANDING DISK

Your table saw can be converted into an excellent disk sander by mounting a sanding-disk attachment in place of the saw blade. Two different grit sandpaper disks can be cemented to the wheel sides, for versatility. The standard table insert on some saws must be replaced with a special one designed for using a sanding disk (Fig. 9-2). The blade guard is not used with the sanding disk.

The abrasive used on the disk will depend upon the work. Garnet can be used for all types of woods (both soft and hard). The abrasive can be somewhat coarser than that used for surfacing. A 60 grit disk cuts rapidly to a fairly smooth surface. Do finish sanding with a 120 grit disk so that abrasive scratches will not show. The abrasive paper is mounted on the disk attachment as directed by the manufacturer of the paper.

Operating the Disk Sander. Sanding work to be done on the disk sander can be fed freehand, can be guided with the miter gauge, or can be fed along the rip fence. In all cases, however, the feed should never be forced (the paper will clog and burn). Gently engage the moving disk, applying only enough pressure to keep the abrasive cutting. In other words, a smooth, light feed should be practiced. Avoid heavy pressure. Remember sanding is done on the "down" side of the disk; working on the opposite side would lift the work from the table and also throw dust up into the operator's face.

When you are sanding edges longer than the diameter of the disk, take particu-

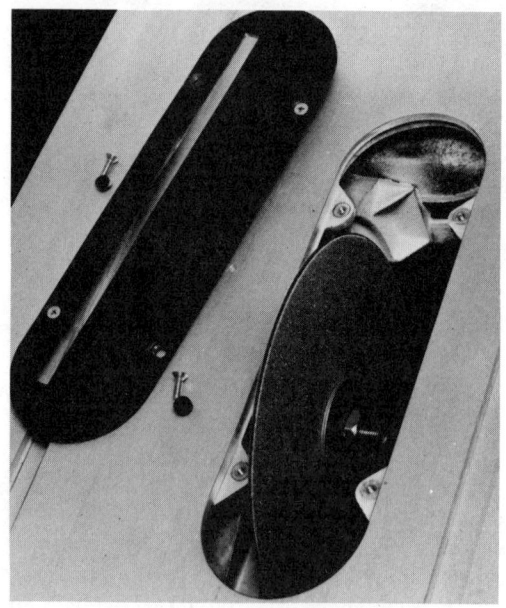

Fig. 9-2: Sanding disk in place on table saw.

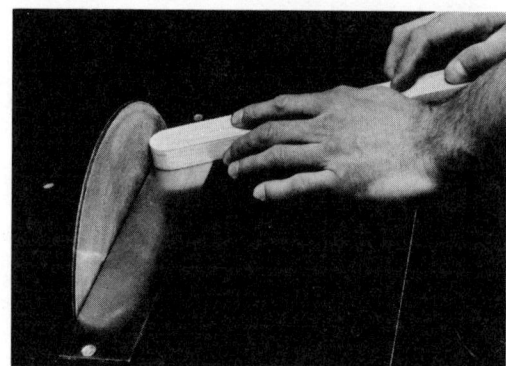

Fig. 9-3: Feeding work into sanding disk.

lar care to prevent the disk edge from digging into the work. The best approach is to start the end of the workpiece at the down side of the disk and, with gentle pressure, feed the full length across the face (Fig. 9-3). Keep the work moving at all times when it is in contact with the abrasive.

A miter gauge can be used to advantage when sanding square or mitered ends. Where miters are being sanded, the preferred position is as shown in Fig. 9-4A. This position permits better handling than the reverse position shown in Fig. 9-4B. Square ends are sanded by moving the work along the miter gauge until it contacts the disk (Fig. 9-4C). Sanding to exact length can be done by presetting a stop rod at the required distance. The rod is free to slide into the hole at the end of the gauge. The exact length is set when the rod comes to a stop at the bottom of the hole.

Circular work should always be sanded with the use of a pivot jig. Top and bottom views of a simple jig for this task are shown in Fig. 9-5. The cleat on the underside slides in the miter-gauge slot of the saw table. The dovetail sliding strip of the jig can be set at any position. It is locked into place by pushing down on the locking arm, the end of which works like a cam. In use, the work is first band-sawed to shape, after which it is mounted on the pivot point. The sliding strip is locked at the required distance from the sanding disk. Pushing the table into the disk sets the cut, and the rotation finishes the entire edge to a perfectly circular shape. The jig can be clamped to the table or simply held with one hand while the other hand rotates the work.

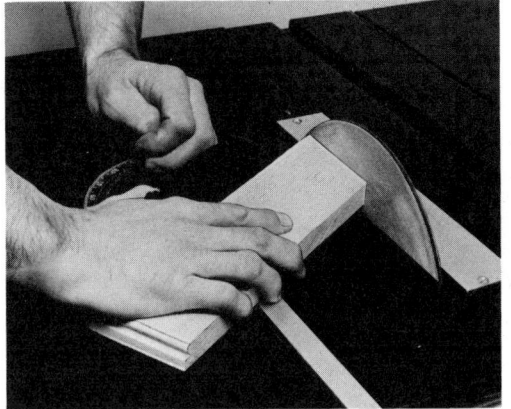

A

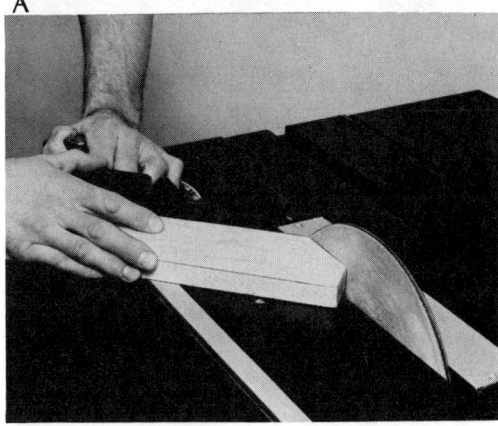

B

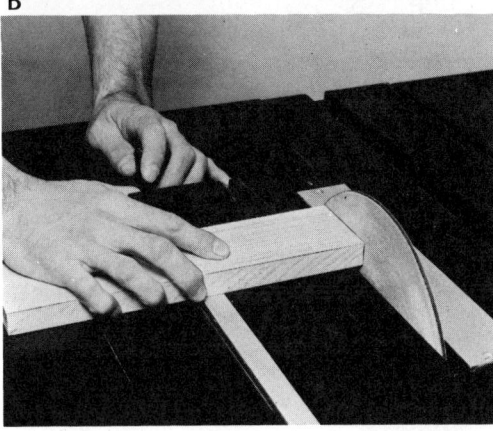

C

Fig. 9-4: Disk sanding using a miter gauge.

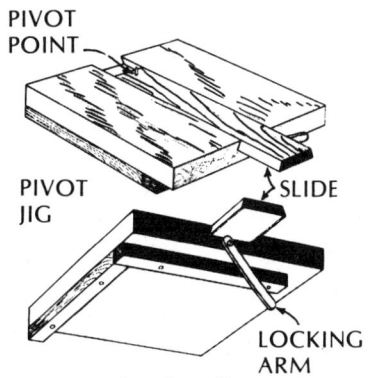

Fig. 9-5: Views of a pivot jig.

109

Any other style of pivot jig will work equally well. The simplest setup is a brad driven into a board which is clamped to the table at the required distance from the sanding disk (Fig. 9-6).

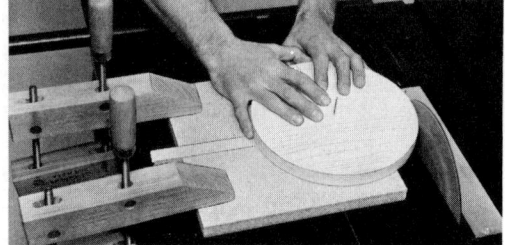

Fig. 9-6: Simple pivot jig in use.

The sanding of corners is allied to circular work in that the edge being worked is part of a true circle. Most work of this nature can be done freehand, by sweeping the corner of the work across the face of the sanding disk two or three times until the desired round is obtained. More accurate results are possible if the pivot jig (Fig. 9-5) is used in the manner illustrated in Fig. 9-7. The sliding strip is first locked in place at the required distance from the face of the sanding disk. A pencil mark is then drawn on the table of the jig. This mark is the same distance from the pivot point as the pivot point is from the sanding disk, as shown in Fig. 9-7A. The work is placed against a guide fastened to the rear edge of the jig, as illustrated in Fig. 9-7B, and is brought down on the pivot point in alignment with the pencil mark. Rotating the work rounds the corner (Fig. 9-7C). Figure 9-7D shows how the jig table can be marked with pencil lines as a guide in placing work of any radius.

In production work, a pattern can be used to ensure perfect sanding. A thin but rigid strip of metal is screw-fastened to one side of a wooden table. The table is clamped in place over the regular table, as shown in Fig. 9-8. The guiding edge of the metal strip should be about 1/8 inch from the surface of the sanding disk, and the pattern should be made 1/8 inch undersize to correspond. Anchor points permit fastening the pattern to the work, after which the work is band-sawed about 3/16 inch outside the edge of the pattern. The work is then sanded smooth, the pattern being held in contact with the metal guide as the work is moved into the sanding disk.

Metals and plastics are finished on the disk sander in practically the same way as wood, except that an aluminum-oxide abrasive disk must be used.

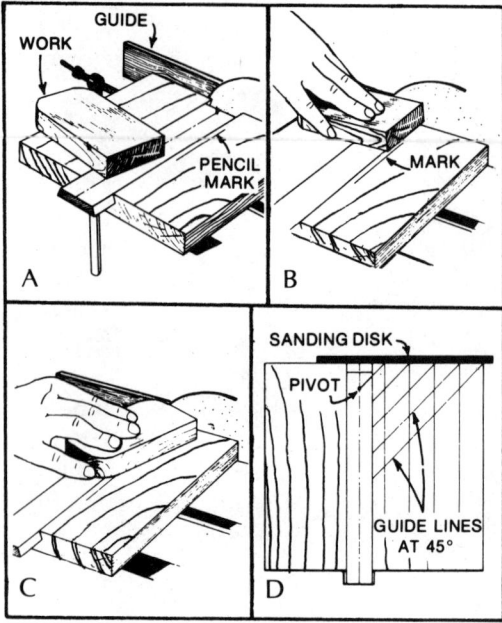

Fig. 9-7: Method of round corners.

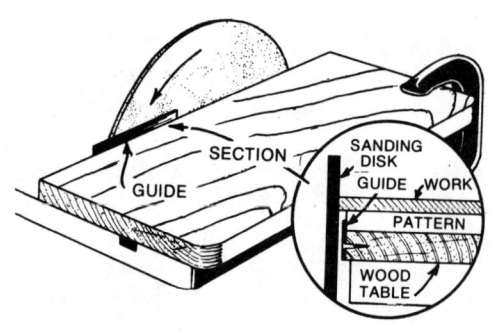

Fig. 9-8: Sanding with the use of a pattern.

Chapter 10

SHARPENING SAW BLADES

Today, blade sharpening in the home workshop hardly pays because the professionals do an excellent job at reasonable prices. But, for the purist who wishes to do everything, this chapter describes how to sharpen your own saw blades.

The sharpening operation of a table saw blade may be divided into four parts—jointing, gumming, setting, and filing. All these operations, however, need not be done every time a saw needs sharpening. Since all the teeth on a saw blade are subject to the same amount of wear, a worn blade will have no teeth to serve as original patterns. It is therefore a good idea to make a paper pattern of each new saw blade that you acquire (Fig. 10-1). Note the tooth set data on the pattern, and keep it for reference when sharpening the blade.

JOINTING

Jointing means bringing the point of every tooth to exactly the same distance from the center or arbor hole in the saw. This is generally not required until the blade has been filed several times, and the length of the teeth may have become unequal.

Reverse the saw blade on the arbor so that it runs backwards. Lower the blade so that it is below the table. Place a medium-grit oilstone in place as illustrated in Fig. 10-2. Turn on the saw and while firmly holding the stone down, carefully raise the blade until its teeth just scrape the stone. The miter gauge with an auxiliary face can be used to help keep the stone from moving. This causes plenty of sparks to fly, indicating that the points of the teeth are

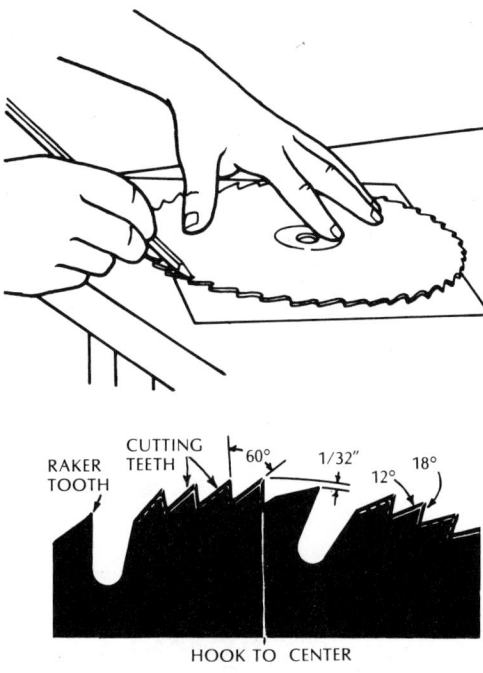

Fig. 10-1: Make a pattern of each new saw blade.

being ground down. Stop the saw after a few seconds and examine the points of the teeth while revolving the saw by hand. When every tooth has a bright spot on its point, the jointing operation has been completed. If some of the teeth have not been touched by the sharpening stone, raise the blade a little and repeat the process.

GUMMING

Gumming means increasing the depth of the gullets between the teeth to carry the

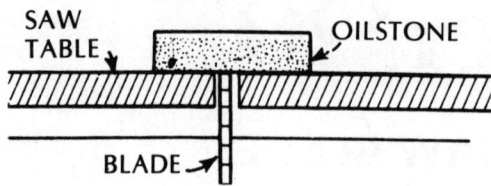

Fig. 10-2: The jointing process.

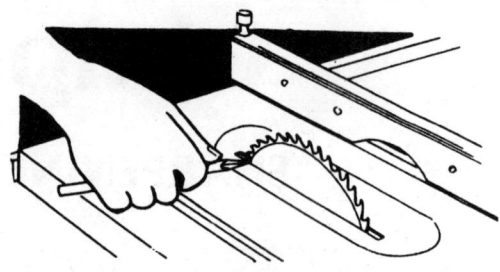

Fig. 10-3: The gumming process.

sawdust away. It is usually necessary to do this after a blade has been jointed, since that operation shortens the teeth and makes the gullets shallower. Also, when checking the blade against its pattern and if the gullets have decreased more than 1/16 of the original, the blade must be gummed. A poorly shaped gullet can quickly cause a blade to crack.

With the blade on the arbor, mark a pencil line on the side of the saw blade so that all the gullets may be filed to the same depth. To do this, rotate the blade by hand while the pencil is held as shown in Fig. 10-3. Then remove the blade from the saw and place the blade in a special saw vise (Fig. 10-4).

To make this vise, use a 1- by 6-inch board rounded at one end and bored to admit a 5/8-inch bolt. Make a short front jaw, boring it to match and hinging it to the first board. With a blade held between the jaws by the bolt, the vise can be clamped against any suitable support or in a bench

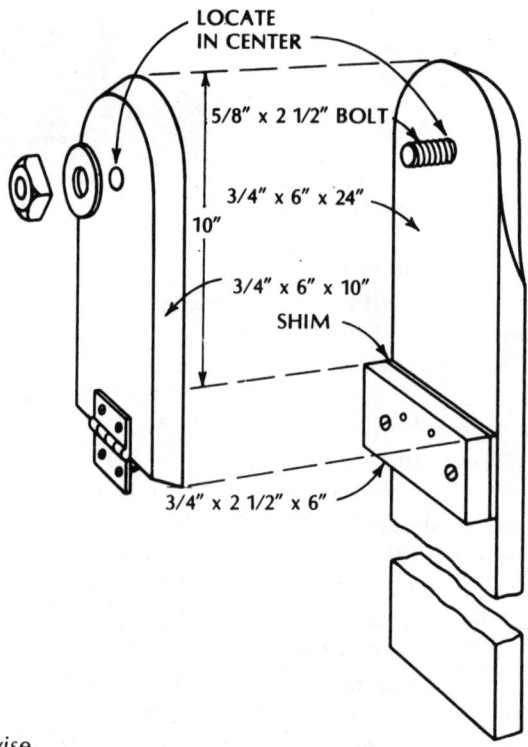

Fig. 10-4: A saw-filing vise.

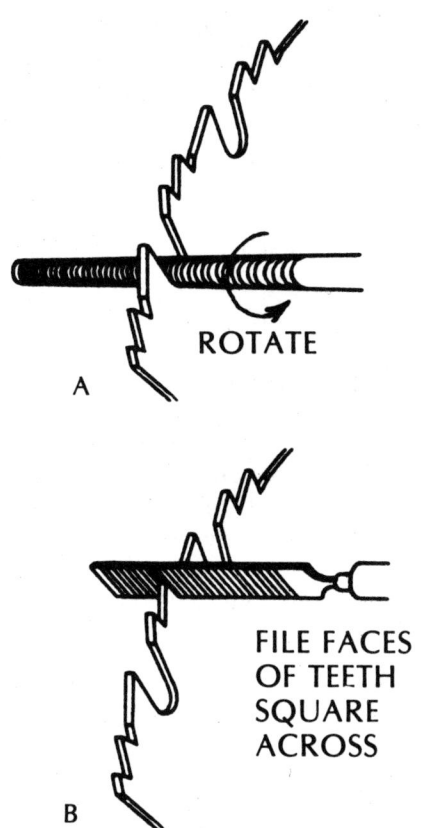

Fig. 10-5: Filing the saw's teeth.

vise while the blade is filed. Be sure the saw vise is held rigidly enough to prevent chatter during filing.

Before starting to file, clean the gullets with a rattail file or the tang of another file (Fig. 10-5A). Holding the rounded edge of the file down, file the gullets to the depth of the line. The remaining teeth should be filed, as per the original pattern (Fig. 10-5B). The angle of the front of each tooth, called the rake, must be maintained when gumming a saw. To find the rake, mark a circle on the saw blade halfway between its center and its edge, and draw a line from the front of any one of the teeth tangent to this circle.

Shape the corresponding teeth all around in sequence. Then do the remaining teeth in sequence. This equalizes any stresses set up in the blade by filing. Do all filing straight across (no beveling) until the jointing flats have disappeared and the teeth have the correct shapes. When gumming or shaping round gullets, rotate the file slightly while stroking to follow the contour.

For crosscut teeth, use a 6- to 8-inch fine-slim, extra-slim, or double extra-slim taper file, as required by the tooth size. For round gullets use a 6- to 10-inch fine round or rattail file. For all other needs, use a 7- to 12-inch fine mill file.

SETTING

Setting a saw means to bend some teeth to one side and others to the opposite side. All blades except those which are hollow-ground and those which are swaged must be set. When a saw is properly set, it cuts a kerf or groove wide enough for the blade to go through without binding. In other words, the saw cuts "freely" without binding.

To accomplish this, a setting jig (Fig. 10-6) should be made, as follows. Use a 5/8-inch bolt to fasten the blade to a block of wood screwed to a base block that holds the anvil. The anvil is also a bolt with half of its head beveled to the angle of set. To set a rip-saw blade, adjust it so that each tooth projects one-third over the beveled part of the anvil. Mark a tooth that has been bent away from you with a piece of chalk, place it on the anvil, hold a flat-ended punch on it, and strike a blow with a hammer (Fig. 10-7). Skip the next tooth, but set the following one as before and continue setting every other tooth until the one with the chalk mark has been reached. Now, reverse the saw on the setting jig and set those teeth which were skipped before. Be sure not to set more than one-half the length of the teeth or more than one-half the tooth thickness, because a saw can cut itself free only with the points of its teeth. Also, if the teeth are set too much, the saw offers resistance

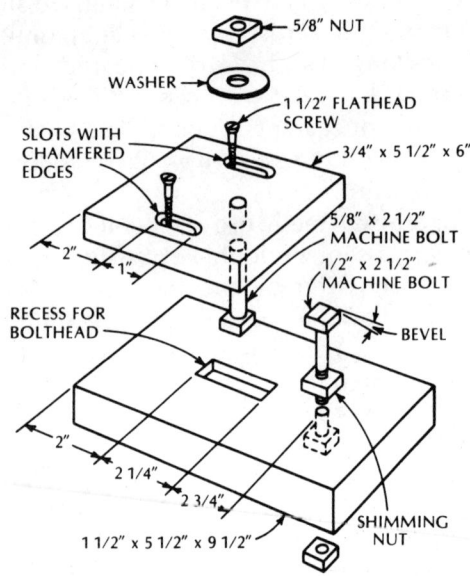

Fig. 10-6: A setting jig.

To file a *rip blade*, begin by filing the front edge of each tooth square to its sides, (If the saw has just been gummed, this operation will have been done in the gumming process.) Then, file the top edges of the teeth. Start on a tooth set away from you and file it so that its top edge is in line with the original pattern. File the teeth straight across. If a good deal of material has to be filed away after a joining operation, go over the saw twice to be sure that all the flat points have disappeared.

A *planer* or *hollow-ground blade* has groups of four crosscut teeth with a rip or raker tooth between. The raker is filed square 1/64 to 1/32 inch shorter than the others and is not set. As the fronts and backs of the teeth must be filed separately, a cant file—a triangular file with two sides

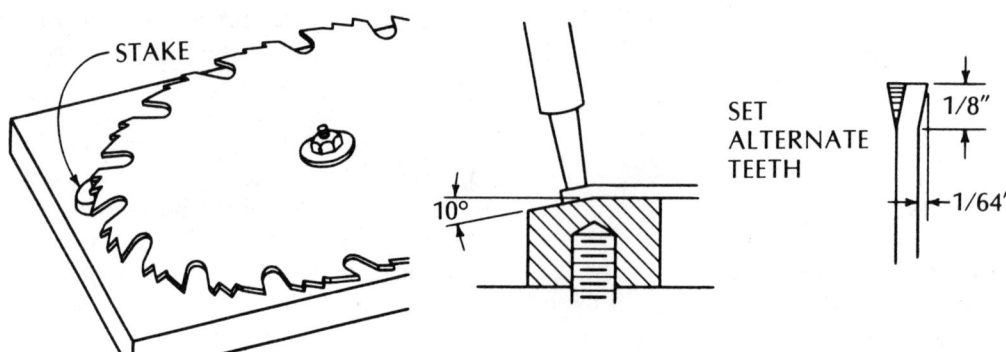

Fig. 10-7: The setting process.

to the wood and does not cut as well. The set should be maximal for soft, resinous woods or for fast, rough cutting and minimal for hard, dry woods or extra-smooth cutting. Thin-rim blades have a very slight tooth set for extra-smooth and less wasteful cuts. Hollow-ground blade teeth have no set.

FILING

This is the final sharpening operation and is done while the blade is held in the filing vise. Use the same files for gumming.

longer than the third—should be used. If an ordinary taper or blunt saw file must be used, be careful to press only on the tooth being sharpened. Test the saw after filing it by making a shallow cut across the grain of a piece of waste wood. If the cut is not smooth, the raker teeth are too long. When the cut is right, it should be flat on the bottom, but two fine parallel lines should be scored by the crosscut teeth.

A *combination blade* is filed in the same way as a hollow-ground blade except that the crosscut teeth are beveled on alternate sides, the fronts 18 degrees, the backs 12 degrees, with the fronts radial.

DADO HEAD

When sharpening a dado head observe the following:

1. If the spurs (or cross-cut teeth) need jointing, the two outside cutters should be placed on the arbor as shown in Fig. 10-8A and an oilstone should be located over the dado table insert as shown in Fig. 10-8B. Holding the stone in place, the spurs are jointed by turning the arbor by hand. *Be sure the machine is disconnected from its power source.*

2. The rakers are jointed by a crosswise motion, after raising the saw arbor 1/64 inch (Fig. 10-9). The inside cutters are jointed at the same setting as the rakers.

3. When setting spurs, use the setting stake and set all spurs in one group in the same direction as shown in Fig. 10-10. The next group should be set the opposite way.

4. When filing the outside cutters, file the cross-cut teeth to the same bevel as the dado set was when received from the factory. File the raker teeth (large teeth) square across their faces, and keep them

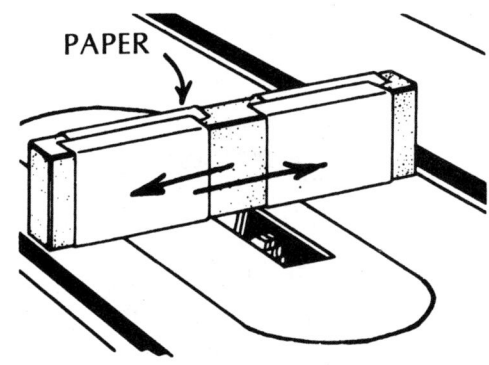

Fig. 10-9: Jointing the rakers.

Fig. 10-10: Setting the spurs.

1/64 inch lower than the cross-cut teeth (Fig. 10-11A). File the spurs with a square file maintaining the original angle (Fig. 10-11B). When filing, take the same amount off of each tooth to preserve the balance of the saw. This may be done by counting file strokes.

On the dado head's inside cutters, file the top fo the teeth only (Fig. 10-12). Do not touch the face of the teeth with the file except to remove the burr left when the tops are filed. The inside cutters, when

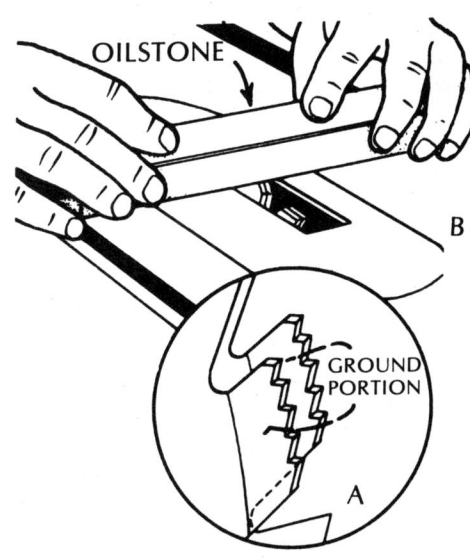

Fig. 10-8: Jointing the spurs.

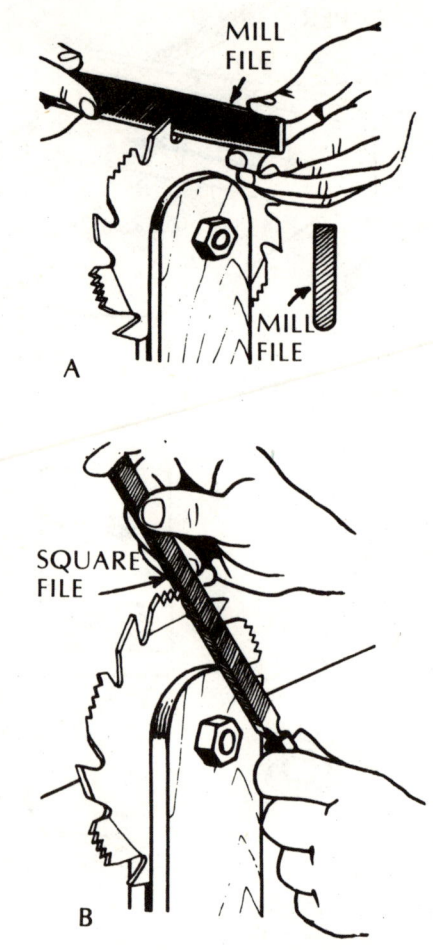

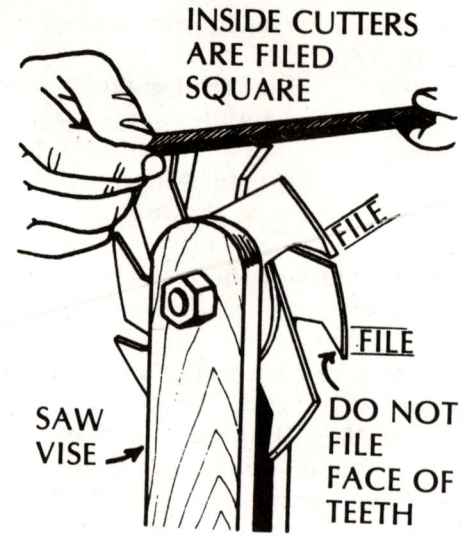

Fig. 10-12: Filing the inside cutters.

CLEANING A SAW BLADE

Saw blades that are used for cutting woods containing a considerable quantity of resin and pitch will have the gullets and sides of the teeth filled with sawdust that adheres tenaciously to the metal. Using a blade in this condition not only results in overloading the motor but may be the cause of a burned blade. The pitch and hardened sawdust can be removed readily by immersing the blade in a container of solvent such as kerosene or turpentine. Allow the blade to remain in the liquid for 8 to 12 hours. Then, when the sawdust has softened, it can be removed with a brush. If the first treatment is not sufficient, repeat. *When using solvents be sure there is good ventilation in the room.*

SHARPENING MOLDING HEAD CUTTERS

Molding head cutters must be kept as sharp as possible. This is done with several special sharpening stones. A flat Arkansas oilstone approximately 2 by 6 inches or a slipstone made of the same material about 4 inches long and tapering from 1/8 to 3/8 inch in thickness, with rounded edges, is

Fig. 10-11: Filing the rakers and spurs.

placed on the arbor of the saw, should be the same length as the raker teeth on the outside cutter; that is 1/64 inch shorter than the cutting teeth. As with the outside cutters, you should be careful to take the same number of file strokes on each side of a cutter, to preserve the balance and the same diameter of all the cutters. Figure 10-13 shows both a good and bad dado head cut.

Carbide-tipped blades should be resharpened only by properly equipped specialists.

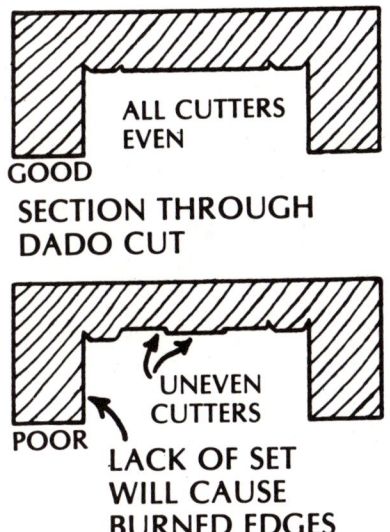

Fig. 10-13: Example of a good and bad dado head cut.

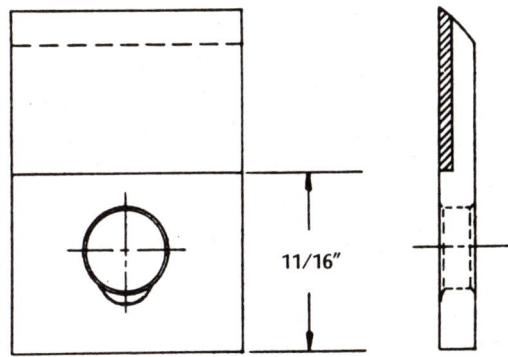

Fig. 10-14: To sharpen the molding cutterhead knives, grind the cross-section portion only.

needed. Also, an oilstone or a slipstone about 4 inches long and 1/4 inch square and another 4 inches long, 2 inches wide, and 3/8 or 1/2 inch thick should be available. Another convenient oilstone to have is a triangular sectional one with each face 1/16 inch wide and 3 inches long. With this collection of oilstones it is possible to sharpen almost any cutter used in the molding head.

The knives are ground in such a manner that sharpening is accomplished easily by whetting the flat side and removing the burr formed from the beveled edge. To preserve the same shape of molding cutter knives with involute bevels grind them on their flat side only. If the knives are in good shape and need only to be touched up, they can be sharpened by hand. Do this on any oil stone. On the other hand, if the knives have nicks in them and are in poor shape, grind the blades on the front surface only (Fig. 10-14).

The high speed molding cutter knives used on most table saws are made in sets of three which means each set must be kept together to insure even cutting. If one cutter of a set becomes broken or lost purchase a new set since each cutter of a set is matched to have the same shape and weight.

INCH/MILLIMETER CONVERSIONS

INCHES TO MILLIMETERS
Multiply inches by 25.4

MILLIMETERS TO INCHES
Multiply millimeters by 0.03937

INCHES	MILLIMETERS	INCHES	MILLIMETERS	MILLIMETERS	INCHES
.001	.025	17/32	13.4938	.001	.00004
.01	.254	35/64	13.8906	.01	.00039
1/64	.3969	9/16	14.2875	.02	.00079
.02	.508	37/64	14.6844	.03	.00118
.03	.762	19/32	15.0812	.04	.00157
1/32	.7938	.6	15.24	.05	.00196
.04	1.016	39/64	15.4781	.06	.00236
3/64	1.191	5/8	15.875	.07	.00276
.05	1.27	41/64	16.2719	.08	.00315
.06	1.524	21/32	16.6688	.09	.00354
1/16	1.5875	43/64	17.0656	.1	.00394
.07	1.778	11/16	17.4625	.2	.00787
5/64	1.9844	.7	17.78	.3	.01181
.08	2.032	45/64	17.8594	.4	.01575
.09	2.286	23/32	18.2562	.5	.01969
3/32	2.3812	47/64	18.6531	.6	.02362
.1	2.54	3/4	19.050	.7	.02756
7/64	2.7781	49/64	19.4469	.8	.0315
1/8	3.175	25/32	19.8438	.9	.03543
9/64	3.5719	51/64	20.2406	1.0	.03937
5/32	3.9688	.8	20.32	2.0	.07874
11/64	4.3656	13/16	20.6375	3.0	.11811
3/16	4.7625	53/64	21.0344	4.0	.15748
.2	5.08	27/32	21.4312	5.0	.19685
13/64	5.1594	55/64	21.8281	6.0	.23622
7/32	5.5562	7/8	22.225	7.0	.27559
15/64	5.9531	57/64	22.6219	8.0	.31496
1/4	6.35	.9	22.86	9.0	.35433
17/64	6.7469	29/32	23.0188	1 CM	.3937
9/32	7.1438	59/64	23.4156	2 CM	.7874
19/64	7.5406	15/16	23.8125	3 CM	1.1811
.3	7.62	61/64	24.2094	4 CM	1.5748
5/16	7.9375	31/32	24.6062	5 CM	1.9685
21/64	8.3344	63/64	25.0031	6 CM	2.3622
11/32	8.7312	1.0	25.4	7 CM	2.7559
23/64	9.1281	2.0	50.8	8 CM	3.1496
3/8	9.525	3.0	76.2	9 CM	3.5433
25/64	9.9219	4.0	101.6	1 DM	3.937
.4	10.16	5.0	127.0	2 DM	7.874
13/32	10.3188	6.0	152.4	3 DM	11.811
27/64	10.7156	7.0	177.8	4 DM	1 Ft., 3.748
7/16	11.1125	8.0	203.2		
29/64	11.5094	9.0	228.6		
15/32	11.9062	10.0	254.0		
31/64	12.3031	11.0	279.4		
1/2	12.7	1 Ft.	304.8		
33/64	13.0969				

ABBREVIATIONS
MM-Millimeter(1/1000)
CM-Centimeter(1/100)
DM-Decimeter(1/10)

Index

Abrasives, 108
Abrasive wheels, 7, 107-110
Adapter, cord, 12
Adjustable dado heads, 8, 34
   cut-off stops, 68
Adjustments, 14-18
Aluminum-oxide wheels, 7, 110
Angle irons, 73, 78
Anti-kickback fingers, 2, 21, 24, 40, 95
Auxiliary face boards, 32-33, 34, 35, 36, 58, 59, 90, 91, 96
   fence, 10, 27, 30, 43, 47, 60, 63, 95-96, 98, 99
   table fence, 27-29, 38, 44, 60

Band saw, 30, 58
Bare faced tenon, 74, 76
Bench type saw, 1, 2, 3
Bevel angle sawing, 36-38
   crosscutting, 1, 23, 38, 45
   miter, 1, 23, 38
   rabbet, 46-47
   ripping, 1, 23, 36-37, 45
Beveled polygon joints, 52, 53-54, 85
   segments, 52
Blade alignment, 15-17
   changing, 18
   cleaning, 119
   guard, 2, 4, 21, 23, 24, 40, 95, 108
   blade-table alignment, 14-17
Blind dadoes, 43
   doweling, 69, 70
   grooving, 43, 44
   splined miter joint, 83-84
   wedged tenon, 75, 76
Box joints, 90-91
Butt joints, 54, 69-73

Carbide-tipped blades, 5, 6, 8, 58, 118
Casters, retractable, 11
Chamfer cutting, 45
Clamp attachment, 8, 62-63
Combination blades, 6-7, 58, 116
   miter joints, 85-86
Compound angle cutting, 45, 52-55
Concealed haunched tenon, 74, 76
Cogged dado joint, 76, 77

Corner blocks, 56
   cutting jig, 67
   dadoes, 43, 77
   lap, 78, 79, 80
Cove-cutting, 45, 56-58, 100-101
Corrugated fasteners, 78, 82
Cross lap, 80
Crosscut blades, 5
   gauge, 33, 34
Crosscutting, 1, 5, 6, 8, 11, 21, 22, 23, 31-34, 42
Cuttoff wheels, 7, 107-108
   operation of, 107-108

Dado-and-rabbet, 77
Dado heads, 7-8, 39-44, 47, 71, 73, 77, 86, 97, 98, 116-117
   adjustable, 8, 34, 36
   operation of, 39-44
   sharpening, 117-118
   standard, 7-8, 34-35
Dado joints, 76-78, 86
Dadoing, 39, 40, 42-43
Dentil molding, 59-60
Dovetail dado, 77
   joint, 81-82
   lap, 80, 82
   tapers, 51-52
Dowel joints, 69-71
   pops, 70, 71
Dowels, 69-71, 73, 82, 100
   cutting, 100
Doweling, 69-71
   jig, 71
Drawer joints 89, 101-103
Drill press, 51, 73

Edge grooving, 44
Edgewise cross-lap joint, 79
Electrical requirements, 12-13, 19, 20
End grooving, 44
   lap, 78-79
Extension cord, 13, 20

Featherboard, 29, 30, 41
Filing dado head, 117
   saw blade, 114

Flatground blades, 5
Floor type saw, 2, 3
Full dovetail dado, 77
　dovetail lap, 80-81

Glue joints, 100
Grooves, 39
Grooving, 39, 40, 41-42, 71-72
Gumming dado head, 117
　saw blade, 111-114

Half dovetail dado, 77
　dovetail half-lap, 80, 81
Handsawing, 30
Hard-tip blades, 6
Haunched tenons, 74-76
Hold-downs, 63-64, 99
Hollow-ground blades, 5, 69, 116
Housed dado, 76

Installation of saw, 11

Jig board, 63
Jointer, 12, 99
Jointing wood, 103-104
　saw blade, 111, 113

Kerfing, 45, 58-59
Keyed miters, 63, 84
Kickback, avoiding, 20, 22, 24, 32, 41
Kidproofing saw, 13

Lap on rabbeted frame, 79
Lapped joint with groove, 79
　joints, 79-81
　miter, 84-85
Laying out dowels, 70-71
Line cord, 12-13
Lock corner joint, 91-92
　miter joint, 86, 92

Maintenance, saw, 19
Masonry cutting, 108
Metal cutting, 107-108
　slitting blades, 7
Mending plates, 73
Middle half lap, 79

Milled joint, 88
Miter crosscut, 31
　gauge, 1, 2, 3, 8, 9, 16, 17, 20, 21, 31, 35, 38, 44, 52, 61, 62-63, 65, 66, 73, 109
　jigs, 36, 61-63
Mitered end lap, 79
　joints, 36, 54, 61, 82-86
　polygon joints, 52, 53-54, 85
　segments, 52
　tenon, 74, 76
Mitering, 1, 23, 35-36, 61-62
Mortise-and-tenon joints, 73, 74, 75, 76
Molding cutterhead, 10, 47, 63-64, 95-106
　end grain, 99
　head sharpening, 119
　operation, 95-106
　shapes, 96-98
　straight edge, 98
Moldings, 45, 59-60, 104-106
Motor arrangement, 1
Motors, 3, 4

National Electric Code, 12
Nonferrous-metal blades, 7
Notched jigs, 65-67
　stop blocks, 42, 43, 76

Oblique half lap, 79
Octagonal cutting, 45
On/off switch, 13
Ornamental molding, 45, 59-60
Open doweling, 69-70, 71
　mortise-and-tenon, 75, 80

Panel raising, 58, 100
Parallel ruler jig, 56-57
Pattern sawing, 45, 48, 64
Pivot jig, 109-110
Planer blades, 6, 27
Planning, 103-104
Ploughing, 41-42
Plywood, 6, 23-24, 27
　blades, 6-7
Polygon miters, 52, 53-54, 85
Power switch, 13
Push board, 26-27
　block, 26
　stick, 26

Rabbet groove joints, 88-90
　joints, 86-90

Rabbeted miter joints, 86-88
Rabbeting, 39, 45, 46-45, 100, 103
Raised-panel cutting, 47, 100
Resawing, 29-31
Rip blade 5-6, 58, 116
    Fence, 1-2, 17, 19, 20, 21, 22, 25, 42, 65, 95, 98
Ripping, 1, 2, 17, 19, 20, 21, 22, 23, 24-31, 41, 47
    long stock, 29
    narrow stock, 25-27
    wide stock, 24-25
Roller support, 28, 29, 32-33
Router, 51, 73

Saber saw, 58
Safety goggles, 10, 21
    tips, 21
Sanding disks, 10, 107, 108-110
    operation of, 108-110
Saw blade changing, 18
    blade setting, 114-117
    blade sharpening, 111-116
    blades, 5-7
Saw capacity, 1, 4
    cut moldings, 45, 59-60
    filing vise, 113
    maintenance, 19-20
    size, 1
Setting jig, 115
    saw blade, 114-117
Shaper, 51, 99
Shop vacuum, 10, 12
Sliding table jig, 64-65
Slip feathers, 84
    feather miter joint, 84
Spline joints, 71-72, 85
    miter joints, 82-83
Splines, 71, 72, 76
Splitter, 2, 19, 20, 40, 95

Square legs, 50
Squaring boards, 64-65
Stake pointing jig, 66
Standard dadoes, 76-77
Stop blocks, 33, 34, 35, 42, 43, 68, 73, 76, 107
    dadoes, 43, 44
    rods, 9, 33, 34, 42, 73, 109
Strip moldings, 99
Stub tenons, 75, 76

T-half lap joint, 79, 80
T-straps, 73
Table extensions, 9-10
    inserts, 10, 49, 99
Taper jigs, 48-51
    legs, 48, 50-51
    ripping, 45, 48-51, 64
Tenon with long and short shoulders, 75, 76
    splines, 75, 76
Tenoning jigs, 9, 44, 45, 63, 66, 73, 84
Tenons, 67, 73-76, 100
Thin-rimmed blades, 5
Three-way lap, 80
Through-wedged tenon, 74, 76
Tilt angle scale, 19
    mechanism, 15-17
    scale pointer, 15-17, 20, 36
Tongue and groove joints, 78, 100
    and rabbet joints, 77
Troubleshooting guide, 19-20
Tubing cutting, 107

V-blocks, 47, 107
V-groove cutting, 47-48

Wedge cutting jigs, 67